Governing Animals

Governing Animals

Animal Welfare and the Liberal State

KIMBERLY K. SMITH

OXFORD
UNIVERSITY PRESS

OXFORD
UNIVERSITY PRESS

Oxford University Press, Inc., publishes works that further
Oxford University's objective of excellence
in research, scholarship, and education.

Oxford   New York
Auckland   Cape Town   Dar es Salaam   Hong Kong   Karachi
Kuala Lumpur   Madrid   Melbourne   Mexico City   Nairobi
New Delhi   Shanghai   Taipei   Toronto

With offices in
Argentina   Austria   Brazil   Chile   Czech Republic   France   Greece
Guatemala   Hungary   Italy   Japan   Poland   Portugal   Singapore
South Korea   Switzerland   Thailand   Turkey   Ukraine   Vietnam

Published by Oxford University Press, Inc.
198 Madison Avenue, New York, New York 10016

www.oup.com

Oxford is a registered trademark of Oxford University Press

Library of Congress Cataloging-in-Publication Data
Smith, Kimberly K., 1966–
Governing animals : animal welfare and the liberal state / Kimberly K. Smith.
    p.   cm.
Includes bibliographical references and index.
ISBN 978-0-19-989575-5
1. Animal welfare—Government policy. 2. Animal rights—Government policy.
3. Liberalism—Social aspects. I. Title.
HV4708.S62   2012
179'.3—dc23   2011046913

9 8 7 6 5 4 3 2 1

Printed in the United States of America
on acid-free paper

Contents

Preface

IN 2005, SHORTLY after Hurricanes Katrina and Rita devastated the Gulf Coast, I began thinking about animal welfare. Granted, this was not an obvious move in response to the Gulf Coast tragedy, nor to the problems of poverty, racial oppression, and environmental degradation that it uncovered. Social inequality and environmental management are arguably the major challenges of the twenty-first century. Why, at this moment, should we be thinking about animals?

One answer, of course, was famously formulated by Claude Lévi-Strauss: animals are good to think with.[1] Thinking about animal welfare may help us to extend and enrich liberal political theory, to make it more relevant to the deeply interconnected social and environmental problems we face. That is part of my project. But I hope this book makes the case that animals are also an interesting and important subject of public policy in their own right. They deserve greater attention by political theorists and, indeed, by the general community of policy makers, activists, and ordinary citizens. This book, then, is intended for that broad audience. It aims to introduce readers to some of the tools and concepts that political theorists use to think about political obligation, the role of the government, and related issues as they apply to animals. But because I don't think political theorists have all the answers, the book attempts to bring others, such as historians and legal scholars, into the conversation. You will find here a lot of theoretical argument but also a lot of excursions into history, law, and public policy—excursions that will, I hope, encourage some creative and critical engagement with the theory presented. We need to improve our ability to govern the natural world, to make the world a better, richer, more sustaining habitat for humans and other species. This is a collective project, and thinking together about our political relations with animals is a good place to start.

Thus although this book focuses on animal welfare, it does so with the understanding that human welfare matters and that animal welfare matters to us largely because all of us are deeply interdependent with animals. I *don't* assume that pursuing animal welfare will necessarily be helpful to human welfare. There are ways of protecting animals that could make social inequality among humans even worse. But there are also ways of not attending to animals that could make life worse for the socially marginalized. My goal here is to consider how we can design political practices and institutions to improve the welfare of the mixed human/animal community overall. In particular, I try to be attentive to the fact that humans' life chances are still too greatly determined by race, class, gender, and ethnicity. These inequalities affect our relations to animals, and the politics of animal welfare will affect these inequalities one way or another. Ultimately, I hope that by investigating the political morality of our treatment of animals, we can figure out how to design practices and institutions that protect the most vulnerable members of our society. In short, this work asks how we can make of our shared world a more fitting home for human lives—lives that embrace the nonhuman beings and phenomena to which we are so deeply, intimately, and variously connected.

I had quite a lot of help writing this book. I benefited considerably from conversations on these issues with Sheri Breen, Ted Clayton, Andrew Rehfeld, Kerry Whiteside, Melvin Rogers, and Jennifer Rubenstein. Jane Caputi, Gavin Van Horn, Adrienne Cassel, Bryan Bates, David Keller, and the other members of the 2009 NEH summer workshop on Aldo Leopold were also very helpful. And I would like to thank my many readers for their generous and insightful feedback. They include Tun Myint, Clara Hardy, David Schlosberg, Rebecca Potter, Annette Nierobisz, Chris Heurlin, Lester Spence, David Schraub, Daniel Groll, Breena Holland, and most of the members of the Environmental Political Theory section of the Western Political Theory Association, as well as the anonymous reviewers for Oxford University Press. Mike and Shane Peterson, Marlene Halverson, and Charlotte Laws generously agreed to be interviewed for this book, and Carleton College, as always, provided the vibrant and supportive intellectual community in which the work took shape. Finally, I am grateful to Don Herzog and Dale Jamieson, whose scholarship, in different but complementary ways, inspired this project.

Introduction

[A] human being is by nature a political animal.
—ARISTOTLE, *Politics*

[A] land ethic changes the role of Homo sapiens from conqueror of the land-community to plain member and citizen of it.
—ALDO LEOPOLD, *A Sand County Almanac*

IN 2002, SENATOR Jesse Helms proposed an amendment to the federal Animal Welfare Act with the aim of preventing the US Department of Agriculture from extending the Act's protection to certain classes of animals. The Act, first passed in 1966 and amended several times since, sets standards of care for warm-blooded animals used by breeders, dealers, exhibitors, and researchers. It mandates, among other things, humane care, training for those who handle animals, and supervision of animal experimentation by Institutional Animal Care and Use Committees. But in 1972, the US Department of Agriculture, which is responsible for enforcing the Act, adopted regulations exempting birds, rats, mice, horses, and farmed animals from its coverage, leaving a relatively small class of animals protected. The regulation was supported by the scientific research community but strongly criticized by animal welfare advocates as unfair and inhumane to the excluded animals. The animal welfare advocates very nearly won their point: In 1998, a lawsuit brought by the Alternatives Research and Development Foundation, a subsidiary of the American Antivivisection Society, resulted in a settlement with the USDA providing that rats, mice, and birds would be brought under the statute's mandate. But before the regulation could be changed, Senator Helms persuaded his colleagues to amend the statute to preserve the exclusion.

Helms's principal argument in favor of the amendment was to "make sure that none of the important work taking place in the medical research community will be delayed, made more expensive, or be otherwise compromised by regulatory shenanigans on the part of the US Department of Agriculture." He stressed the importance of animal research to human health and dismissed the proponents of the regulation as "professional activists who delight in creating mischievous controversies like this." But he did not neglect the animal welfare argument: Noting that the NIH already imposes regulations on the humane care of all vertebrate research animals, he insisted that "a rodent could do a lot worse than live out its life span in research facilities. Isn't it far better for the mouse to be fed and watered in a clean laboratory than to end up as a tiny bulge being digested inside an enormous snake?"[1] His colleagues apparently agreed, and the amendment passed.

The debate over the AWA suggests that our political relations with animals involve complex ethical judgments. Our laws reflect in part the interests of human beings, but ethical arguments revolving around duties to animals are not out of place in the legislature. Indeed, such arguments resurfaced a few years later, in June 2005, when air force officers had to decide whether Air Force Technical Sergeant Jamie Dana could keep her dog. Rex, a military working dog trained to detect bombs, had worked with Sergeant Dana for three years, until a roadside bomb left Dana critically injured. Dana, no longer on active duty, wanted to take Rex home with her, but Rex was still several years away from his official retirement age. (German shepherds work until they are ten to fourteen years old.) The law was clear: Section 2583 of Title 10 of the US Code permits military working dogs to be adopted by their handlers, but only when they are no longer useful to the military. The law was a recent one; from 1949 until 2000, military working dogs were classified as "equipment" and were therefore kept until they were no longer useful, then "disposed of" (euthanized).[2] That law was amended in 2000 to allow adoption, and Rex's case led to another amendment, in 2006, to allow early retirement for working dogs after traumatic events.

Representative Roscoe Bartlett, speaking in support of the 2000 amendment, focused on the community's duties to these dogs. He told the heart-rending story of Robby, an eleven-year-old Belgian Malinois suffering from missing teeth and arthritis. No longer deployable, he was scheduled to be euthanized. Such a policy defied "normal logic," according to Bartlett. Surely Robby should "have the opportunity to experience the comforts and joys of normal companionship." He had "faithfully served [his] country" and enjoyed a "special bond" with his handler that deserved to be respected. Bartlett's argument carried the day and won him his colleagues' praise for "looking out for those who cannot speak for themselves."[3]

Representative Bartlett was making an appeal to our ethical intuitions, but the ethical judgments involved in these policy debates are not always straightforward and obvious. For example, in St. Paul, Minnesota, citizens have been discussing how to respond to a growing population of feral cats. Milder winters may account for the increase, which is packing animal shelters to capacity. The chief justifications for trying to reduce the population are the beliefs that feral cats can spread harmful diseases to humans, that they kill a significant number of songbirds and other desirable wildlife, and that life in the wild simply isn't good for cats. But some officials suggest that the problem is overstated, and measures to stabilize the population are controversial. Minnesota law treats feral cats as a nuisance animal that may be shot, like gophers and skunks—but a measure allowing feral cats to be hunted recently failed in neighboring Wisconsin, despite significant public support. Animal rights advocates insist that shooting strays is not humane and will not stabilize the population (because cats' reproductive rate is so high). They propose instead trapping the cats, then spaying or neutering, vaccinating, and releasing them. Several animal welfare organizations in Minnesota have already begun trap-neuter-release programs, which reportedly can be effective in controlling feral cat populations, at least after the programs have been in place for several years. In 2007, St. Paul became the first municipality in the state to adopt such a program.[4]

A similar but more multifaceted problem was the controversy over the navy's decision in 1977 to exterminate the feral goat population on the navy enclave of San Clemente Island. The navy was implementing a decision by the US Fish and Wildlife Service, which concluded that eradicating the goats was necessary to protect endangered plants and animals on the island. The navy planned to shoot the goats from helicopters.

The navy's proposal was challenged by the Animal Lovers Volunteer Association (ALVA), which filed a federal lawsuit on the grounds that the navy's environmental impact statement (required by the National Environmental Policy Act) was woefully inadequate. The court never reached that issue, though; it decided that the association lacked standing to challenge the navy's decision. The group had no special interest in the goats, the judges argued—that is, no interest lying within the "zone of interests" that the National Environmental Policy Act was intended to protect. Goats are not an endangered species; members of ALVA do not, and indeed are not permitted, to visit the island and see the goats; and their general interest in preventing inhumane treatment of animals is not specific enough to count as a legally cognizable injury.

After the lawsuit failed, the navy exterminated most of the estimated fifteen thousand goats. A small number, though, were removed and resettled, or adopted as pets. The American Livestock Breeds Conservancy managed to secure a small breeding population, and the San Island Goat Association is now attempting to preserve what it calls a "critically-endangered heritage breed."[5]

These cases, all examples of political practices under attack or in the process of reform, are complicated because they raise questions of animal ethics intertwined with questions of political theory. Is Senator Helms a better representative for animal interests than the "mischievous" professional activists? Should Representative Bartlett be confined by his role to considering only human military personnel, or does he have a duty to represent the interests of military working dogs as well? If so, when does a dog cease to be military property and become a fellow soldier? More generally, how and when does an animal's welfare become the responsibility of the political community, with a valid claim on the public treasury? If animals' interests are relevant to policy decisions, who should represent those interests in legislatures, city council meetings, and courts? How do we decide what is fair, what is morally and politically appropriate, in the government of animals? To be sure, certain answers—certain ethico-political principles—are implicit in our practices, but it takes some work to discover what those principles are, whether they are the right principles, and whether our practices adequately instantiate them.

It might seem natural to look to the ethical literature on animal welfare and animal rights for answers to these questions. Since the 1960s, ethicists have developed a large body of scholarship arguing persuasively that animals and humans have morally relevant similarities, that animals can have moral standing, and that we as individuals have important moral obligations to animals.[6] Moreover, many of these ethicists have pressed the political system to recognize these duties, with a fair degree of success. This literature is an important foundation for my study, but unfortunately it does not address directly the questions I'm asking. Ethicists typically focus on the moral duties we have as private individuals rather than the political duties we have as citizens. But my questions concern *political* obligations. Specifically, I'm concerned with whether and how the state, and more specifically the liberal state, can defend animal welfare. To illustrate the difference: We may agree that you have a private moral duty not to lie to your spouse, but that doesn't mean the state can legitimately punish you for doing so. Similarly, we may agree that we have individual moral obligations not to inflict wanton harm on animals, but it takes further reasoning and argument to determine what the state's role is in enforcing that duty—not to mention the numerous related questions, like who should represent animal interests in the political and legal systems or whether the state should recognize property rights in animals.

This work of determining whether a liberal government can defend animal welfare and what tools it can use to do so is the proper domain of liberal political theory. The liberal tradition in political theory is of course a bit difficult to define, but its touchstones include the early social contract theorists (like John Locke) and their heirs (from the American founders to contemporary philosophers such as John Rawls). It is generally characterized by (1) an assumption of human equality and (2) a concern with preserving human liberty, usually (but not always) conceptualized as preserving individual rights from government power. Unfortunately, its focus on human liberty and human equality means that liberal political theory has been remarkably unhelpful on animal governance. Indeed, liberal theorists rarely mention animals except to assert in what respects humans are different from them. Animals (we are told) are those creatures without reason, without language, without autonomy or freedom—and therefore without interests, rights, political status, or representation. Political theory, it seems, can have little to say about such creatures.

Happily, a few political theorists are beginning to challenge that view. Martha Nussbaum, Elizabeth Anderson, Alisdair MacIntyre, Marcel Wissenburg, and Robert Garner have addressed important subjects like whether animals can be members of the social contract and how liberal citizens ought to value animals.[7] But thus far none of them have offered a fully developed version of liberal political theory that takes seriously the moral status of animals. Indeed, some have suggested that liberalism is too focused on a narrow conception of human freedom to be helpful in protecting animal welfare. I think that conclusion is too hasty. This book attempts to develop liberal political theory so that it can answer the kinds of questions posed above. Specifically, I take up three key liberal concepts—the social contract, property rights, and representation—and explore how they should be understood when applied to animals. I argue against the skeptics that liberalism properly understood can recognize the moral status and social meaning of animals, and it can give us guidance in fashioning animal welfare laws. Liberalism may not take us as far as the more radical defenders of animal rights would like, but it does, I believe, support broader protections for animal welfare than any nation currently provides.

But the skeptics do have an important point about the limits of liberalism. The philosophical problem is this: Liberal theorists typically begin their investigations by dividing the moral universe neatly into people and things. People have moral status and are both the subjects and agents of politics; things, by contrast, have neither intrinsic moral status nor agency of any sort.[8] Since animals serve primarily to mark the boundary between moral subjects and things, liberal theory would seem to be wedded firmly to maintaining a bright line between humans and (nonhuman) animals and to treating animals as things.

This dualistic moral universe is of course merely a model—an admittedly simplified conception of the world it is meant to explain—and is perfectly valid to the extent that it is useful for making sense of political phenomena. No doubt it would be adequate if the political community did not have such extensive, complex, and meaningful dealings with animals. But these dealings, I contend, make it impossible to treat animals as mere things, even for the limited purpose of explaining our political world. Animals (a term I will use to encompass not only mammals but also birds, fish, reptiles, and insects)[9] are too deeply involved in the political sphere—as subjects of regulation, members of families and communities, and even workers—to be treated as mere undifferentiated, nonsentient, inanimate things. They are best understood as neither human persons nor mere things but *fellow creatures*, co-inhabitants of our ecological and social spaces. They form a wildly diverse set, differing among themselves in terms of physical, emotional, intellectual, social, and, accordingly, moral characteristics. Our laws and practices must attend to those differences, as well as their similarities to and differences from humans.

So a liberalism suitable for a state committed to animal welfare cannot be grounded on a strict metaphysical distinction between persons and things. But I won't be arguing that we should simply replace that metaphysical distinction with a different metaphysical foundation. On the contrary, I don't believe liberalism needs a metaphysical foundation per se; our liberal theory can be based on a broad *social* consensus about the status of animals. This book follows the approach taken by John Rawls in *Political Liberalism*: We are trying not to discover universal political truths but to develop a public philosophy for a particular pluralist community—namely (for reasons explained below), for the contemporary United States. In such a community we can expect to find many different comprehensive moral and religious doctrines, reflecting different metaphysical assumptions. So, as Rawls puts it, this public philosophy "should be, as far as possible, independent of the opposing and conflicting philosophical and religious doctrines that citizens affirm." Instead, it should be supported by an "overlapping consensus" of such doctrines.[10] The liberalism on offer here depends on an overlapping consensus (explained and defended in chapters 1 and 2) that some animals are members of the social contract. A liberal state that enjoys such a consensus has a sufficient social foundation for animal welfare policy, even if citizens disagree about the metaphysical principles supporting it.

This nonmetaphysical approach may worry some readers: After all, what if our social consensus is faulty? Perhaps we mistakenly value some animals more than others, or perhaps we overvalue them. How can we be sure our social practices are justified without delving into metaphysical questions about what sorts of beings have moral status? I address in the following chapters how we can critique, justify, and reform our social practices without resolving these deeper philosophical questions. I leave such philosophical inquiry to others. My aim is more limited: to show that there is a coherent version of liberalism, grounded on a widespread social consensus, that makes sense of the animal welfare policies found in the United States (and many other twenty-first-century industrial democracies). This liberalism is consistent with several plausible animal welfare and animal rights ethics, but it is not based on any particular one.

This point is worth emphasizing: This book is an exercise in political theory, not moral philosophy. Scholars in these respective fields often work on the same problems, including liberal theory and animal rights. But political theory tends to be less abstract, appealing more to empirical data and history than to metaphysical principles. We theorists are more interested in institutions and practices than metaphysics, and we are more likely to treat politics as distinct from other realms of ethics. Moreover, political theory arguments don't always aim for an analytical rigor that compels assent; they may aim instead for a richness that fosters new insights and may change the way one understands the problem. Whether I achieve such richness is for the reader to judge.

More specifically, this book is not a defense of animal rights in the traditional sense. That is, I am not going to spend a great deal of time in this study rehearsing the ethical arguments supporting our direct moral duties toward nonhuman animals. Much has been written about the mental and emotional lives of animals; debates about their cognitive capacities, their ability to feel pain and pleasure, and their sociability and autonomy are rich and ongoing.[11] As interesting as those debates are, I would like to move beyond them to explore the political questions that these ethical arguments raise. Thus, for the purposes of this study, I will simply take as settled that animals can have moral standing. That standing may be based on their capacity for suffering, the fact that they are subjects of a life, or their social relationships with humans. Although they are not moral agents, they can be what Tom Regan calls "moral patients"; they can be not only harmed but also *wronged*.[12] For our purposes it is not that important that we settle on one philosophical basis for moral standing. What matters is that virtually all of those doctrines support, one way or another, moral duties to animals. To be sure, different subcultures have different practices of animal husbandry; in some communities, animal sacrifice is consistent with showing respect for animals, while in others, animal sacrifice is abhorred but hunting is acceptable. But defenders of these practices typically have no trouble acknowledging that animals deserve respect and consideration; they differ on the meaning of the practice at issue, not the moral status of animals.[13] Thus the moral standing of animals is a *political* fact, a widespread and enduring consensus that supports our laws and public policies.

I will also take as settled that animals can have interests. The concept of interest—understood either as a rational desire or as that which is objectively good for an individual—looms large in liberal theory. Animals may lack the sort of rationality implied by a subjective concept of interest; most of them probably do not weigh alternatives and choose which ends to pursue. But surely in many circumstances they do have an objective good. As Regan puts it, things can go well or ill for them.[14] Animals vary quite a bit in the kinds of interests they have, of course. An animal's degree of sentience and intelligence, and our social relationships with it, all have a significant bearing on whether we (as citizens) must attend to its interests, and on which interests we must attend to. So, for example, I will argue in the following pages that we do *not* have political duties toward all animals; dolphins and deer are after all quite different from dogs and cats, and these differences are critical in the political sphere.

Finally, I will assume that we can usually with a reasonable degree of confidence figure out what animals' interests are. Admittedly, the chief difficulty with according political status to animals is the communication barrier; we can't just ask them what they want. But that barrier must not be overstated. The animals with whom we have the most significant social relationships (pets and livestock) are precisely those with whom we are best able to communicate and whose needs we are best able to satisfy. Otherwise, they would not thrive under our care. In fact, the needs and capacities of many animals may be less difficult to decipher than the more complex needs and capacities of humans. There is always a degree of uncertainty in determining any subject's true interest; the question is whether that uncertainty is so great that it defeats any attempt to satisfy that interest. This issue will surface later, in the chapters on the social contract and representation, where we will consider in greater depth what political difference the social bond and the communication barrier make. But we should begin our investigation with confidence that there is no impenetrable epistemological barrier standing in our way.

But before beginning that inquiry, I would like to consider some general objections to this project. I see four principal concerns: One might object that liberal political theory is primarily concerned with justice, and animals cannot be subjects of justice; that our relationship to animals isn't, properly speaking, "political"; that improving our ethical relationships with animals isn't a liberal value; or that our relationships with animals are too unequal for liberal political theory to apply. If any of these reasons holds water, then animals should *not* be part of the liberal model of politics. That conclusion would not, of course, be equivalent to saying that animals are moral ciphers. Animals might be among those things that can be very important to our moral lives but that needn't appear in our theory of politics, like God or Gaia. But I argue the contrary: Unlike God or Gaia, animals are distinctive subjects of political duties and political concern.

I. Are Animals Subjects of Justice?

Few would deny that to be cruel to animals is a moral failing of some sort. At the very least it is a failing of charity or compassion, and we should be ashamed of it. But the claim that we owe animals justice is thought to be stronger than the claim that we should be kind to them. Regan, for example, argues that "kindness is not something we *owe* to anybody, is not *anyone's* due. To be the beneficiary of a kind act no doubt generally is to be blessed, but no one has a claim on anyone else's kindness." He insists instead that animals are subjects of justice—more precisely, that they have rights we *must* attend to.[15] Justice is not supererogatory.

Of course, as an empirical matter, it is probably not true that justice is a stronger claim than compassion. The animal welfare movement has been remarkably successful in making appeals to compassion, while the animal rights movement, when it appeals solely to our sense of justice, meets considerably more resistance. I'm not sure it is true as a philosophical matter, either, that "kindness is not something we *owe* to anybody." But much of the scholarly literature on animal ethics accepts Regan's argument that our task is to defend duties of justice and not just an ethic of kindness to animals.

A lot of ink has been spilled over this point. Arrayed against Regan we find theorists such as R. G. Frey, who insists that animals cannot have rights because they cannot have interests, and they cannot have interests because they cannot have desires—they lack the cognitive capacity for formulating the beliefs necessary to have desires.[16] A more sweeping attack on the idea of justice toward animals comes from David Hume, who claims that only beings

who are roughly equal in power can owe justice to one another. As he writes
in *Enquiry Concerning Morals*:

> Were there a species of creatures intermingled with men, which,
> though rational, were possessed of such inferior strength, both of
> body and mind, that they were incapable of all resistance, and could
> never, upon the highest provocation, make us feel the effects of
> their resentment, the necessary consequence, I think, is that we
> should be bound by the laws of humanity to give gentle usage to
> these creatures, but should not, properly speaking, lie under any
> restraint of justice with regard to them. . . . Our intercourse with
> them could not be called society, which supposes a degree of
> equality; but absolute command on the one side, and servile obedi-
> ence on the other.[17]

He goes on to describe animals as beings that are "servilely obedient" and
therefore not subjects of justice. And, finally, there are theorists who conceptualize justice as *reciprocal* obligation. Under this view, we respect the rights of
others because we expect them to respect our rights in return. These theorists
conclude that subjects of justice must therefore have moral agency, which
animals lack.[18]

   This debate is of great interest and importance to philosophers. But it
doesn't seem to matter at all to Representative Bartlett, who spoke quite
confidently and successfully about what we *owe* to military working dogs.
What Bartlett understands is that even if we define justice so narrowly as to
exclude duties to moral patients, we may still have political obligations to
them. Whether we call these duties of quasi justice, metaphorical justice, or
simply compassion, they still fall within the domain of political morality
and are therefore a proper subject of political theory. As Joseph Raz help-
fully reminds us, the sphere of political morality extends beyond rights and
justice. It consists of all the principles that should guide political action.[19]
Those principles must include the ones underlying our political relations
with animals.

II. Do Humans Have Political Relations with Animals?

This conclusion that animals can be subjects of justice only invites a broader
attack: We might consider that we have duties, even duties of justice, to animals but still deny that those duties fall within the political sphere. They are

(we could argue) purely a matter of personal ethics, not considerations relevant to state action or to being a good citizen. After all, one hallmark of liberalism is the principle of limited government. As I suggested above, the political system does not concern itself with everything that should be done, only with the things that should be done by political actors and institutions. Like religious duties in a secular state, duties toward animals may be important but not relevant to public policy.

Of course, that comparison reveals a major difficulty with the concept of limited government; after all, political actors cannot simply ignore the fact that citizens have religious duties. Even if a set of duties falls entirely within the private sphere, we still need to think about how to fashion public policy to maintain that private space. But I want to make a more general claim: There is an important sense in which we can achieve political relations with (some) animals.

There is of course a long tradition in Western letters of using political terms to describe human/animal relations. When Aldo Leopold suggested that we are "plain member[s] and citizen[s]" of the biotic community, he was challenging the more common notion of humans as rulers, holding dominion over animals. Hector St. John de Crèvecoeur, in the eighteenth-century classic *Letters from an American Farmer*, followed a standard literary convention in having his narrator use such terms to describe how he "governs his cattle," acting as "a bridle and check to prevent the strong and greedy from oppressing the timid and weak."[20] Indeed, some animal behavior is best understood using political terms, like "dominance" and "submission" among canines or primates.[21]

Is all of this just an appealing metaphor, or do we really have political relations with animals? In the most ordinary sense of the word "political," certainly we do. Government actors, in their political capacity, make public policy concerning animals and use the machinery of the state to implement those policies. But when normative theorists use the term "political," they're usually up to something more than simply describing what governments do. They want to show why what legitimate governments do isn't the same as tyranny, or armed robbery. "Political," in this sense, means something deeper and richer than merely "concerning government."

Aristotle, for example, reserves the term "political" for rule over equals— over free-born citizens who can rule in turn. Rule over slaves, by contrast, is mastery, which is also the form of rule that tyrants exercise over their subjects. Political rule, for Aristotle, is *good* rule (for equal human beings), and it is possible only under certain kinds of constitutions and by citizens with the right sort of character. John Locke's definition, which closely tracks our modern, liberal understanding of "political," also contains an element of aspiration: Political power is "*a Right* of making Laws with Penalties of Death, and consequently all less Penalties, for the Regulating and Preserving of Property, and of employing the force of the Community, in the Execution of such Laws, and in the defence of the Common-wealth from Foreign Injury, and all this only for the Publick Good."[22] Political rule thus has to do with certain functions (regulating and preserving property, defending the community, serving the public good); it is exercised through rules backed by force (penalties); it is principally the domain of the state or government (employing the force of the community); and—a key point—it is the exercise of legitimate or justified power (it is a "*Right*"). This is consistent, too, with Max Weber's definition of the state as the entity that claims a monopoly on the *legitimate* use of force within its borders.[23] For both Locke and Weber, the concept of the political is deeply attached to the act of *justifying* the use of force.

To be sure, Locke's and Weber's focus on the state may be too narrow; feminist theorists have argued persuasively that we can talk about political relations within the family and can identify exercises of social power and relations that take place in the private sphere but are intimately connected to political status.[24] But we face a deeper problem: Can our exercise of power over animals be considered "political" even in Locke's narrower sense? Is it the exercise of *legitimate* power?

Joseph Raz's discussion of authority helps us think this through more clearly. Raz defines "authority" as the ability to impose an obligation to obey.[25] This is a useful way to differentiate between a thug and a police officer: You obey the thug out of fear, not because you have a moral obligation to obey him. He has power, but not *legitimate* power. The police officer, by contrast, has authority: you recognize that in some cases, he can impose on you a moral obligation to obey his orders. If we accept this distinction, it is clear that one can have authority *only with respect to a rational, moral being*—that is, someone capable of being obligated, of understanding what "authority" and "obligation" mean. Animals, we assume, don't understand these things. Since they don't have the capacity to recognize and follow obligations to obey,[26] it seems inappropriate to say we have authority (much less political authority) over them.

Of course, the notion of authority with respect to animals is perfectly coherent when we find the state defending its right to exercise power over an animal against the claims of another human actor. For example, an animal control officer might have to defend her authority over a dangerous dog against the claims of the dog's owner. But in this case, although we might say that the officer has authority over the dog, what we mean is that the officer has authority over the owner with respect to the dog. That is, she can impose an obligation on the owner to obey her orders.

But Raz points out that authority and illegitimate power aren't the only options. What the animal control officer has with respect to the dog is, according to Raz, *justified power*. This term covers those cases in which one may justifiably exercise power over another while the other still has a right to resist (or, more precisely, no duty to obey). For example, as Raz says, "I do not exercise authority over people afflicted with dangerous diseases if I knock them out and lock them up to protect the public, even though I am . . . justified in doing so." Interestingly, he adds, "I have no more authority over them than I have over mad dogs."[27]

Political rule, then, can refer to the exercise of justified power by the government (and perhaps by others, if we use the term "political" more broadly) with respect to animals. But that possibility raises another quandary: When we exercise power over animals, to whom do we justify ourselves? We might think that we have to justify ourselves to the animal, but only in an "as if" sense. That is, we might consider that an act is justified only if the animal could agree to it, if the animal were in fact capable of reasoning about such things. (In chapter 2 I will argue that, odd as it sounds, this is precisely what we should do.) But it is also possible that those actors might simply be concerned about justifying their actions to other humans, especially humans who sympathize with the animal.

For example, in the case of the San Clemente Island goat extermination program, the dispute turned on whether the navy's killing of the goats was justified with respect to the goats, but it was ALVA and the courts to whom the navy had to justify itself. However, the chief issue *for ALVA* was whether the policy constituted humane treatment of the goats—or, more precisely, whether the goats' interests were given sufficient weight in developing the program.[28] My point is this: Whether we are justifying government actions to the animals themselves or to sympathetic humans, the justification will have to take into account the fact that we believe animals have moral status. That is, the justification will have to refer somewhere to the animal's interests, rights, or welfare (even if those aren't the deciding consideration). Our beliefs about our moral duties to animals play an important role in justifying the use of state power against them.

Let us say, then, that a person (or institution) can have authority over other persons (or institutions) with respect to animals, and can have justified power over animals with respect to the animals themselves. But only when the justification of power includes reference to the animals' welfare, interests, or rights does our rule deserve to be called "political" in the sense suggested by Aristotle and Locke, as something to be achieved by the best regimes. Under this view, Representative Bartlett's relations with the military working dogs he defended can properly be called political, and so can Senator Helms's relations with the lab mice (although, in my view, to a lesser extent). To refuse to consider the welfare of these animals at all would have been (with respect to the animals) acting like a tyrant or a thug.

Defending that claim, and developing a fuller account of what political rule over animals looks like, will be the task of the rest of this book.

III. Is Achieving Justified Relations with Animals a Liberal Value?

It is possible, of course, that it simply isn't the job of a liberal state to look after animal welfare. Liberalism is first and foremost aimed at protecting liberty, usually understood as individual autonomy: the capacity to make reasonable choices and live life as one chooses. Animals do not have the capacity for that sort of freedom, so perhaps liberal states need not concern themselves with animals' good.

I address this point in more depth in chapters 2 and 3, but here I can briefly offer three reasons liberal states should concern themselves with animals' welfare: First, relations with animals are important to many persons' visions of the good life; they can even figure centrally in a person's life. If the liberal state seeks to preserve and expand citizens' abilities to pursue their own conceptions of the good life, it must give some attention to making possible meaningful, morally justifiable relations with animals.[29] The possibility of such relations depends on a background of social practices and beliefs in which such relations can develop. The state may have a role to play in supporting those practices and beliefs, and it may need to regulate institutions and practices—like the mass marketing of animals or animal experimentation—when they erode the more positive and enabling social background we are trying to preserve.

Second, animal lives may have some of the features we value in a free human life. They enjoy a *kind* of natural freedom, or freedom from domination, that many humans find valuable and worth respecting.[30] Animals may be guided more by instinct than by reason, but they still have ways of dwelling intelligently in the world. Indeed, aspects of that freedom are shared by humans; humans, too, may act according to habit, emotion, and other nonrational drives in socially valued ways. This sort of behavior is also included in our liberal conception of a life free from domination.[31] I would suggest, then, that there is nothing inconsistent or illiberal about including animal liberty among our public values.

Finally, the fact that a liberal state privileges human autonomy does not mean it is free to neglect other values, like kindness and compassion. Such neglect could lead to an inhumane sort of liberalism that leaves no place for communal and spiritual values. Of course, serving other values can sometimes promote and sometimes undermine human autonomy; certainly, many measures to promote animal welfare could detract from human liberty. So we need to think carefully about how to fashion liberal institutions and practices to maximize all the values the state must support in order to create a community conducive to a flourishing human life. Our question is whether we can protect animal welfare and promote enriching animal/human relations in a way that serves—or at least does not undermine—what we value in human liberty. That, certainly, is a proper subject for liberal theory.

IV. Can a Democratic Regime Govern Nonequals?

The discussion above invites a final concern about including animals in liberal theory: Would a strong commitment by the liberal state to animal welfare erode our commitment to human equality? We may be, as Leopold suggests, "plain member[s] and citizen[s]" of the biotic community, but the fact remains that we're the governing class. If nonhumans are part of the political community, they are a considerably less powerful part. Our political relations with them must accordingly differ considerably from our relations with coequal citizens. Would recognizing animals as a kind of second-class quasi citizen undermine our hard-won egalitarian norms?

This question brings us into conversation with the literature on recognition and identity politics, which has a vexed relationship with the animal rights movement. Most animal rights advocates emphasize similarities between human and nonhuman animals (sentience, reasoning, emotional life, and so on), and these similarities become the grounds for arguing for similar treatment under law and policy (like granting them rights). But that approach often leads animal rights activists to compare animal and human suffering, which in turn seems (to some) to trivialize human suffering. Should factory farms be compared to the Holocaust, and zoos to prison camps? Doesn't calling our treatment of animals "slavery" simply reinforce the pernicious stereotype of African Americans as beastlike? More generally, if we make room for a class of politically unequal creatures, isn't it too easy to put some humans in that category?

I think these are valid concerns. Animals are similar to us but also different from us in morally and politically relevant ways, and clearly those differences need to be recognized. Good policy would incorporate animals into the political system in appropriate ways—ways that respect both their similarities to and their differences from humans. The question is, can we build the institutions and cultivate the habits and dispositions necessary to govern mute, powerless animals, and also fully realize our egalitarian ideals? Surely this too is a proper subject for liberal theory.

Nevertheless, theory may not be the best guide to answering any of the theoretical questions posed above. They are difficult to answer in the abstract because they involve practical issues of institutional design and civic education. We must look, in part, to our actual practices. This is why I focus my argument on one country, the United States. I expect that many of the arguments in the following pages will be generalizable to other industrialized liberal democracies to some extent, but I want to keep the theoretical argument firmly grounded in the laws and practices of a particular political community. That is, I'm exploring the variety of liberalism that seems to be reflected (albeit somewhat inconsistently) in these laws and practices, rather than trying to develop a liberal public philosophy from a set of abstract principles. This approach will, I hope, ensure that the resulting philosophy is practical and relevant to contemporary issues.

I've chosen the United States partly for convenience; it is the case I know best. But it is also a good test case: The United States is famously, or notoriously, liberal.[32] True, it's not the most progressive of the industrial democracies, and it doesn't go as far as many European nations to protect animal welfare. On the other hand, as I argue in chapter 1, it does have a long-standing commitment to and a broad, bipartisan social consensus in favor of protecting animal welfare. As a result, in the United States we have a complex body of decidedly liberal laws, institutions, and practices that govern animals, with more or less success. Moreover, the United States is an influential case; its wealth and power ensure that American policies (and especially corporate practice) will affect animal welfare all over the world. In short, the United States has an important set of liberal animal welfare practices. Our task here is to surface the principles that underlie these practices, to view them critically and see how they fit with liberalism generally, and also to consider how both the principles and practices might be improved upon. The following chapters attempt to do that.

Chapter 1 begins with a historical account of our changing political and ethical relationships to animals in the United States. My goal here is to make sure the rest of the book is grounded in a concrete understanding of the complex relationship between animals and the state. Specifically, my account challenges some of the conventional wisdom about the development of the animal rights/welfare movement:[33] I argue that rather than thinking of the rise of this movement as the natural outgrowth of the expansion of our sphere of moral concern, we should understand it as a consequence of the expansion of the liberal welfare state. That expansion, I argue, generated the set of issues the animal rights/welfare movement is concerned with. Accordingly, addressing those issues requires not just a new individual ethic but a new public philosophy, suitable for the liberal animal welfare state.

Chapter 2 argues, against several liberal theorists, that animals can be members of the social contract. This argument isn't as radical as it might sound, however. It depends on a quite narrow understanding of the social contract as a kind of heuristic for liberal rulers and citizens to guide their exercise of political power—that is, a public philosophy rather than a comprehensive moral doctrine. I make no claims about the nature of political or moral obligation generally. I do contend, however, that the social contract model is quite useful for thinking through what political duties we owe to animals and to which animals we owe them.

Chapter 3 takes up liberal property theory, addressing whether we can have property rights in animals, what those rights mean, and whether the state can restrict commerce in animals. I argue—this time against several animal rights advocates—that human ownership of animals is not necessarily ethically problematic. The property status of animals does need some reform, but it is *mass commerce* in animals, resulting in their commodification, that deserves our concern.

Chapter 4 turns to the representation of animal interests in political and legal institutions. Liberal theories of representation tend to assume that beings with no agency cannot be represented in the political process. I argue to the contrary that representation of animal interests not only can be but is institutionalized in ways that can facilitate good deliberation and even create for animals a kind of political agency.

Finally, chapter 5 concludes by considering the potential tensions between liberal values and pursuing social reforms aimed at greater protection for animal welfare. I point out that certain kinds of reform strategies can, in fact, pit animal interests against human interests and can undermine liberal values like racial equality and respect for cultural differences. To avoid such conflict, I counsel against relying too heavily on criminal prohibitions and sanctions to protect animals. I emphasize instead the potential of creating new social practices and institutions that bring animal and human interests into harmony. Along these lines, I suggest (again following Raz) that animal rights are best understood as devices to protect collective goods—that is, the *common culture* we need to realize our ideals—rather than devices to protect individual interests. Animal rights rest on the animals' interest in their own welfare, but that interest is best realized in a public culture in which good, enriching human/animal relations flourish. Therefore, our primary goal in promoting animal rights and welfare should be to develop and maintain good institutions and practices of animal husbandry and fellowship.

Governing Animals

1

Trials

The good of the (human) polis depends on the happiness of animals.
—VICKI HEARNE, *Animal Happiness*

IN 1973, THE US Congress passed the Endangered Species Act (ESA), which directs federal agencies to protect endangered species and declares their conservation a national policy goal. According to Roderick Nash, this statute codified a new ethical consensus that nonhumans can enjoy rights, or at least moral status.[1] Granted, according to the preamble, it protects endangered species only because such species are valuable *to humans*.[2] Still, the ESA, along with the many other federal environmental statutes passed during this era, does seem to reflect a new sensibility, a sense that the nonhuman world has greater value than we had recognized and deserves greater protection. This new sensibility is particularly evidenced in American attitudes toward nonhuman animals. Not only have we developed a substantial and relatively well accepted body of laws aimed at protecting animal welfare, but a 2003 Gallup poll shows that the vast majority of Americans (96 percent) believe animals deserve some protection from harm and exploitation. Many think they deserve even more protection than they currently receive; a surprisingly high percentage of respondents (35–38 percent) supported the extension of laws protecting laboratory animals, and 62 percent supported the passage of strict laws protecting farm animals. Twenty-two percent were even willing to support a ban on hunting.[3]

Nash sees this new sensibility as an instance of ethical evolution, even ethical progress: the extension of our moral sensibilities to include nonhumans. He explains the ESA as evidence of "the relatively recent emergence of the belief that ethics should expand from a preoccupation with humans (or their gods) to a concern for animals, plants, rocks, and even nature, or the environment, itself."[4] Behind his claim is a familiar story: For most of the history of Western society (according to this story), animals were not accorded moral status. A few enlightened souls excepted, Western Europeans did not recognize moral duties toward animals at all. Happily, we've all advanced in our moral sympathies. We have gradually come to recognize the moral status of more groups of humans (notably blacks and women), and now we recognize duties to animals as well. Our laws and policies have accordingly evolved to reflect that new, more enlightened consensus. Giving legal protections to nonhumans is simply another step in this process of ethical extension. As Nash says, it marks "the farthest limits of American liberalism."[5]

This is a clear and concise account of the relationship between ethics and public policy, neatly accounting for animals' changing relationship to the liberal state. And it isn't entirely wrong. Contemporary animal ethics *are* different from the ethics in play in Europe in, say, the mid-sixteenth century, and so are our laws and policies. But the story of that evolution, I think, is not so simple. This chapter offers a different account: The development of our animal welfare laws has less to do with the expansion of our "sphere of moral concern" than with the expansion of the liberal welfare state. This expansion generated a new set of questions about the political community's relationship to animals—questions that the rest of this book will attempt to address. My aim here is to offer a more sophisticated and nuanced explanation of the development of the American animal welfare state, but also to show that the questions of animal ethics we are wrestling with today are rooted in a specific political and institutional context. Accordingly, addressing those questions requires us to develop not only our individual moral sense but our liberal public philosophy.

I. Medieval Animal Trials

E. P. Evans's 1906 classic *The Criminal Prosecution and Capital Punishment of Animals* describes the prosecution of weevils (or *charançon*) that were ravaging the vineyards of the French hamlet of St. Julien in 1545. The complaint was brought by the wine-growers to the procurator of the ecclesiastical court, who duly appointed counsel for the insects. The lawyers argued their respective cases quite ably, but the court decided not to issue a sentence. Instead, he admonished the community to seek relief through prayer: "Inasmuch as God . . . hath ordained that the earth should bring forth fruits and herbs, not solely for the sustenance of rational human beings, but likewise for the preservation and support of insects . . . therefore it would be unbecoming to proceed with rashness and precipitance against the animals now actually accused and indicted."[6] Accordingly, the court ordered High Mass to be celebrated on three consecutive days and the host carried in solemn procession around the vineyards. The program was carried out, and the insects soon disappeared.

Unfortunately, in 1587 the insects returned. Again they found themselves subject to legal proceedings. This time the case went to trial, the petitioners asking the court for a writ of excommunication against the insects. The insects were represented by Pierre Rembaud, who argued that the insects were well within their rights to inhabit the vineyards. He cited the book of Genesis, in which God explicitly bade the living creatures to be fruitful and multiply—which command he would not have given if he had not intended that these creatures eat plants to support themselves. Moreover, Rembaud argued that it was unreasonable to invoke civil and canonical law against brute beasts, which are subject only to natural law and their own instincts.

The prosecutor responded that the animals, although created before man, were intended to be subordinate and subservient to him. The book of Genesis made it clear that animals had no other purpose but to minister to man and should therefore refrain from ravaging his vineyards. The defense, however, replied that the subordination of the lower animals did not involve the right of excommunication and that the prosecutor had failed to show that the civil and canonical law applied to animals.

The trial promised to drag on, so the villagers took another approach. They held a public meeting at which they designated another field outside the vineyards for the use of the insects. They authorized this compromise by vote and agreed to draw up a conveyance of the field (with certain rights reserved) to be delivered to the insects. The defense rejected this generous offer, however, declaring the land in question too sterile to provide support for the animals. Sadly, the outcome of the case is unknown, the final page of the record having been destroyed by insects.[7]

Animal trials were not uncommon in Europe during the Middle Ages.[8] Evans notes that both the secular and the ecclesiastical courts prosecuted animals; the secular courts usually handled domestic animals, while ecclesiastical courts were asked to deal with pests and vermin. The practice reached its peak during the fifteenth through seventeenth centuries and then declined (although instances occurred as late as the late nineteenth century).[9] Scholars have offered many interpretations of what seems, to modern readers, a very

odd use of the legal system. Evans himself dismissed the theory that such procedures were intended to impress on a weakly disciplined populace respect
for the law, by teaching men to respect even the lowly insect. He thought it
more likely that such trials represented a "barbaric" sense of justice and efforts
by the ecclesiastical establishment to extend its power even to insects.[10] Walter
Woodburn Hyde, discussing the practice in a 1916 law review article, took a
more anthropological approach, arguing that such trials were survivals from
primitive ceremonies for inflicting revenge and averting evil fortune. They
were intended not to punish the animal itself but to cast out the evil demons
that evidently had entered into it and caused its bad behavior.[11]

Later scholars have largely endorsed Hyde's view. J. J. Finkelstein's detailed
study, for example, agrees with Hyde that the "trials" of pests and vermin were
purely ritualistic, usually resulting in spiritual punishments: anathemas, excommunication, and the like. But he notes that domestic animal trials were
not, strictly speaking, trials at all; the judicial process consisted merely of
stating the facts of the case and pronouncing how the animal was to be exe-
cuted. The beast received no formal defense.[12] Nevertheless, he does not suggest that we view this practice as comparable to our modern administrative
procedures for "putting down" unwanted or dangerous dogs.[13] Finkelstein
instead characterizes animal executions as a way to expiate the public's horror
at an animal that was "a living rebuttal of the divinely ordained hierarchy of
creation"—again, emphasizing the ritualistic nature of the punishment.[14]

Esther Cohen's treatment of the subject, by contrast, gives more attention
to the significance of using *legal* procedures; she suggests that the animal trials
indicate a view of justice as a universal attribute, applicable to all nature. "If
man was to rule nature, he must do so according to the same principles that
governed his relationships with fellow humans. . . . The strict observance of
judicial (not necessarily human) procedure according to the letter of the law
carefully exonerated these trials from any appearance of a lynching. The animals got their just due."[15]

On one point, at least, most scholars agree: Putting animals on trial did
not imply that these animals had moral agency in the same sense that human
beings do. Indeed, it appears that medieval views of animals' rational and
moral capacities were not so different from our own views. Nor, *pace* Evans,
do animal trials suggest that medieval folk lacked compassion or a sense of
moral obligation *to* animals. On the contrary, the trials of vermin and the
procedures surrounding the execution of domestic animals suggest that animals were deeply involved in the web of ethical and spiritual relations that
constituted these medieval communities.

Rather, what made these trials a more meaningful practice in the 1500s than they would be today was the religious and institutional background. To the people who prosecuted the weevils of St. Julien, courts had not just earthly but also spiritual power. And animals, although lacking moral agency themselves, could be host to evil spirits or could, quite innocently, be agents of God's will, inflicting a much-deserved trial on their human neighbors. Courts and other legal procedures (like the contract offered by the residents of St. Julien) were appropriate ways to exercise spiritual power against beings with whom the human community had social and moral relations. Judicial proceedings showed respect for animals as God's creation and acknowledged that humans' relationship of dominion over animals was defined and limited by man's duties to his Creator. Given this context, it made sense for the villagers of St. Julien to use legal procedures to govern their relations with animals. Cohen's argument is on point here: The trial and contractual negotiations helped to constitute the villagers' ethical relations with the weevils. Although these legal practices were not unproblematic—they raised difficult questions about the nature of man's dominion, and his own culpability in disturbing his harmony with nature—the procedures apparently were useful in incorporating the insects into the ethical community.

We should not, however, forget Evans's cynical notion that the trials were merely attempts by the Church to extend its power beyond all reasonable bounds. Perhaps the villagers of St. Julien were *encouraged* by an aggrandizing Church to bring insects within the circle of their ethical sensibilities and thus within the ambit of ecclesiastical jurisdiction. Government institutions, after all, are not simply ciphers to be deployed at will by members of the public; they can be actors in their own right, shaping public opinion and social practices to serve institutional interests.

II. Modern Animal Trials

Modern Americans do not typically bring suit against animals. But animals sometimes bring suit against humans. For example, in 1993 a dolphin named Kama sued the New England Aquarium and the US Navy. The suit, initiated by Citizens to End Animal Suffering and Exploitation (CEASE), the Animal Legal Defense Fund, and the Progressive Animal Welfare Society, was aimed at stopping Kama's transfer from the aquarium to the navy. Following what has become a fairly common practice, they named Kama as the lead plaintiff.

Kama was born in captivity at Sea World in San Diego and was transferred to the New England Aquarium in 1986. In 1987, the aquarium concluded a

deal to sell Kama and another dolphin, Rainbow, to the navy, which intended
to study their sonar capabilities. The animal welfare organizations brought
suit under the federal Marine Mammal Protection Act, which prohibits the
"taking" of marine mammals without a permit. The defendants had no permit,
but they argued that the statute applied only to animals "taken" from the wild,
not to animals born in captivity. The court, however, never reached that issue.
It dismissed the case on the grounds that neither Kama nor the animal welfare
organizations had standing to bring suit under the statute in question.[16]

Do animals have the right to bring suit in federal courts? The court noted
that there was little case law on the issue. Although federal courts had enter-
tained lawsuits involving animal plaintiffs, in only one case, *Hawaiian Crow
v. Lujan*,[17] was the animal's standing challenged. The Hawaiian crow lost, as
did Kama. The court in Kama's case first noted that the question of standing
to sue under the Marine Mammals Protection Act[18] was governed by the federal Administrative Procedure Act, which provides that "a *person* suffering
legal wrong because of agency action . . . is entitled to judicial review thereof."[19]
The court then, without much argument, concluded that the term "person"
does not include animals. "If Congress and the President intended to take the
extraordinary step of authorizing animals as well as people and legal entities
to sue, they could, and should, have said so plainly."[20] It also considered the
relevance of Federal Rule of Civil Procedure 17(b), which deals with the capacity of an individual to sue. This rule has been used to allow corporations
and other legal entities to bring suit in federal courts, but the court was unwilling to apply it to "other non-human life." It noted that animals are usually
treated as property of their owners, and that fact (in the court's opinion)
weighed against according animals standing in their own right.

The court went on to determine that, under the rather arcane principles of
standing doctrine, the animal welfare organizations also were not allowed to
bring suit. The court concluded that the members of these organizations were
not being harmed (in a legally recognized way) by Kama's transfer, because
none of them had a particular, personal relationship with the dolphin that
was threatened by its sale. They "do not, and evidently cannot, state that they
ever observed Kama in particular, as opposed to dolphins in general, at the
Aquarium. . . . The fact that neither [party] knows if she actually observed
Kama belies any possible assertion that either of them had established a relationship with Kama."[21] The court noted that after the transfer, there were still
other dolphins in the aquarium for the parties to look at. The lawsuit was,
accordingly, dismissed. (The court didn't pause to consider whether there was
some tension between its conclusions that, on one hand, a dolphin is not a

person but, on the other hand, one can have a personal relationship with a particular dolphin—a point to which we will return below.)

The New England Aquarium considered the lawsuit frivolous, but not, interestingly, because the plaintiffs included a dolphin. Rather, they thought the animal welfare organizations had their facts wrong. The welfare organizations claimed that Kama had been captured from the wild and that the dolphin was being mistreated, neither of which (according to the aquarium) was true. In fact, the aquarium and the animal welfare groups largely agreed on humans' basic ethical duties to dolphins. Their quarrel centered on whether it is acceptable to hold some dolphins in captivity for educational and political purposes, with the aim of promoting support for their protection.[22] The animal welfare organizations were probably also concerned about the navy's apparent interest in using dolphins in warfare. None of those issues, of course, came up in the court's opinion.

The issue of Kama's standing was not, however, unimportant or frivolous. Admittedly, it was and is controversial: Many people think the idea of according legal standing to animals displays a fundamental confusion between animals and persons.[23] But clearly the legal world is not divided up so neatly between human persons and nonhuman things. Corporations, after all, are not natural persons, but they can sue and be sued. The judge himself acknowledged that the legislature could, if it wished, confer on animals the right to sue, just as it has conferred that right on other nonhuman entities.[24] Of course, the court or the legislature would then have to make some difficult decisions about who is authorized to represent the animal in question (an issue I will address in a later chapter). But conferring standing on animals does not require us to embrace novel philosophical conceptions of moral agency. As the court recognized, it is not a question of philosophy but of policy: Would this be the best way to ensure appropriate enforcement of laws intended to protect animals?[25]

Gary Francione thinks it is. Francione has been arguing for many years that animals' legal status as property prevents the proper enforcement of many statutes (like the Endangered Species Act, the Animal Welfare Act, and the Marine Mammals Protection Act) intended to protect their welfare. It's a reasonable point: If standing doctrine prevents animal welfare organizations from bringing suit on behalf of animals, and animals themselves cannot be named as plaintiffs, then in many cases no one is in a good position to ensure aggressive enforcement of these statutes. He and a number of other legal scholars would like to see the law reformed so as to express more consistently and effectively the concern for animals expressed in many of our statutes.[26]

On the other hand, courts have reason to be wary of recognizing animal plaintiffs. To do so might give better protection to animals' welfare, but it would also empower certain human persons or groups to bring suit to enforce these statutes. This is the issue that troubled E. P. Evans about the medieval animal trials: Letting animals into court extends the power of the court, and the power of those well placed to use the court. Is this what Congress intended in passing these statutes? Since federal court judges are not elected and enjoy life tenure, extending their power raises issues of democratic legitimacy. Do we want animal welfare policy driven by federal judges and litigants, or by elected representatives and their constituents?

The same concern lies behind the Supreme Court's efforts to restrict the standing of animal welfare and other public interest groups. Justice Antonin Scalia has been a leading voice in this effort, arguing in a 1983 law review article that a more generous standing doctrine threatened to turn courts into "political forums." Courts, according to Scalia, should simply protect individuals whose rights are harmed by application of a law. Allowing people with no particular, concrete injury to bring suit to enforce statutes would convert courts from their "traditional" role as defenders of individual and minority rights against the majority into "an equal partner with the executive and legislative branches in the formulation of public policy" (a role he believes they are too undemocratic to perform well).[27]

Although there is much to admire in Scalia's penetrating analysis of the larger implications of standing doctrine, there is also much to criticize in his effort to restrict the standing of public interest groups to enforce animal welfare statutes. For example, his reasoning is at odds with the long tradition of court/legislature partnership in creating public policy. Although it may seem somewhat undemocratic, judges' policy-making role is in fact a central feature of the Anglo-American common law tradition, and the American constitutional tradition. But let us leave that issue aside. I want to make a different point: Standing doctrine in the area of animal welfare is not driven solely by concerns over who should enforce federal statutes. It also, quite consistently, recognizes the meaning and importance of the human/animal bond. In Kama's case, for example, the court noted that a human would have standing to bring suit if he or she personally observed and studied Kama—if she knew Kama, as it were, *personally*. Merely observing or wanting to observe any old dolphin at the aquarium was not sufficient; the plaintiff must allege harm to a *personal relationship* with the particular animal. Disruption of this relationship can constitute a harm (to the human) of which the Court can take cognizance. Thus this personal relationship, this bond between an individual human and animal, is the value on which the Court's standing doctrine in this area is based.

The Ninth Circuit Court of Appeals reasoned similarly in *Animal Lovers Volunteer Association (ALVA) vs. Weinberger*. As discussed in the introduction, this suit concerned the navy program to eradicate goats on San Clemente Island in order to protect certain endangered species. The court denied ALVA standing to bring suit on behalf of the goats. The members' distress over the shooting of the goats, the court concluded, did not constitute a sufficient injury to confer standing, principally because the members of ALVA were not personally acquainted with the goats and wouldn't witness their killing. "ALVA has not differentiated its concern from the generalized abhorrence other members of the public may feel at the prospect of cruelty to animals."[28] The reasoning assumes, even takes for granted, that humans can form meaningful personal relationships with animals and that those relationships are worth protecting.

In short, standing doctrine in this area has evolved (without much explicit argument on the point) to protect a particular kind of human/animal bond. Someone who studies an animal, interacts with it regularly, and develops an emotional connection to it will probably be allowed to bring suit to protect that animal. This, apparently, is the sort of relationship that can give rise to the concrete, particularized *human* injury the court is accustomed to addressing. That is, of course, an institutional value, but it also expresses a public value— the value of a certain way of relating to animals. Rather than affording legal protection to one's general, impersonal sympathy with or sense of justice toward animals, standing doctrine protects *social relationships between humans and animals*. And although the court is interested in the value of these relationships to humans, it is not implausible that this recognition could also be the basis for finding that some animals, at least, are legal "persons": They are persons to us because we relate to them as members of our social community.

This discussion suggests that both the medieval and the modern animal trials use legal procedures to incorporate animals into the ethical community, to express and to protect the moral significance of our relations with animals. As different as these practices are, neither of them displays any fundamental confusion about animals' moral status or rational capacities. That is, neither practice asks us to assume that animals are moral agents. At the same time, both practices suggest a deeply felt need for morally justified relations with animals and a belief that legal institutions can play a role in achieving that. But clearly these medieval and modern legal practices have vastly different meanings, reflecting different views about the way courts and the law can mediate our relations to animals. How should we understand these differences? How should we explain the evolution of our moral and political relations with animals?

III. A Critique of Ethical Extensionism

Roderick Nash calls his theory of moral evolution "ethical extensionism." Under this theory, the evolution of our moral and political relations with animals—more specifically, the contemporary animal rights movement—reflects the expanding sphere of our moral sympathies. Thus, according to Nash, during the Middle Ages "nature did not fare well in Western ethics. Increasingly people assumed that nature, animals included, had no rights, and that nonhuman beings existed to serve human beings. There was no extended ethical community. It followed that the appropriate relationship of people to nature emphasized expediency and utility."[29] He then traces what he calls the gradual extension of ethical relations to animals and then to the rest of nature over the eighteenth, nineteenth, and twentieth centuries—an evolution evidenced by our increasing willingness to entertain the notion that nonhumans have rights.

Nash's argument builds on a respectable tradition. Peter Singer, for example, cites W. E. H. Lecky's *History of European Morals*, first published in 1869: "At one time the benevolent affections embrace merely the family, soon the circle expanding includes first a class, then a nation, then a coalition of nations, then all humanity and finally, its influence is felt in the dealings of man with the animal world."[30] Nash himself draws on Darwin's theory of the evolution of morals, which also posits a process of ethical extension: "Over time [according to Darwin], humans broadened their ethical circle to include 'small tribes,' then 'larger communities,' and eventually 'nations' and 'races.' They gradually reached out still farther 'to the imbecile, maimed, and other useless members of society.' Finally, humans would put aside 'baneful customs and superstitions' and might eventually reach 'disinterested love for all living creatures.'"[31] Aldo Leopold, supporting the Darwinian view, famously argues in "The Land Ethic" (1949) that the processes of ecological evolution have driven the "extension of ethics" from the relations between individuals, to the relations between individual and society, and finally to the relations between human society and the land, animals, and plants.[32] Largely as a result of Leopold's influence, this theory of ethical extension has become a commonplace in environmental ethics. Environmental ethicist Baird Callicott, for example, also supports the Darwinian view of the evolution of morals and finds in this process of ethical extension an explanation for the contemporary rise of animal rights and environmental ethics.[33]

Of course, even its advocates would agree that the extension of ethical sensibilities has not been as consistent as these passages suggest. Many ancient communities may have included some animals but excluded many humans, for example. More generally, the circle of moral sympathy seems to expand and contract in ways that the theory does not explain. Nash himself recognizes that at least one Roman jurist accorded legal status to animals, in the form of the *jus animalium*—an idea that continued to inspire some legal theorists throughout the Middle Ages but was rejected by jurists in the seventeenth century.[34] Still, theorists like Nash and Callicott believe it is reasonable to assume that ethics are confined by the boundaries of the social community, whatever it is, and that over the course of human history we can discern a pattern of expanding the social community, bringing more entities under the sphere of ethics.

But this theory leaves too much unexplained. To begin, what counts as having "ethical sensibilities" or being "within the sphere of ethics"? "Expediency" seems easy enough to define: It is expedient to close one's office door to avoid being distracted, just as it is expedient to close the blinds to diminish the sun's glare on one's computer screen. Neither action involves consideration of others' interests. By contrast, refusing to cheat a customer (even if you could get away with it) seems to be an other-regarding act, and thus purely a matter of ethics. Still, there is a great deal of gray area between those extremes. For example, consider two communities that engage in warfare and trade with one another. They may observe certain rules of conduct toward one another—rules designed to ensure productive trade relations—but also consider one another enemies, subject to torture and summary execution, when they are at war. Do they have "ethical relations" with one another? Or is their apparently ethical behavior purely a matter of expediency? There is a good deal of complexity to explore here.

A related question is how we define "community." In some accounts of ethical extension, it seems that the social community is defined as those beings with whom we recognize ethical relations—but then ethical extensionism just leads us in circles: As the community to whom we recognize ethical duties expands, we recognize ethical duties to more beings. For ethical extension to work as social theory, it seems that something like the state or economic system must determine the bounds of the community and, accordingly, our ethical sentiments. Those questions thus lead to another key question: What *drives* ethical extension? Does the state play a role in expanding the moral community, or does public policy simply follow changing public sentiment? Should we look to other large-scale social forces, like the economy, to explain this extension, or focus our attention on the individual level, asking why and how a human is moved to recognize obligations to nonhumans?

Stephen Quilley's version of ethical extension proposes an interesting and instructive set of answers to these questions, drawing on Norbert Elias's theory of "the civilizing process." Elias, an early twentieth-century sociologist, was trying to explain how certain classes in Western Europe came to think of themselves as "civilized." He links this development to two interrelated trends that shaped Western society from the Middle Ages onward. First, a certain habitus—a psychological disposition to restrain one's impulses—became characteristic of court society and was eventually adopted by the middle class. In other words, people enjoying social privilege internalized rules of "polite" behavior, identified first as court etiquette and later, more generally, as good manners. At the same time, an expanding urban economy fueled the increasing power of the central state, which had greater access to this economy than did the landed aristocracy. As a result, what was once an independent warrior class (the landed aristocracy) became a dependent upper class of courtiers—who were defined by their embrace of court etiquette. Quilley calls this process a "virtuous cycle," whereby "greater pacification [of the warrior class] facilitated trade and economic growth, which in turn underwrote the economic and military power of the state." The expanding urban economy created greater economic and social ties, which increased the conscious interdependence among social groups, and those interdependent relationships were smoother and more productive for those who internalized the pattern of self-restraint we call good manners. Good manners thus became "second nature," backed by social norms, law, and commercial incentives.[35] Quilley goes on to suggest that a similar pattern of increasing conscious interdependence with the non-human world could fuel a similar "virtuous cycle," which would account for the extension of ethics to nonhumans.[36]

Quilley's analysis is useful in several respects. First, he characterizes the ethical attitudes we are talking about as "manners" or "etiquette," which helps us specify what exactly we mean by "ethical relations": We're talking about the circle of persons to whom we feel obliged to show good manners. And since good manners are a social practice, not a sentiment (much less a fundamental belief about a being's moral status), it makes sense that they are context-dependent. So what counts as ethical relations (or good manners) with animals will vary according to one's relationship with the animal and the social situation.

Similarly, Quilley's analysis helps us understand how we can talk about the spread of certain ethical norms that are, nevertheless, still widely violated (especially, as he notes, "behind the scenes").[37] Good manners are those patterns of behavior that people display in public when they are trying to win social approbation and avoid being shamed. So we may see the spread of good manners but still lament the constant violation of these norms when no one is looking. Finally, Quilley usefully directs our attention to the interaction between civil society and the state in explaining how good manners evolve. The state, responding to changing economic forces and pursuing its own institutional interests, may play an important role in rewarding good manners and, eventually, writing them into law.

On the other hand, Quilley's theory does not give us much insight into why and how the *content* of good manners changes—why, for example, it was once proper to appoint legal counsel to insects, and it is now socially acceptable in some circles to throw a birthday party for a dog. We will need to reach beyond Elias's civilizing process to explain such transformations. Similarly, his theory strikingly fails to explain why the "civilizing" European society simultaneously embraced human slavery as a mode of production. Reliance on race slavery grew deeper and more pervasive from the fifteenth to the eighteenth centuries, and even into the nineteenth century in the United States. How does that development square with the notion of ethical extension?

This final question points to a basic difficulty with Quilley's logic: He assumes that increasing interdependence with another group will lead to the extension of ethical attitudes (or good manners) toward that group. But it might also have the opposite effect. A community might *dehumanize* those beings on whom it depends, in order to control and exploit the subordinate group more effectively. In other words, the community might fall into a vicious cycle instead of a virtuous one: Dehumanization and brutal behavior toward a group (like enslaved Africans) undermines the feasibility of voluntary cooperation and ethical relations with them, making it necessary to adopt increasingly more violent means of control.

This is just to say that increasing interdependence doesn't make ethical extension inevitable (a point on which Quilley would probably agree). Nor does a community consistently choose one path over another. Rather, we should expect complex societies to be, frankly, complicated, with shifting and conflicting ethical dynamics. Similarly, we should understand ethical relations as involving more than the extension of a standard pattern of behavior we call "good manners." Clearly the difference between the weevils' trial in 1587 and Kama's case in 1993 is not captured very well by the theory of ethical extension.

I argue instead for a less neat, and less progressive, story. First, I think we must endorse Quilley's view that the evolution of ethics is connected to the evolution of the state. The ethics of our relations with animals change in conjunction with changes in the social, intellectual, and institutional context in which those relations unfold. And the political context is particularly important; indeed, the concept of animal rights would hardly make sense before we had a concept of the state as a guarantor of individual rights, just as the concept of animal welfare depends on the concept of the state as a guarantor of individual welfare. Thus the development of the liberal welfare state changes the context of our ethical relations with animals—not by raising the question of whether animals are members of the moral community but by posing the question in a new and distinctive way. The liberal state does not ask whether animals have souls, are inhabited by demons, or have been sent as a punishment from God. Instead it asks, What responsibility does the state have for their welfare? And do animals have something like natural rights that the state must respect?

Second, we must complicate the story of moral progress. To be sure, our ethics toward animals change as our practices and background beliefs change. But change does not always happen in one direction. The age of industry and modern science has created a host of new ways to degrade and destroy animals—factory farming, genetic modification, even species extinction through climate change. These practices are not simply failures to meet our ethical standards. They, too, can be taken as evidence of our evolving egalitarian and liberal ethical sensibilities; after all, these practices are often justified by the importance of providing inexpensive food to the poor, or by the benefits of economic development to human happiness and self-realization (a value that has developed along with, and sometimes in tension with, our concern with animal welfare). So our moral sympathies do not simply expand to embrace more beings. They expand and contract, and our priorities shift, in complex ways over time.

Moral progress of a sort is certainly possible. We are constantly aiming for an elusive coherence that would make our lives fully meaningful and justifiable; some individuals, and societies, may achieve that coherence better than others. But we shouldn't expect ever to achieve a stable state of ethical perfection. We must constantly monitor our laws, practices, and beliefs to ensure that they continue to hang together and make sense.

IV. A Brief History of the Liberal Animal Welfare State

The specific change we are dealing with here, the rise of the animal welfare/ animal rights movement and the extension of animal welfare laws in the United States, is best understood in the context of the development of the modern liberal welfare State. By "State" I mean the semiautonomous set of institutions, along with the laws and practices by which they operate, that claims a monopoly on the legitimate use of force in a territory. (For the sake of clarity, in this section I will capitalize "State" when I use it in this comprehensive sense, to distinguish it from the governments of particular American states.) The American State includes federal, state, and local governments, but like any concept, it has messy borders. Some civic organizations (like the Humane Society) may take on State functions, and sometimes an agent of the State (like a forest service officer) might muddy the distinction between her role as government agent and her role as private citizen. Still, the State is distinct from civil society and public opinion. It has some autonomy; it may act independently of the public, or influence public opinion rather than simply reflecting it.

As Nash noted, over the course of the nineteenth and twentieth centuries, the American State extended civil and political rights to more segments of civil society, creating a direct relationship between individual citizens as rights-bearers and the State as the primary guarantor of those rights. At the same time, the State took on more responsibility for protecting the vulnerable, not just by preventing others from violating their rights but through the delivery of a wide array of services (education, welfare benefits, and so on) intended to improve their welfare. This second development involved the creation of administrative agencies, giving us the vast administrative State we have today.[38] Clearly, all of these developments helped to structure how we think about our ethical relations with animals. Our attempts to make livestock production more humane, for example, assumes the existence of administrative agencies to oversee their welfare, and the idea of granting legal rights to animals assumes a host of judicial procedures that would make those rights meaningful.

More precisely, we can identify four principal trends, from the late eighteenth through the twentieth centuries, that shaped the relationship of animals to the emerging American liberal welfare State and how we understand our ethical duties toward them: (1) the institutionalization (in animal welfare organizations, traditions of pet-keeping, and other practices) of a strong social ethic of kindness to animals; (2) the political organization of those with recreational interests in animals (particularly hunters, but also bird-watchers and outdoor enthusiasts), and the development of industries around those interests (such as gun manufacturing and tourism); (3) the increasing commodification and industrial production of animals (as markets for animal products and pets expanded); and (4) the expansion of the State's capacity to manage animals, principally in pursuit of military, economic, and public health objectives. These trends sometimes worked in different and even conflicting directions, so the evolution of animals' relationship to the American State is a long and fascinating story. I can offer only a brief summary here, but even this very general overview should help to orient us and ground the discussion in the remainder of the book.

From the Colonial to the Early Republican Era

Communal control of animals is nothing new, of course. To be sure, with respect to wild animals, American colonists enjoyed considerable freedom from the restrictive hunting laws common to European polities. Moreover, unlike the natives (who traditionally hunted for subsistence and for local trade only), the European colonizers established vast trade networks, an apparently unlimited market for animal products, and a commercial economy, all of which helped to displace preexisting native hunting practices and promote overhunting. The British government had little interest in restricting such market hunting; on the contrary, by the second half of the sixteenth century, the fur trade had become critical to the colonial economy.[39] Colonial governments did grow concerned about the diminishing supply of game, and all but Georgia had established closed seasons on fish and deer by 1776. However, it was hard to enforce these laws, and the vast frontier beyond the colonies remained open to commercial hunting throughout the colonial period and well into the nineteenth century.[40]

The colonists seemed to view wild game animals principally as commodities (or, in the case of predators like wolves, as nuisances) and did not dwell on any ethical obligations they might have toward these creatures. But domestic animals had a more secure place in the seventeenth-century ethical universe. As Virginia Anderson explains, the European colonists viewed animals through the lens of Christian beliefs and a rich body of folklore. Domestic animals were created by God to serve humans, but humans had a stewardship relationship toward them. Colonists were routinely instructed by preachers and agricultural experts to treat their animals gently. Massachusetts even included in the Body of Liberties some liberties for "bruit creatures."

> No man shall exercise any Tirranny or Crueltie towards any bruite Creature which are usuallie kept for man's use.
> If any man shall have occasion to leade or drive Cattel from place to place that is far of, so that they be weary, or hungry, or fall sick, or lambe, It shall be lawful to rest or refresh them, for a competent time,

in any open place that is not Corne, meadow, or inclosed for some peculiar use.[41]

We should note that we have no evidence of any prosecutions under this law; it was enforced, if at all, through social pressure, as were most of the other norms governing New England society.[42] Indeed, the general dearth of colonial statutes protecting animal welfare does not necessarily indicate the absence of an ethic of stewardship; it merely indicates greater reliance on nonlegal means of controlling behavior. Of course, judicial proceedings were occasionally used in New Englanders' relations with animals, but in a typically seventeenth-century way: Although the English colonists did not put animals on trial, they did engage in ritual executions of unruly dogs or livestock suspected of being cursed or housing malevolent spirits.[43]

In general, domestic animals were well integrated into colonial social communities and a major concern of colonial governments. We see the greatest degree of communal control in New England, where town governments were well organized and the settlers practiced mixed husbandry. Raising livestock and crops together, in close proximity to human habitation, required close control of animals. Thus in addition to requiring farmers to pay for damages caused by wandering livestock, town governments typically took responsibility for providing pasture, paying herders' fees, and ensuring that crop land was adequately fenced. In fact, the New England colonies developed a complex set of land use practices designed to keep livestock separate from crop lands and under strict control.[44] Some towns even regulated livestock breeding, appointing officials to determine which bull calves would be allowed to breed.[45]

Communal control of livestock was less developed in the southern colonies, where the settlers adopted free-range husbandry, letting their pigs and cattle roam in the woods most of the year. This style of husbandry made it difficult for the colonial governors even to enforce property rights in livestock; despite draconian penalties, theft was common.[46] Nevertheless, the free-range system depended on a suitable legal structure. For example, in contrast to New England, South Carolina made farmers responsible for fencing their crops to protect them from roaming livestock. It also provided for registration of brands and earmarks so that wandering animals could be identified.[47]

So when we speak of the development of the American State's authority over animals, we are not necessarily speaking of an increase in community concern and control of animals from the seventeenth to the twentieth centuries. Rather, we are referring to a change in how the community exercises that concern and control: through an increasing use of statutes and judicial decisions, as opposed to social pressure; the development of new institutions like police forces and administrative agencies to exercise State authority over animals; the evolution of civil society to include numerous organizations devoted to animal welfare and management; and the gradual movement of responsibility for animal management from the local to the state and federal level.

These institutional changes were, of course, related to changing beliefs about animals. Anderson notes that animal folklore was steadily modified by advancing Protestant orthodoxy over the sixteenth and seventeenth centuries. Those views were further affected by the rise of a more secular, scientific worldview among the American elite in the eighteenth century. Eighteenth-century natural historians, such as Thomas Jefferson, were immersed in the scientific study of animals. But secular, scientific perspectives probably were not widely shared among the general public. Indeed, the public apparently retained a more spiritual and folkloric view of animals well into the nineteenth century.[48]

Changing beliefs about animals, I would suggest, do not entirely explain the demise of practices like the ritual execution of animals. We must also consider changing beliefs about law and the courts. Blackstone's *Commentaries on the Laws of England* was published in 1765 and had a profound influence on American law. In the *Commentaries* we see clear evidence of a shift away from the worldview that made sense of animal trials and ritual executions. Blackstone's worldview is rigorously rationalist: His God created the universe but then left it to be governed by the laws of nature; he leaves little room for divine agency in everyday affairs. Only man has free will and therefore moral agency—the *Commentaries* make no mention of the possibility of demonic possession.[49] Blackstone was also an eighteenth-century rationalist in his understanding of the role of civil courts, whose purpose is confined to redressing invasions of rights.[50] They wield no supernatural power and can be of use only to rights-bearing agents seeking compensation from other moral agents. He also recognized ecclesiastical courts, whose primary purpose seemed to be imposing uniformity on church doctrine, but he was clearly hostile to what he saw as their pretensions to nearly despotic authority and had little to say about their spiritual role.[51] This understanding of law and the courts is, of course, consistent with the principle of separation of church and state, a value that took root in the United States in the early years of the republic. In short, changing understandings of nature, law, and government, promoted by the intellectual and social elites and reflecting colonial experience and evolving institutional practices, are all relevant to explaining the evolving relationship between animals and the State.

Some aspects of the animal-State relationship, however, were dictated by the needs of the State itself, largely independent of mass or elite opinion. The military, for example, relied heavily on animals. While mounted soldiers played a relatively minor role in the Revolutionary War, soldiers did use horses for transportation, and draft animals and livestock (provisions on the hoof) were critical to eighteenth- and nineteenth-century warfare.[52]

Thus, it is fair to say that managing animals was not just a concern but a *major* concern of government during the colonial era. While the need to control livestock was probably the most significant animal-related factor in State development throughout this period, the promotion of market hunting and use of draft animals and livestock by the military were also significant. These factors continued to be vital to State development throughout the nineteenth century, but they were accompanied by the emergence of a civil society deeply concerned with moral reform, or what Quilley calls the "civilizing process."

The Nineteenth-Century Era of State-Building and Reform

In 1815, a reorganization of the army eliminated the cavalry, on the grounds that mounted units were of little use in forest warfare with the Native Americans. But that decision was reversed when the army began to encounter the mounted warriors of the Great Plains.[53] Cavalry units were rapidly reinstated and continued to play an important role in warfare and law enforcement in the West throughout the nineteenth century. The invention of newer, lighter artillery that could be drawn into place with horses also increased their importance to the military.[54] Indeed, the Civil War was, in historian Russell Weigley's words, "largely a war of animal power." Horses, mules, and oxen, numbering in the hundreds of thousands, provided most of the army's transportation, while the cavalry and horse artillery used thousands of horses as well.[55] Herds of cattle followed the Union armies as a mobile food supply, and the Confederate Army even created a "cow cavalry" to bring cattle from Florida to the Georgia rail system.[56] But while the military depended on livestock, livestock also benefited, in some ways, from a strong military. The South's defeat, for example, had serious consequences for southern livestock. Hunger, disease, lack of labor, and general social disorder caused the South to lose about half its population of hogs and about 15 percent of its cattle during the Civil War.[57]

The military's intense use of animal power was characteristic of the industrializing age in general. Until the invention of the internal combustion engine, animals were a critical source of industrial power. They were also heavily exploited for their meat and fur: During the nineteenth century, hunters and, eventually, farmers and ranchers invaded the Great Plains, with drastic consequences for the animal population. Hunting continued largely unregulated on the frontier through the nineteenth century, contributing to the striking depletion of game animals throughout the country. The bison's story is well known: From 1830 to 1870, bison skins were the most marketable commodity in the Great Plains, and the market was dominated by one organization, the American Fur Company (which owed its success in part to the federal government's protectionist policies, which freed it from British and French competition). The American Fur Company made efforts to maintain stable prices for bison skins but did nothing to restrict hunting or to counter the bison's decline.[58] The spread of ranching throughout the West (a development also supported by State action) further impaired their numbers.

Even in the more settled eastern states, a culture of unrestricted hunting took root. State governments enacted four kinds of hunting regulations: bounties on predators, a closed season on certain game species, restriction of the hunting privileges of certain social groups (usually blacks or Native Americans), and regulations of trespass. But these were hard to enforce, particularly in less settled areas, which included most of the South and West. The state and local governments simply lacked the means—revenue, personnel, and administrative structures, not to mention the knowledge—to engage in anything like effective game management. Moreover, restrictions on hunting were widely considered elitist. Indeed, unrestricted hunting probably contributed to the democratization of society in North, by undermining the traditional European notion that hunting was an aristocratic privilege.[59]

Unrestricted hunting also, in more subtle ways, probably reinforced the patriarchal characteristics of the American State by associating masculinity with violence. This is a complicated subject that deserves deeper exploration than I can offer here, as is the relationship between hunting, racial hierarchy, and the State. In the South, for example, aristocratic values persisted; hunting was a way to display social status and signal one's willingness to use force to maintain that status. This status display undoubtedly played a role in managing the slave population and therefore in maintaining the racial order of the State. (Slaves usually participated in formal hunts as well, but in a subordinate role.) It is worth noting, too, that methods of controlling livestock (like branding) were also used on slaves. Thus some of the State and social capacity to manage a large slave population is probably due to the Euroamerican settlers' experi-ence with livestock management.[60]

That capacity to manage livestock continued to evolve during the early years of the Republic. For example, Spanish cattle-ranching spread from northern Mexico into what would become the American West, bringing with it a highly developed set of practices and laws governing livestock production. Indeed, the story of early State development in the American West is in large part the story of establishing and managing ranching.[61] But livestock were critical to the development of the State and civil society in the East as well. Agricultural societies began to proliferate in the early 1800s, and they intro-duced the first cattle shows. Already common in England and France, the cattle show was intended to interest farmers in improving breeds; they spread rapidly between 1815 and 1830. Livestock were already a commodity, of course, but exhibitions and auctions of pure-blood stock helped to invest them with greater social meaning: Breed improvement was touted as an expression of patriotism, and livestock were also becoming consumer items and vehicles for status display—a trend that would also characterize pet ownership later in the century, as I will discuss below.[62] More insidiously, this early concern with livestock breeds and patriotism foreshadows the later American obsession with racial purity (leading to antimiscegenation laws) and the early twenti-eth-century eugenics movement, both of which also are relevant to the racial-ization of the American State.

To return to the cattle shows, however, we should note that the line between civil society and the State is a bit blurry here. The agricultural soci-eties that sponsored cattle shows depended on aid from state governments and tended to collapse when such aid was withdrawn. To be sure, such sup-port for agricultural societies was probably a response to pressure from social elites, who made up most of the membership in agricultural societies.[63] Nevertheless, the elites couldn't maintain these societies on their own; the State played a critical role in developing these proto–animal welfare institu-tions. Indeed, the State played an even more important, if less direct, role in sparking interest in breed improvement when the federal government, from 1807 to 1810, adopted policies to inhibit foreign commerce. The trade em-bargo stimulated the domestic textile industry, creating a strong demand for merino wool. As a result, by 1814 American farmers were intensely interested in sheep breeding—an interest that fell off when peace with Britain brought an end to the trade embargo.[64] Such State influence on markets would con-tinue to be (and remains today) an indirect but very important element in the relationship between animals, civil society, and the State.

Another factor indirectly affecting this relationship was the increasing urbanization of the young republic, which created higher concentrations of animals in urban centers. As cities grew larger and more numerous, the local State extended its traditional concern with livestock control, using nuisance law to regulate the locations of liveries and slaughterhouses. Eventually, in the 1860s and 1870s, cities began creating boards of health with some regulatory power over these animal-related businesses.[65] These boards were principally concerned not with the animal welfare but with protecting property owners from noise and odors. But they represented a new institutional approach to State regulation of livestock.

The State's role is less apparent in the establishment of the "cult of pets" in the mid-1800s. Historian Katherine Grier notes that by 1820 a modern, secular ethic of kindness to animals was fully articulated, and pet-keeping was justified as a way to teach this ethic to children. Pet-keeping became a norm in the United States around that time, promoted as a means to educate children and shape their moral sympathies.[66] Although different sorts of animals were kept for different reasons—cats, usually, for policing rodents; fish for decoration and the study of natural history; and so on—there were some common themes in the nineteenth-century discourse surrounding pet-keeping. As Grier puts it, "The cultivated person [was supposed to have] the capacity for engagement and delight in a rich web of relationships with other people and with other things in the world, including nonhuman beings."[67] What Harriet Ritvo calls "the Victorian cult of the pet" promoted the idea that a pet is a member of the family and deserves affection and respect.[68]

At the same time, however, pets were increasingly treated as commodities. By midcentury, a thriving trade in pet animals had developed, along with advertising and branding (that is, using brand names to market animals).[69] Dog shows (modeled on livestock shows) began in the 1860s, and the American Kennel Club (founded in 1884) soon began to establish standards for breeds of dog. Thus well-bred dogs could serve not only as companions but as luxury items that demonstrated social status. Grier reports that fish, birds, and eventually more exotic animals were also desired for decorative purposes, rather as one desires a new lampshade or style of cookware.[70]

Oddly, despite the popularity of pet-keeping and the trend toward pets' commodification, pet owners enjoyed only uncertain and limited property rights in their animals. Traditionally, criminal statutes only protected livestock. As the Supreme Court opined in 1897 with respect to the most common pet animal,

Property in dogs is of an imperfect or qualified nature. . . . They stand, as it were, between animals *feroe nature* [wild animals] in which until killed or subdued, there is no property, and domestic animals, in which the right of property is complete. . . . They have no intrinsic value, by which we understand a value common to all dogs as such.[71]

Pet owners could recover damages when their pets were wrongfully killed, but they would have to prove the market value of the animal—which was typically nonexistent, except for purebred animals.[72] Thus the commodification of pet animals did not depend on or create a strong regime of property rights.

Of course, the other significant development in civil society during this period was the growth of the animal welfare movement, beginning in the 1860s. Inspired by the London Society for the Prevention of Cruelty to Animals (established in 1824), Henry Bergh founded the American Society for the Prevention of Cruelty to Animals in 1866.[73] It succeeded immediately in winning passage of an anticruelty law, and the fledgling society devoted much of its energy to discovering and reporting violations. But SPCAs also engaged in lobbying, rescue efforts, education, and institution-building. For example, the Women's Branch of the Pennsylvania SPCA prompted Philadelphia to open an animal shelter in 1869 and then lobbied the mayor for control of the local dog pound. They not only developed new, more humane methods for capturing and euthanizing strays, but also regularized the accounting process for dog fines. Bergh's organization was similarly creative, inventing the first ambulance service for injured horses.[74] The ASPCA was joined by the American Humane Association in 1877, and both organizations acquired official power to investigate and prosecute animal abuse, thus becoming quasi-State actors.[75]

It is tempting to see in the rise of the animal welfare movement a new ethic, or what Nash would call evidence of ethical extension. Nash points to the granting of civil and political rights during this period as evidence of an expanding sphere of moral concern: American slaves were emancipated in 1863, women received voting rights in 1920, Native Americans were granted full citizenship in 1924, and so on.[76] But there are several problems with that theory. First, women, natives, and even slaves were clearly subjects of ethical duties well before the nineteenth century, even though they did not enjoy full civil rights. And livestock, as we have seen, were already subjects of a stewardship ethic in the colonial era. Indeed, Bergh's concern about horses probably reflects not a new ethic but a response to the more intense use of draft animals as a result of the quickening pace of industrial development. (By 1900 there would be over 3 million horses in American cities, and the first anticruelty laws typically focused on these draft animals.)[77] I would suggest that the ASPCA is best understood as an innovative way to enforce older standards of care in a new, more urban and industrial age. Indeed, that was the opinion of the court in *Broadway Stage Co v. ASPCA*, one of the early cases concerning the new anticruelty statutes. The New York Court of Common Pleas opined that cruelty toward animals was an offense at common law, which suggests there was a long-standing communal norm against mistreating animals; the statute merely improved the procedure for enforcing it.[78]

Second, Nash is wrong to characterize social interest in the welfare of women, blacks, animals, and so on as expanding in some sort of sequence. Rather, nineteenth-century moral reformers were interested in making society more humane and (in Quilley's terms) "civilized" *in general*. Their reforming zeal took aim, often concurrently, at a host of social ills, from alcoholism and prostitution to slavery and animal abuse. During this same period (roughly 1830–1900), state governments were creating a host of new institutions aimed at caring for the dependent and vulnerable: reforming the penal system, creating asylums for the insane, and establishing public schools, to name a few. And the federal government was beginning to develop the first federal welfare programs.[79] In short, the animal welfare movement was an integral part of the development of the American welfare State, supported by a civil society pursuing a comprehensive ideal of humane behavior.

A final difficulty with Nash's account concerns the link between rights and welfare. Nash suggests that we see the extension of civil rights as reflecting increased ethical concern for the new rights-holders. But the relationship between becoming a subject of government welfare and becoming a holder of civil rights is not straightforward. When the rights of black men were given legal protection during the Reconstruction era, for example, this development became for many a justification for *reducing* public responsibility for their welfare. A similar dynamic is apparent in the case of the early women's suffrage movement; when women received the vote, some judges concluded that legislation designed to protect them was no longer constitutionally justified.[80] Once a subordinated group has equal rights, it seems, we must treat them as independent actors capable of taking care of themselves. (For this reason, children's rights are always limited and qualified; having rights seems inconsistent with their dependent, vulnerable status.) Moreover, the extension of civil rights can create conflict as new social groups become competitors for government resources. The tensions between the women's rights movement (historically dominated by white women) and the civil rights movement (historically dominated by black men) turned in large part on this issue. This conflict can undermine a general public commitment to the welfare of these groups.

On the other hand, the first federal welfare program was directed not at the most vulnerable or dependent members of society but at soldiers who had served in the Civil War,[81] and subordinated groups have often cooperated in seeking government reforms that would benefit everyone.[82] So I do not mean to say that granting some legal rights to animals would necessarily work against expanding public responsibility for their welfare. Much depends on how those rights are justified and institutionalized. My point here is merely that, historically speaking, receiving legal rights is not always the straightest path to receiving greater welfare protections.

In fact, in some respects the expansion of the welfare state did not work in favor of animal welfare. For example, local governments, in pursuit of public health goals, often organized campaigns to eradicate nuisance animals. Concern about rabies supported very active government intervention in controlling the dog population. Early efforts at control involved organizing hunts in which stray dogs were brutally beaten to death (despite protests from animal lovers). Less bloody methods of animal control were also invented: Philadelphia called for a "dog census" as early as 1809, and many states introduced licensing, dog taxes, leash laws, and laws requiring unleashed dogs to be muzzled and unmuzzled dogs destroyed over the course of the nineteenth century. The control of dogs and, later, cats has been a persistent area of state action; while humane societies have taken the lead in developing control strategies involving spaying and neutering, adoption programs, shelters, and euthanasia, local animal control officers also play a key role in managing the animal population.[83]

Finally, the nineteenth century witnessed the beginning of government support for scientific research on animals, with the creation in 1862 of the federal Department of Agriculture and the land-grant universities, both of which were measures to promote scientific knowledge to increase agricultural productivity. In 1887, the Hatch Act provided federal funds for agricultural experiment stations, helping to institutionalize agricultural science in the nation's universities. Both the Department of Agriculture and universities have typically focused their research on increasing agricultural productivity and fighting diseases, and these concerns continue to characterize most federally and state-supported agricultural research today.[84] Whether this development has been, on the whole, good or bad for animal welfare is a moot point, but it does implicate the State in most contemporary animal research.

In sum, during the nineteenth century we see different and apparently conflicting trends: On one hand, rapid industrialization and the expansion of markets results in more intense exploitation and commodification of animals, both wild and domestic. On the other hand, we see the rise of new institutions of civil society devoted to animal welfare. The State's interest in animals during this era centered on facilitating their commercial exploitation (which has typically been the principal aim of government-supported scientific research on animals), using them for military operations, and controlling them in urban areas. But the increasingly democratic State was also responsive to the demands of the new animal welfare movement and cooperated in creating new institutions to protect them. As the next section suggests, however, these trends were not always at odds with each other. In some ways, the animal welfare movement has served to promote the more effective industrial exploitation of animals.

The Twentieth-Century Era of State Expansion and Consolidation

By World War I, the military was phasing out the use of horses. But the military continues to depend on animals in a variety of ways, from transportation in foreign operations to the use of dogs for bomb detection. Kama the dolphin is just one of the millions of animals affected by the State's and society's creative efforts to find new ways to make use of animal power and animal minds. Those efforts have, over the course of the twentieth century, resulted in the expansion and, to some extent, centralization of the State's responsibility for maintaining and managing animal populations.

Most notably, the era of unrestricted hunting came to an end with the rise of contemporary game management practices. This development was heralded by the appearance, in the late nineteenth century, of the Audubon Society, the Boone and Crockett Club, and other civic organizations devoted to protecting wild animals—a movement based in large part on concerns of hunters and gun manufacturers over diminishing numbers of game animals, but also drawing on growing sentiment against hunting. By 1915, most states had game laws and administrative agencies devoted to enforcing them. Congress, despite its limited constitutional authority in the conservation area, passed the Lacey Act in 1900 (prohibiting the interstate shipment of illegally taken wild animals), and the Weeks-McLean Migratory Bird Act in 1913 (giving responsibility for protecting migratory game birds to the Bureau of Biological Survey).[85] In 1939, Congress moved the Bureau of Biological Survey from the Department of Agriculture to the Department of the Interior, merging it with the Bureau of Fisheries to create the Fish and Wildlife Service, the federal agency principally responsible for enforcing laws to protect wild animals.

The conservation movement is usually given chief credit for the creation of these federal administrative structures, and it deserves much of that credit. However, we should recognize that administrative agencies do more than enforce laws; they engage in educational and even lobbying efforts to advance their mission. Thus conservation agencies, like the Fish and Wildlife Service, have often helped to organize and coordinate conservation groups. As it did in the early nineteenth century, the State has helped to create a civil society that embraces the values and goals of its professional personnel.[86]

Nevertheless, it is fair to say that early American conservation policy was oriented toward serving hunters. Hunting remains highly valued by the State today; some states even give it constitutional protection.[87] Indeed, just as the State was heavily involved in killing stray domestic animals, it has also encouraged the slaughter of wild animals: Preserving game, in the early twentieth century, meant eradicating predators. Thus the Bureau of Biological Survey instituted a predator control program in 1915, working to eliminate wolves, coyotes, lions, and bobcats from the West. This approach to game management drew protests from scientists as early as 1924 and eventually gave way to strategies more firmly rooted in an ecological understanding of the predator/prey relationship. But the US Fish and Wildlife Service remains deeply involved in managing predators (in some cases, the very predators the agency is trying to reintroduce into the ecosystem).[88]

If preserving game has been an important goal of conservation policy, preserving livestock has been a principal aim of government animal policy as a whole throughout the twentieth century. While the routine use of animals for transportation has diminished, domesticated animals still serve as a critical source of food, fiber, drugs, and other products. To take just one illustrative statistic, the United States currently slaughters about 34 million head of cattle each year (compared to 887,611 in 1919).[89] This more intensive production of livestock was one of several factors increasing the federal government's involvement in animal management during the twentieth century: mass production of livestock created public health concerns. Before the twentieth century, the federal government's contribution to animal welfare protection was limited to the passage of the 28-Hour Law, providing that animals being transported by rail must be unloaded every twenty-eight hours for rest, water, and food. But *The Jungle*, Upton Sinclair's 1906 exposé of the meat-packing industry, prompted passage of the federal Pure Food and Drugs Act and the Meat Inspection Act (both administered, initially, by the Department of Agriculture). These Acts did not directly regulate the treatment of livestock, but they provided for inspection of meat and other food products, and the inspectors appointed to administer these Acts would eventually be given responsibility for enforcing humane slaughter regulations.[90]

These regulations were one of the chief victories of the twentieth-century animal welfare movement. Buoyed by its success in winning passage of animal welfare laws at the state level, the movement by the 1950s was pressing the federal government for a general animal welfare statute. Their first success came in the area of traditional government regulation: livestock. The federal Humane Slaughter Act (to be enforced by the US Department of Agriculture) was passed in 1958. Its first section is worth quoting in full:

> The Congress finds that the use of humane methods in the slaughter of livestock prevents needless suffering; results in safer and better working conditions for persons engaged in the slaughtering industry; brings about improvement of products and economies in slaughtering operations; and produces other benefits for producers, processors, and consumers which tend to expedite an orderly flow of livestock and livestock products in interstate and foreign commerce. It is therefore declared to be the policy of the United States that the slaughtering of livestock and the handling of livestock in connection with slaughter shall be carried out only by humane methods.[91]

The Act thus begins with a strong declaration of public interest in preventing animal suffering. Although concern with animal suffering was hardly new in 1958, this is the first federal policy explicitly articulating a State interest in addressing it. (The 28-Hour Law, although clearly intended to prevent cruelty, did not include an explicit statement of the federal government's interest in animal welfare.)

At the same time, however, the statute makes it clear that State protection of livestock welfare is expected to further their industrial and commercial production—to make them more valuable commodities. Such statements of economic interests in animal welfare are probably intended to satisfy any doubts about the federal government's constitutional authority in this area.[92] Nevertheless, the linking of animal and commercial interests obviously complicates any simple story of moral progress in this area. The same conflicting interests mark the next major statement of federal animal welfare policy in

1966, the federal statute that would become the Animal Welfare Act (AWA). The Act was prompted by an investigative report on a new phenomenon, the mass production of dogs for commercial sale (or "puppy mills")—a phenomenon that was, ironically, encouraged by the Department of Agriculture itself, which had counseled farmers to increase their income by breeding pet animals for sale.[93] The AWA applies to wholesale dealers, exhibitors, and federally funded research facilities, and authorizes the Department of Agriculture to enforce standards of care for all warm-blooded animals. It excludes livestock and poultry, however, and the Department has also chosen to exclude research mice, rats, and birds from its regulations.[94] These animals receive some protection from other federal laws; nevertheless, their exclusion from the AWA reflects the federal government's reluctance to promote animal welfare at the expense of commerce or scientific research.

Still, despite their limitations, the AWA and Humane Slaughter Act, along with more comprehensive state anticruelty statutes, constitute the primary legal foundation of the contemporary animal welfare State. Less prominently, changes in tort, criminal, and even family law are gradually extending greater protection to animals. The most significant developments concern companion animals: For example, many courts have questioned the rule that disallows pet owners from recovering damages for emotional distress or loss of companionship when their pets are killed, and at least one state has altered that rule by statute.[95] Most states have criminalized the theft of pet animals, and several have enacted statutes to make it easier to establish trusts to care for pets after the owners' death. Recognizing these trends, many judges are reluctant to treat pets as mere property in divorce disputes, using instead a "best interest of the pet" standard to decide custody.[96]

Despite (or perhaps because of) these successes, animal advocacy has grown more radical in recent decades, as witnessed by the publication of Peter Singer's *Animal Liberation* in 1975 and Tom Regan's *The Case for Animal Rights* in 1983. These are the best-known articulations of the ideology of the American animal rights movement: that is, the claim that humans have a duty to give animals not just compassion but also justice—a claim that can be framed as respecting their rights (Regan) or avoiding inflicting any unnecessary suffering on them (Singer). Discussing our relations with animals in terms of rights and justice linked the movement (philosophically, if not in practice) to the other radical rights movements of the era. Importantly, it also helped to justify the adoption of more radical measures on behalf of animals, such as protests and civil disobedience. Of course, one consequence of this radical activism was to bring groups devoted to animal rights to the attention of state and federal law enforcement, further complicating the State's relationship to the animals under its jurisdiction. When animal liberationists started staging illegal rescues of lab animals, it became clear that community responsibility for animals could be not only a reason for extending State authority but also a reason for *resistance* to State authority.

The emergence of the modern environmental movement in the 1970s has also affected the State's relationship to animals. Environmental modernization in the United States included a variety of federal environmental laws aimed at protecting wild animals, including the Endangered Species Act (1973), the Marine Mammals Protection Act (1972), the Wild Free-Roaming Horses and Burros Act (1971), the Refuge Recreation Act (1962), the National Wildlife Refuge System Act (1966), and the Convention on International Trade in Endangered Species (CITES; 1973). These measures were supported by domestic conservation groups and reflected a fairly strong public opinion in favor of species conservation. But the CITES treaty puts American conservation efforts in an international context; since its adoption, American policy toward endangered species has had to accommodate State foreign policy interests as well as satisfying domestic constituencies.

Indeed, the constituency for animal rights is no longer purely domestic. By the 1990s, an international animal rights movement had emerged, winning several victories in the European Union. For example, in 1999 the European Union banned the use of battery cages in poultry production; in 2002 Germany amended its constitution to make the State responsible for protecting animals; and in 2006 Great Britain extended its animal welfare protections, authorizing the administering agency to draft detailed standards of care for domestic (non-farm) animals.[97] Some nations are even extending constitutional protection to nonhuman entities. It is not yet clear how these "rights of nature" constitutional provisions will be interpreted, but they seem to be based on an inclusive conception of the political community that includes nonhuman animals.[98]

Consistent with this international trend, the American political community has also developed an extensive administrative regime aimed at protecting the welfare of animals, supported by a widespread consensus that the political community has some responsibility for both domesticated and wild animals. At the same time, though, the State still supports an extensive industrial production system that commodifies livestock, game, research animals, and pet animals. The State imposes some regulations on those industries, but it also allows new systems of production, like large-scale contained animal feeding operations, that are hard to reconcile with a strong commitment to animal welfare.

Thus we are now grappling with questions that could not have been conceived three hundred years earlier—like whether a dolphin should have standing in federal court to challenge the decision by a private aquarium to transfer the dolphin to the navy for use in sonar experiments. That question arises not, I think, simply because we care more about dolphins than we once did. It arises because we have a much greater understanding of dolphin minds than we did three hundred years ago, along with a much greater capacity for the scientific study and exploitation of dolphins. The question also reflects profound changes in our military and our judicial and public educational institutions, all of which make it possible to contemplate a judicial resolution to the conflict between the animal welfare groups, the aquarium, the navy, and Kama himself.

Kama's case barely scratches the surface of the ethico-political issues we face in our government of animals. How should governmental and nongovernmental organizations divide responsibility for managing the local population of feral animals? How should pets be allocated in divorce proceedings? Should the State fund research on genetic modification of animals? How should animal welfare and protection of endangered species be weighed against other government priorities? More generally, how would recognizing animal rights affect the community's responsibility for an animal's welfare? At what point does caring for an animal constitute unjustified infringement on its autonomy? How should we distribute responsibility for care, and what sort of caring relationships deserve legal protection? Of course, similar debates about rights, welfare, community responsibility, and individual autonomy occur in many other policy domains. They are endemic to the modern liberal welfare State.

We have traveled some distance from Nash's theory of ethical extension. It is understandable, of course, why so many animal advocates like to describe the contemporary animal rights movement as evidence of the gradual dawning of a new, enlightened ethic that needs only a few legal reforms to become fully realized in our society. That story puts the animal rights advocates on the right side of history and suggests an obvious strategy (i.e., pass more laws) to realize its ends. The problem with this story is not that it is wrong; *all* theories are simplified models of reality and are therefore to some extent incomplete. The problem with the idea of ethical extension is that it is misleading and unhelpful, at least insofar as it is used to explain the progress of animal rights in the United States.

My story is less optimistic but, I hope, more instructive: I suggest that the animal welfare/rights movement has been, in part, fighting against the forces of industrial exploitation and commodification in an attempt to preserve a traditional ethic of animal stewardship, but also, in part, inventing new forms of meaningful association with animals. Under that theory, the movement is fighting both old, outmoded ways of thinking *and* new, innovative ways of exploiting animals and the natural world. To make sense of our relationships with animals in this changing landscape, we do need a deeper, richer ethic for our treatment of animals—an ethic appropriate to their biological, ecological, and social natures. But we also need a public philosophy that explains the respective roles of government, civil society, and private individuals in governing the mixed human/animal community, along with new practices and institutions that facilitate meaningful and justifiable relations with our fellow creatures. We need a public philosophy that recognizes, as Vicki Hearne says, that the good of the human polis depends on the happiness of animals. The next chapter begins the project of articulating such a public philosophy.

2

Contracts

CAN A LIBERAL government legitimately protect animal welfare? Despite the ubiquity of animal welfare laws and a broad social consensus in their favor, it is not all that easy to justify them in liberal political theory. For hundreds of years liberal theorists have insisted that the purpose of government is to protect *human* welfare, and extending that principle to animals—including animals in the liberal "social contract"—poses some challenges.

Those challenges were starkly on display when Hurricane Katrina hit the Gulf Coast near New Orleans on August 29, 2005. The resulting flood, along with the government's inadequate response, led to the deaths of thousands and the displacement of hundreds of thousands of residents. One near-victim was Molly, a Labrador retriever belonging to Denise Okojo. Okojo was blind and suffering from cancer, and Molly had been her guide dog and companion for six years. But when Okojo was airlifted to Lake Charles Memorial Hospital, the coast guard officers told her that no animals were allowed on board. "I screamed and yelled," she said. But they pulled Molly away from her and left the dog to fend for herself in the rising floodwaters.

Okojo, however, refused to abandon her dog. She told her story to a nurse at the hospital, who contacted the Louisiana Society for the Prevention of Cruelty to Animals (LSPCA). The LSPCA saved over 8,500 pets during the first two weeks of the flood and helped other organizations save 7,000 more. After hearing about Molly, four volunteers from the LSPCA and ASPCA took a flatboat to Okojo's New Orleans East neighborhood and started searching. One of the volunteers smashed a window to gain access to the apartment complex and swam through the building, calling for Molly. They found her on the second floor, cold, hungry, and frightened—but alive.[1]

Many pets and pet owners weren't so fortunate. Thousands were forced to abandon their pets by the coast guard, national guard, and other government officials involved in the rescue effort. Others reportedly stayed behind, risking their lives to protect their pets.[2] The risks borne and resources spent by volunteers to rescue animals affected by Hurricane Katrina contrast strikingly with the refusal of government actors to do anything to help rescue pet animals or livestock. Private citizens acted as though they had a duty to their animals that justified risks to their own welfare. But government officials, particularly the military and paramilitary officers charged with conducting the rescue, put humans first.

The officers were of course just following orders. What passed for a rescue plan in the weeks following the storm made no provisions for pets. The Red Cross did not allow animals (except service animals) in their shelters, and the Federal Emergency Management Administration (FEMA) had no plan or even authority to rescue pets. This lack of attention to animal welfare should not be surprising. Government actors are reluctant to spend taxpayer resources protecting animals when human lives are at stake. People are supposed to take care of their own pets.

But clearly there are circumstances in which citizens can't fulfill that responsibility without public assistance. Recognizing this reality, one of the first major legislative responses to Hurricane Katrina was the Pet Evacuation and Transportation Standards (PETS) Act. Enacted by Congress in September 2006, the Act mandates that emergency preparedness plans include provisions for pet rescue. It also authorizes the use of federal funds to create pet-friendly emergency shelters and allows FEMA to assist pet owners and the animals themselves after a major disaster.[3] Supporters of the Act cited the health and safety problems attendant on leaving pets behind during disasters, but the most common argument for the Act was the sheer inhumanity of forcing pet owners to abandon their animals. Congressman Tom Lantos (D-CA), the bill's chief sponsor, explained that the purpose of the bill was to ensure that people "would never be forced to choose between being rescued or remaining with their pets." A representative of the Humane Society of the United States supported the bill with the claim that "the bond between people and their pets is so great that it becomes nearly impossible to separate the human rescue and relief effort and the animal rescue effort."[4] Moreover, while legislators expressed concern about the pet owners' suffering, they also seemed concerned about the pets themselves. Representative Christopher

Shays (R-CT) argued that "the plight of the animals left behind was truly tragic." Dennis Kucinich (D-OH) insisted that this bill was an expression of compassion not only for our fellow human beings but also for "our gracious household pets and service animals."[5] Indeed, the experience of Katrina suggests that drawing a sharp distinction between human and animal welfare may be misguided. Humans and their pets are often too integrally connected to make such a distinction. In some cases, the government must treat humans and the animals in their care as a single unit.

But the bill did have critics. Representative Lynn Westmoreland (R-GA), for example, declared himself a dog lover but nevertheless called the bill "silly." He worried that it would distract the federal agencies from their primary mission of saving human lives.[6] He raises a reasonable point: Is it fair to other citizens for the government to rescue pet animals? What if making room on the rescue chopper for Molly means that a human being doesn't get rescued as quickly, or that there isn't as much money to help humans needing food and shelter? Sentimental appeals aside, is the PETS Act a legitimate exercise of government power?

Certainly it doesn't seem right to spend more public resources on Denise Okojo than on other citizens simply because she has a dog, as opposed to some other sort of special possession, like family photos or a prize orchid. What makes Okojo's bond with her pet more important than her bond with other things to which she is integrally connected? Of course, Molly isn't just an ordinary possession; she's an animal. Maybe government officials see Molly as a creature with welfare interests they are bound to protect, quite apart from the dog's contribution to Okojo's welfare. That would make sense of the policy, but Westmoreland would still have a valid objection: It is not clear that liberal governments have the right to use public resources to promote the welfare of nonhumans for their own sake. Under traditional liberal theory, the government's job is limited to promoting *human* welfare.

There is a third possibility, however. Perhaps the government has no direct duty to Molly, but it does have a duty to protect Okojo's relationship with Molly. Okojo's duty to her pet may be a purely private matter, like her duty to God, but a liberal state can and should accommodate such private duties. Under this reasoning, giving pet owners a right to have their pets rescued is comparable to giving workers the right to take a day off each week to honor the Sabbath. The state can create policies that support citizens' private duties to their animals, acknowledging as a matter of public policy that such duties are important to many people *without* acknowledging that the state has any direct duty to the animals themselves.

That logic would go some way toward justifying public rescue of animals during a disaster. But it doesn't explain why the government can use its coercive powers to protect animals *from their owners*. It is one thing to accommodate private relationships with pets; it is quite another to punish a citizen for failing to satisfy the government's view of how pets should be treated.

This was the problem faced by Henry Bergh, the founder of the American Society for the Prevention of Cruelty to Animals (ASPCA) and the principal force behind New York's controversial anticruelty statute. The law, passed in 1867, defined as a misdemeanor several offenses, including cockfighting, bear-baiting, impounding an animal without food and water, and mistreating draft animals. The first section runs, "If any person shall over-drive, over-load, torture, torment, deprive of necessary sustenance, or unnecessarily or cruelly beat, or needlessly mutilate or kill . . . any living creature, every such offender shall . . . be guilty of a misdemeanor."[7] Violators could be arrested, held in custody, and fined.

Bergh's law had considerable public support, but it ran into fierce resistance from the stagecoach drivers of New York City. To them, Bergh was the very embodiment of intrusive governmental meddling. He would walk the streets of New York, stopping drivers in order to inspect their horses and pointing out their poor condition and overloaded carts. Even worse, the new law gave him and his ASPCA friends the authority to arrest drivers and drag them into court. Poor Dennis Christie, for example, was driving his coach along his usual route when Bergh called a policeman over to arrest him. Bergh insisted that the horse was lame and Christie was overdriving him. Christie was taken away from his coach and committed to the local police court, where he was eventually acquitted—but not compensated for his loss of time and income.

The stagecoach companies weren't accustomed to this sort of interference. In 1873 they brought several lawsuits against Bergh (including an action by Christie for false arrest). They lost all of them. The Stage Horse Cases offer the first judicial interpretations of the 1867 anticruelty law, and some of the first judicial reflections on using the government's coercive power to protect animals from their owners.

In considering the stagecoach companies' complaints, the court (in the person of Judge Daly) first established that the statute did authorize officers of the ASPCA to arrest people for violating the law. But Daly went on to consider why the government had the power to pass such a law in the first place. He noted that cruelty to animals was a common law offense long before the legislature enacted the criminal statute, explaining that such legislation is not merely governmental meddling in private property rights but has a clear public purpose: "It truly has its origins in the intent to save a just standard of humane feeling from being debased by pernicious effects of bad example, the human heart being hardened by public and frequent exhibitions of cruelty to dumb creatures, committed to the care and which were created for the beneficial use of man."[8] The court classified anticruelty laws as morals legislation, like laws against "lewd prints," public drunkenness, and prizefighting.

Improving the citizens' "humane feelings" isn't widely accepted as a legitimate public purpose today (as I will discuss below), and it wasn't particularly strong grounds for the anticruelty statute even in the nineteenth century. But this moral purpose was not the only rationale for the law. Although the court didn't mention it, stagecoach owners eventually realized that supporting animal welfare laws and the SPCAs was good business. As historian Clay McShane has noted, stagecoach companies actually benefited from the work of SPCAs. These organizations helped to monitor drivers to make sure the companies' horses were well treated, and they also served as disinterested parties who could determine whether a sick or lame horse should be destroyed. "In order to collect insurance for their destroyed property," McShane writes, "owners [had] to cooperate with SPCAs and acknowledge their authority."[9] More generally, in a community heavily dependent on animals, there was a good economic case for protecting their welfare, as Bergh himself insisted. In an 1881 article in the *North American Review*, he estimated that the mistreatment of cattle in rail transit caused losses of 10 to 15 percent, resulting in millions of dollars wasted. "That lesson of humanity to the lower animals," he notes, "should be enforced in the counting-house, as well as in the nursery."[10]

Subsequent animal welfare statutes have followed Bergh's practice, routinely proclaiming some sort of public purpose related to *human* welfare, and particularly human health and prosperity: The federal Humane Slaughter Act is supposed to protect workers and consumers as well as the animals themselves; the federal Animal Welfare Act aims to "prevent burdens on [interstate] commerce"; the Endangered Species Act cites the "esthetic, ecological, educational, historical, recreational, and scientific value" of the protected species to the nation.[11] Similarly, contemporary animal welfare advocates often argue that cruelty to animals is an indicator of a personality disorder that can culminate in violence toward humans and that domestic abuse often involves abuse of pets.[12] Criminalizing animal abuse is supposed to help law enforcement officers address these patterns of violence toward humans.

It is tempting to conclude from all this evidence that human interests constitute the primary political justification for punishing animal cruelty. But we should note that these stated purposes are not necessarily the aims of the animal welfare groups and even the legislators who sponsor the statutes. Supporters of the Humane Slaughter Act declared in congressional debates that it was aimed principally at preventing "needless cruelty" to animals; they made few references to human welfare benefits. Similarly, proponents of the Animal Welfare Act focused on our moral duty to protect laboratory animals from unnecessary pain and suffering.[13] Tom Lantos, sponsor of the PETS Act, is a longtime animal welfare advocate, and Bergh himself was clearly more concerned about the animals themselves than with their owners. Why, then, do government actors insist on citing *human* interests in animal welfare?

The difficulty faced by legislators and judges confronting animal cruelty is this: Cruelty toward animals may be morally repugnant, but it doesn't follow that the state has authority to prevent it. This is one reason an individual animal welfare ethic—an ethic that tells us it is morally wrong to inflict wanton harm on animals—isn't an adequate basis for animal welfare protections in a liberal state. There are all sorts of moral wrongs (adultery, lying, failing to forgive trespasses, foisting bad movies on an unsuspecting public) that are beyond the proper scope of state power. It is a basic principle of liberal government that the state's coercive power should be used only for certain purposes: to make its members safe and healthy and free, not to make them good. In American constitutional law, this principle has served as the limit of state governments' "police power," their general power to protect the health and safety of their citizens. Federal power is even more constrained. The federal Constitution grants Congress only a limited set of specific powers, which do *not* include the police power. Most of its regulations concerning animals derive from its power to regulate interstate commerce.

Animal welfare laws therefore raise a fundamental problem for American constitutional law and for liberal government in general: If the purpose of government is to protect *human* welfare and freedom, on what grounds does the government restrict our freedom to treat animals any way we please? Why does anyone have the right to tell stagecoach drivers how to treat their horses, or require us to pay taxes in order to help other people take care of their animals? Emphasizing broad human interests in animal welfare is one way to answer that question. But that response, I think, does not go far enough. Many forms of animal cruelty (like private instances of neglect) don't seriously threaten the welfare of other humans, and protecting animals from cruelty will inevitably burden human welfare from time to time. Some scientific experiments on animals will be disallowed; taxpayer money will occasionally be spent on animals instead of humans; activities that some humans enjoy (like dogfighting, bearbaiting, and cockfighting) may be prohibited altogether. Why should the government *ever* be allowed to protect animals at the expense of human interests? To answer that question, we need to go beyond the moral arguments for protecting animal welfare and draw on political theory about the proper scope of state power. My answer—the only answer, I suggest, that makes sense in light of the liberal tradition and the practices of modern liberal communities—is that some animals are in fact members of the community that the government is bound to protect. In other words, they are members of the liberal "social contract."[14]

To defend that proposition, I will begin with a brief overview of the liberal arguments concerning political obligation and the limits of state power, which will lead us into social contract theory. It is important to note that I am using the social contract device *not* as a general theory of moral obligation but merely as a way to think about political obligation in a liberal state. That is, I claim that the social contract device is useful in defining and justifying our *political* (as opposed to our private moral) duties to animals. I will then explain my somewhat idiosyncratic interpretation of social contract theory and make the case that animals can be considered members of the social contract. The second half of the chapter turns to what I think are the more interesting questions: *Which* animals are members of the social contract, and how do we decide?

I. Are Anticruelty Laws Justified in Liberal Political Theory?

To be clear, the problem we are addressing is not whether we should continue to protect animal welfare. As chapter 1 argues, anticruelty laws have broad public support, and our legislative scheme for protecting animal welfare is growing ever more comprehensive. I don't expect that trend to reverse anytime soon. If animal welfare laws aren't justified in liberal theory, that is not a problem for the animals; it is a problem for liberal theory. I follow John Rawls in understanding the theorist's project as bringing into harmony our principles of justice and our *considered judgments* about justice (that is, judgments about particular practices, rendered under conditions favorable to the exercise of the sense of justice). If our principles and considered judgments conflict, we must work from both ends, examining our judgment in light of our principles and vice versa, making such changes as are necessary to yield a coherent view (or a "reflective equilibrium," as Rawls puts it).[15] That the state should protect animal welfare is a well-considered, stable, and long-standing judgment, endorsed by most Americans and, indeed, most contemporary liberal societies. If liberal principles of justice don't allow for this sort of state action, we need to reexamine those principles.

So what sort of state action does liberal theory allow? The best way to approach that question is to examine on what grounds, in liberal theory, we can justify *any* government regulation. Or, to put it another way, why are citizens obligated to obey the law? Traditionally, liberal theories of political obligation focus either on consent (we must obey the law because we agreed to do so) or rationality (we must obey the law because it is a reasonable rule for this community). But according to the most influential contemporary liberal theorists, neither approach permits the state to infringe human freedom to protect animal welfare.

Joseph Raz, for example, offers a nicely intuitive nonconsensual theory of political obligation. He argues that there are certain actions that are simply morally wrong, and we have no right to perform those actions in the first place. Normally we rely on our individual judgment to decide which actions are morally justified. But in some cases, it makes sense to accept the authority of laws that are designed to help us act in morally justifiable ways. Raz points in particular to cases in which the difficulties of coordinating collective behavior may require some central decision maker. Other possibilities come to mind: We may learn from experience that individuals routinely miscalculate when faced with certain kinds of decisions, or lack the time to research complex issues. This reasoning might justify requiring drivers to wear seat belts, or prohibiting them from driving while intoxicated, or specifying how much income citizens must contribute to government (mistrusting our ability to figure out our fair share on our own). Laws are justified, then, if they (normally) help citizens act on morally correct reasons.[16]

But that is not the whole story. Raz, like all liberals, is concerned about limiting state action to those areas where it is really necessary. After all, there is always a cost to human welfare and happiness when an individual is prohibited from doing something she wants do, even if the rest of us think it is for her own good.[17] Liberals (naturally) put a very high value on individual liberty and are willing to tolerate a lot of bad individual decision making in the name of preserving autonomy. On the other hand, Raz recognizes that individual autonomy can flourish only in a public culture that supports it and offers many opportunities for individuals to develop their capacities. He argues further that the government has a role to play in promoting such opportunities. Thus the government may legitimately promote the conditions for autonomy by making sure people have plenty of choices. But it should refrain from forcing people to make morally correct choices, except to prevent harm to other autonomous beings (namely, humans).[18]

Under this view, government efforts to rescue animals during a disaster are probably justified, but animal cruelty laws are not. It should be acceptable for the government to use noncoercive measures (subsidies, rewards, and educational and rescue programs, for example) to promote animal welfare. These efforts may be supported by involuntary taxation, because citizens, and therefore the government, have "an obligation to create an environment providing individuals with an adequate range of options and the opportunities to choose them."[19] Supporting good practices of animal husbandry, one could argue, creates a richer public culture that expands the options for living a valuable life in community with animals. This is particularly important in a society struggling with class and racial inequalities that limit opportunities for some groups to enjoy animal fellowship. In New Orleans, for example, the people least able to rescue their animals were the poor, the elderly, and the infirm. A general animal rescue program has redistributive effects, shifting government resources to people with fewer resources of their own, thus making it easier for them to enjoy animal companionship. However, nothing in Raz's theory allows the state to take coercive measures that substantially interfere with human autonomy in order to prevent harm to animals. While Raz recognizes that animals do suffer morally relevant harm when we mistreat them, and even concedes that *some* people believe that we can have moral duties to animals,[20] he would not extend the state's protection to animals.

Why not? Although Raz doesn't explain his conclusion, I suspect it has to do with his concern about protecting individual human autonomy. While apportioning a small amount of taxes to support animal welfare doesn't substantially interfere with—and in fact tends to promote—individual human autonomy, anticruelty statutes are a different story. Minnesota's animal welfare statute, to take just one example, carries a penalty of $3,000 or one year in jail for anyone who intentionally causes great bodily harm to a pet. Harming a service animal can earn one a $5,000 fine or two years in jail, and killing a service animal can result in a four-year prison sentence.[21] As Raz notes, putting someone in prison punishes particular instances of immoral behavior by means of a global and indiscriminate invasion of autonomy. "Imprisoning a person prevents him from almost all autonomous pursuits" rather than simply restricting the perpetrator from abusing an animal in the future.[22] Moreover, these laws punish neglect as well, so they can involve the state in fairly close supervision of how one takes care of one's pets. This supervision necessarily will involve, in some cases, entering a person's private home, perhaps on several occasions, to determine the animal's condition. These are the sort of intrusive, coercive state actions that normally require fairly strong justifications in liberal theory. Raz's theory doesn't provide such a justification.

But perhaps I have misread Raz. Perhaps he's assuming that protecting animal welfare and human welfare are perfectly consistent goals. We have already noted several ways in which animal welfare laws can serve human economic, health, social, and recreational interests. We have also noted that those laws can conflict with human interests (restricting medical research and some uses of animals for entertainment, for example), but perhaps those are minor conflicts that distract us from the larger goal of animal welfare laws: As Immanuel Kant famously argued, promoting good relationships with animals can teach us important social virtues and therefore support the conditions for human freedom and happiness.[23] The *Stage Horse* court, for example, argued that animal welfare laws promote humane sentiments, thus making us better citizens—more rational, more humane, and therefore more likely to respect others' rights. Alisdair MacIntyre has made a similar case with respect to severely disabled humans, arguing that caring for these people can teach us how to care for others, what we owe to those who care for us, how to avoid judging a person's capacity from his or her appearance, and similar lessons valuable to good citizenship.[24] Surely caring for animals can also teach such lessons. Conversely, failing to care for animals might undermine human freedom and welfare. People who claim that violent sociopathic tendencies can be identified by a history of cruelty to animals are making a more limited version of this argument.[25] Perhaps creating a culture of kindness to animals supports human welfare generally, even though human and animal interests might conflict in particular cases.

But Raz does not actually make this argument, and for good reason. It is certainly correct that animal and human welfare can and normally should be mutually supportive. However, the claim that the state can enforce kindness to animals in order to make us better citizens is problematic. Although the state may legitimately promote some citizenship virtues (like tolerance and respect for rights), liberal theorists rightly consider it dangerous to embrace "improving moral character" *generally* as a legitimate public purpose. Such purposes have been cited to justify a host of intrusive, illiberal regulations, including criminalizing homosexuality, banning the marketing of contraception, forbidding interracial socializing, and even restricting bad language. Americans have notoriously poor footing on this slippery slope. To be sure, where we can identify a specific harm to human welfare (like domestic violence) and establish a concrete link to animal welfare, we are certainly justified

YBP Library Services

SMITH, KIMBERLY K., 1966-

GOVERNING ANIMALS: ANIMAL WELFARE AND THE LIBERAL
STATE.
                                    Cloth   207 P.
NEW YORK: OXFORD UNIVERSITY PRESS, 2012

AUTH: CARLETON COLLEGE. STUDY OF HOW LIBERAL POL.
PRINCIPLES APPLY TO ANIMAL WELFARE POLICY.
LCCN 2011-46913
  ISBN 0199895759   **Library PO#** AP-SLIPS

		List	34.95	USD
9395 NATIONAL UNIVERSITY LIBRAR	**Disc**	14.0%		
App. Date 2/12/14 SOC-SCI 8214-09	**Net**	30.06	USD	

SUBJ: 1. ANIMAL WELFARE--GOVT. POL. 2. ANIMAL
RIGHTS--GOVT. POL.
AWD/REV: 2014 CHOS
CLASS HV4708   DEWEY# 179.3   LEVEL GEN-AC

YBP Library Services

SMITH, KIMBERLY K., 1966-

GOVERNING ANIMALS: ANIMAL WELFARE AND THE LIBERAL
STATE.
                                    Cloth   207 P.
NEW YORK: OXFORD UNIVERSITY PRESS, 2012

AUTH: CARLETON COLLEGE. STUDY OF HOW LIBERAL POL.
PRINCIPLES APPLY TO ANIMAL WELFARE POLICY.
  LCCN 2011-46913
  ISBN 0199895759   **Library PO#** AP-SLIPS

		List	34.95	USD
9395 NATIONAL UNIVERSITY LIBRAR	**Disc**	14.0%		
App. Date 2/12/14 SOC-SCI 8214-09	**Net**	30.06	USD	

SUBJ: 1. ANIMAL WELFARE--GOVT. POL. 2. ANIMAL
RIGHTS--GOVT. POL.
AWD/REV: 2014 CHOS
CLASS HV4708   DEWEY# 179.3   LEVEL GEN-AC

in developing regulatory schemes that protect both. So nothing in traditional liberal theory prevents the state from creating better systems for detecting and reporting animal abuse as part of a larger effort to address domestic violence. But simply granting the state a broad, ill-defined power to shape citizens' moral character threatens the very concept of limited government. Anticruelty statutes will need a different justification.

Will a consensual theory of political obligation better support animal welfare laws? Such theories have several points to recommend them. First, consent is, intuitively, one important element of legitimacy: That you consented can sometimes be a reason for obeying a law. For example, that I joined the army voluntarily can be a reason for obeying army regulations, over and above the normal justification that such regulations are necessary and reasonable. Respecting a person's ability to create obligations like this through consent acknowledges the value of allowing a person to "fashion the shape of his moral world," to choose his or her relationships and duties.[26] Second, consent theory complements our concern with the rationality of law. After all, if no reasonable person would consent to a law, it is pretty good evidence the law isn't supported by good reasons. Paradoxically, this point is particularly relevant when the people (or beings) affected by the law can't actually give their consent. Consent theory tells us that in evaluating the rationality of a law, we must pay special attention to the point of view of those affected by the law. When they cannot speak for themselves in a public forum, consent theory tells us to make an effort to discover (or imaginatively reconstruct) their point of view. Finally, consent theories address the need to gain and keep public support for laws. Laws to which the public consented are more likely to be obeyed voluntarily, thus reducing the need for government coercion.

Consent theory may not fully explain political obligation. We tend to think that irrational and unjust laws aren't legitimate even if people do consent to them (a point I'll return to below). Moreover, as Raz argues, we have morally compelling reasons to obey many laws even if we never actually consented to them. Nevertheless, the idea of consent does offer a useful heuristic to help us come up with well-justified and acceptable laws.

Social contract theory is the principal liberal consensual theory of political obligation and the dominant one in the United States.[27] Since we're looking for a public philosophy that is suitable for American society, social contract theory is an obvious choice. Social contract theory holds that governments are created by the consent of the people as part of a (usually implicit) social contract among citizens. The terms of that contract are those that one would normally expect other rational citizens to accept. In other words, we (through the government) can impose obligations on other citizens that we would reasonably expect them to consent to, as members of a community seeking to live together in relations of mutual respect and cooperation.

The social contract specifies the legitimate ends of government authority. Surely (one would imagine) under this theory, the people could consent to a government that cared for the welfare of animals and therefore make animal welfare laws legitimate. We can even point to contemporary instances of such consent. The German people, for example, amended their constitution in 2002 to specify that the government "has responsibility for protecting the natural foundations of life and animals in the interest of future generations."[28] Granted, the wording is bit ambiguous—it could mean that the government can protect animals only to the extent they serve human interests—but some supporters of the amendment read it as authorizing the government to protect animal rights even at the expense of human interests (by restricting the use of animals in medical research, for example).[29] If that is the common understanding, then isn't it fair to say that the German people have agreed to a social contract that allows the government to restrict human liberty in order to protect animal welfare?

Not necessarily. In the first place, the amendment was adopted by the German legislature, not by a popular referendum, and it wasn't unanimous. So we can't say that all of the citizens actually consented. Of course, it may be that they agreed at some point to be bound by the decisions of the majority. But even so, the majority should still assure themselves that imposing obligations on people who didn't consent to them is reasonable—that they *should have* consented, or at least that they had good reasons to consent. Similarly, the German people must assure themselves that those who did vote for the amendment really understood what they were doing. Did they understand that this provision might seriously compromise medical research that could relieve human suffering and save human lives?

So consent really means *rational* consent, and "rational consent" is interpreted against a background understanding of what constitutes a reasonable restriction on one's freedom. In classic social contract theory (as represented, for example, by Locke's *Second Treatise of Government*, and the dominant ideology of the American founders), the only kind of restrictions that seem reasonable are those that promote individual humans' opportunities to enjoy their natural freedom and autonomy, conceptualized (usually) as their natural rights. This natural rights background is problematic for animal welfare, because none of the classic social contract theorists recognize animals as having rights in the same sense that humans do. Animals appear in these theories merely as resources for humans, and government has an interest in their welfare only to the extent that their welfare is related to human welfare and freedom.

Obviously, much of the ethical literature on animals—most notably, Tom Regan's defense of animal rights[30]—challenges this exclusion of animals from the social contract. If animals do have something like natural rights, and protecting natural rights is the chief end of government, that would seem to give us reason to support animal welfare laws. But even if we recognize that animals may have natural rights, we still must grapple with the fact that the social contract is usually considered to protect only the rights of its members—of those capable of entering into such a contract. That would seem to exclude even rights-bearing animals.

I am going to argue against that conclusion; I think some animals are members of the social contract, properly understood. However, I am not going to say much in the following section about animal rights. There are several ways of thinking about moral rights, political rights, and the relation between them. But rights are not the whole of political morality, and I think it is possible to separate social contract theory from its natural rights background. In short, even if we don't want to grant that animals have something like natural rights, we may still want to recognize duties toward them and design our institutions and practices to satisfy those obligations. The question here is whether our obligations toward animals are *public* duties, responsibilities carried not only by private individuals but also by the government and ourselves in our role as citizens. I believe we can answer that question without resolving the issue of natural rights.

II. Some Animals Are Members of the Social Contract

Theories of political obligation are useful for two purposes: to explain to citizens why and to what extent they should obey the law, and to tell governors what sorts of laws deserve to be obeyed. Obviously we're not concerned about explaining to animals why they should obey the law. We are interested mostly in the second purpose, thinking through what sort of laws we humans, in our role as governors of animals, should enact. We will of course also feel obligated to obey those laws. But I want to focus in particular on social contract theory as a kind of rule of thumb for lawmakers, a useful way to capture principles of political obligation that should guide us in using government power. As Rosemary Rodd suggests, social contract theory is most helpful as a method for making justifiable, impartial moral decisions (rather than serving as a comprehensive theory of moral obligation).[31] Social contract theory is helpful to us because it focuses our attention on critical questions with regard to animals: Which animals are members of the social and political community? How do the rules and institutions we use to govern them affect their welfare? And, most important, what do our rules and institutions look like from the animal's point of view?

In other words, I am using social contract theory here as a normative "midrange" theory,[32] a guide to thinking about political phenomena as we attempt to govern at the practical level. A midrange theory offers some general rules that have proven useful for certain kinds of question. It doesn't attempt to answer deep metaphysical questions about the nature of humans or the foundations of justice and is in fact compatible with many different answers to those questions. As I explained in the introduction, John Rawls calls this sort of theory a public philosophy, a public basis of justification that can be supported by an "overlapping consensus of reasonable comprehensive moral doctrines."[33] This simply means that although we may hold differing understandings of the deep basis of political obligation—some of us may believe that obeying the law is a religious duty; others may see it as a matter of rational self-interest or a Kantian moral imperative—for practical purposes, we can all think of that obligation in terms of a social contract.

My rationale for including animals in the social contract is this: The social contract, as it is used in political theory and practical politics, usually includes *everyone* in a given political society, even those (like infants and the severely mentally impaired) incapable of consenting. You don't have to sign up; you don't have to give actual consent, either explicit or implicit. If you have significant social relations with other members of the community, you're a member. Of course we often have trouble with marginal cases (immigrants seeking membership, for example). But many animals are not hard cases; they are clearly part of our social community. We have social relations with our pets—or at least an overwhelmingly large number of us do. We communicate with them, recognize duties toward them, interact with them, and recognize the social value of these relationships. Indeed, many people consider pets to be members of the family.[34] I will argue below that many other animals also fall into this category.

At this point, some readers may object that I'm assuming too much consensus on this point. *Many* Americans may think of some animals as part of the social community, but surely there are others (perhaps, for example, some of the dogfighting aficionados we will meet in chapter 5) who do not. But the existence of some disagreement on the precise social status of animals does not necessarily defeat my argument. Of course, if such disagreement were deep and pervasive, then the government could not legitimately treat animals as members of the social contract. But, as mentioned above, all we're looking for is a public philosophy, a practical guide to governing that is supported by an overlapping consensus. That is, treating (some) animals as members of the social contract must seem reasonable (not necessarily true in an absolute, metaphysical sense, but a reasonable approach for the government to adopt), when evaluated by most of the diverse moral perspectives in American society. To be sure, minority groups with radically different views on and practices concerning animals may find this position odd or alien and may wish to see their own views reflected more prominently in our public philosophy. Fashioning our laws to reflect the shifting universe of "reasonable moral comprehensive doctrines" found in the United States is an important and continuing task, and one that I will take up in chapter 5. I claim here only that there is sufficient consensus to claim the existence of a public philosophy concerning animals: Viewing (some) animals as members of the social contract is consistent with and makes sense of most of our laws, our widespread social practices, our typical ways of talking about animals in public discourse, and well-documented measures of public opinion.[35]

Of course, not every consensus is a well-justified consensus appropriate for governing a liberal community. But I believe this one is appropriate and fully consistent with liberal principles. Including some animals in the social contract makes philosophical sense if we conceive of the end of social contract as not protecting natural rights or human autonomy, but as promoting the welfare of all members of the community. As Martha Nussbaum has argued, we can understand the proper end of government as promoting the "characteristic flourishing of beings," which includes promoting the conditions for autonomy for most of us but also caring for the welfare of those who cannot achieve rational self-governance.[36] The contract, according to this understanding, must include all the members whose welfare normally affects other members. Importantly, framing the end of the social contract this way need not expand the reach of the state as far as (for example) "improving citizens' moral character" would. Welfare, and particularly the welfare of animals, can be understood fairly narrowly: taking care of animals' health, preventing undue suffering, and attending to their needs for sociality. (Nussbaum offers a more extensive but still limited definition of human welfare.)[37] Nor does this end diminish the importance of autonomy very much; after all, a proper degree of autonomy is critical to the welfare of most humans. But rational autonomy simply is not a proper goal for most animals (nor for some humans).

This understanding of the social contract is supported by the broad social contract tradition and is consistent with the liberal political tradition generally. For Locke, for example, the end of the social contract was the protection of natural rights, but he recognized that one can exercise those rights most effectively in a stable and flourishing society. He acknowledged that children could not come to enjoy their full autonomy without proper nurture and education, which suggests that supporting education and stable families is a public concern. Similarly, his *Letter concerning Toleration* acknowledges the role that religious communities play in allowing one to exercise one's right to religious freedom. Humans can achieve autonomy only in a supportive social context. Indeed, this is the basic justification for forming the social contract in the first place. So while Locke was careful to protect individual and communal freedom from intrusive government interference, he also accorded government broad powers to legislate for the welfare of the community as a whole. The legislative power, in his words, is aimed at "the preservation of the Society, and (as far as will consist with the publick good) of every person in it."[38]

Admittedly, contemporary social contract theorists usually define the social contract more narrowly than this, to ensure that few people have any reason to object to its terms. For example, in *A Theory of Justice* Rawls attempts to derive a purely procedural theory of justice from the most minimal assumptions about the contracting parties, namely that they are rationally self-interested and not bound by prior, independent principles of right or justice.[39] He wants a contract that any rational person (in the contemporary United States) would have trouble objecting to. So his contractors act solely on rational self-interest behind a veil of ignorance (which prevents them from knowing, for example, whether they are pet lovers or stagecoach drivers). These people would have little reason to consent to a contract that might limit their rights in favor of animal welfare. Thomas Scanlon's version of social contract theory starts from less strict assumptions—he allows his contractors to be motivated by a fairly robust sense of justice and not simply their self-interest. But he also limits the social contract to respecting other humans' rational autonomy rather than promoting their general welfare. And Scanlon, too, would exclude animals from the contract.[40]

These theories are rich and insightful, but unfortunately neither Rawls nor Scanlon can provide a compelling rationale for animal welfare laws. Rawls says virtually nothing about duties to nonhumans, beyond noting that we have them and acknowledging that his theory does not accommodate them. Scanlon also recognizes that we have duties toward animals, but he denies that these duties are part of the social contract (although he is tempted to make an exception for pets, because we tend to treat them as persons).[41] Their failure to explain why the state can criminalize animal abuse requires us to rethink their assumptions. The problematic assumption here is that the sole purpose of the social contract is to protect individual human autonomy.[42]

If we reject that assumption and instead understand the end of the social contract to be the welfare of what Mary Midgley calls the "mixed human/animal community," then we have a good justification in social contract theory for animal welfare laws. Our principles will cohere better with our considered judgments, not only with respect to animals but also with respect to humans who are incapable of achieving rational autonomy. Nevertheless, including any animals in the social contract does raise some theoretical difficulties. The chief of these are that (1) social contract theory centers on the value of freedom, and animals do not have anything like natural freedom; (2) animals cannot consent to a social contract; and (3) even if they could consent, we can't discover what animals would consent to. I will address these in turn and then consider a few more global objections to social contract theory.

III. Objections
Rational Liberty

For many philosophers, the chief reason for excluding animals from the social contract is that they lack freedom. Admittedly, for nonphilosophers, this objection must be puzzling. We've been focusing on whether the government is justified in restricting the liberty of humans to protect animals; whether animals have freedom seems beside the point. But the relevance of animal freedom is clearer when we think about the issue from a different angle—when we use social contract theory to justify restricting the liberty of animals to protect the welfare of humans. For example, may a dog be tied up for several hours a day to suit the owner's convenience? Social contract theory asks us to consider whether this restriction is justified from the animal's point of view. It asks, in essence, would the dog agree to the social contract if the contract permitted this restriction? Using social contract reasoning this way, however, raises an important theoretical objection: If animals are not free in any meaningful sense of the term, it is hard to see why we should worry about justifying such restrictions to them. And the idea of consent also seems inappropriate if animals do not have the liberty necessary to make consent meaningful.

But the philosophers' objection is still puzzling: Surely (we may insist) animals *do* have natural liberty. After all, isn't a wild animal—a lion running on the African savannah, a dolphin leaping in waves—the very image of freedom? Tying a dog up may or may not be cruel, but surely no one would deny that it restricts the dog's freedom. How could anyone dispute this point? The answer to that is found in centuries of philosophical tradition: Western philosophy teaches that animals are not free because they lack the rationality essential to our conception of moral and political freedom. Animals, under this view, lack the higher-order reasoning abilities that would make freedom meaningful to them or that would make their subordination to humans problematic. Liberal theorists emphasize that we value human freedom because it allows us to create and follow a life plan, an experience that seems to be essential to our happiness. It is possible that all animals can be happy without that sort of autonomy, that they are capable of being true "happy slaves." Even vigorous champions of animal rights usually concede that nonhuman animals do not have rationally chosen life plans in the same sense that humans do.[43]

Nevertheless, I think we should trust the intuition that animals *do* have a valuable form of natural liberty. After all, we twenty-first-century Americans do not view animals as Locke did. Twentieth-century developments in our understanding of animal cognition and behavior, and in our own moral sensibilities, challenge the conception of animals as mere unthinking machines.[44] There are both philosophical and scientific reasons for affirming the commonsense view that animals have minds—that they can have beliefs, desires, and intentions.[45] Their minds, to be sure, are different from human minds in important ways, but these ways of knowing may have value precisely *because* they are different from our own. Moreover, we may be overemphasizing the importance of reason to the value of human freedom. Actions motivated by Kantian disinterested rationality are not the only sort of actions that carry moral value. We sometimes value instinctual behaviors, not to mention many forms of nonrational human behavior, precisely because they are disengaged from the realm of reason and the limitations thereof. Such behaviors represent other intrinsically valuable ways of dwelling meaningfully, even intelligently, in the world.[46] Interference with such behavior can sensibly be called control or domination. So we can understand animal freedom as nondomination, in the same way that some theorists define human liberty as, principally, freedom from domination by others.[47] In short, even though animals may have very different ways of reasoning or interacting with the world, this does not mean they do not enjoy something comparable in moral worth to human freedom. They may even have something analogous to a life plan: a way of life that, although partly instinctual, is distinctively their own. That is why tying up a dog for several hours is not the same as leaving a toy in the yard for several hours. The dog, unlike the toy, has a mind, feelings, and intentions that may be frustrated; it has a kind of freedom that is being denied.

In any case, wherever we stand on the philosophical concept of animal freedom, we certainly can recognize that at least some animals—sentient animals, especially those with higher-order cognitive capacity—have welfare interests that deserve respect, and one way to protect animal welfare is to resist treating them as mere means to our ends. All that social contract theory requires is that the contracting parties recognize that other beings—humans and at least some animals—must be treated as though they are not subordinate to one another by nature. Importantly, because we are using social contract theory as a middle-range theory or Rawlsian public philosophy, we do not need to agree on a set of religious or metaphysical principles to undergird this recognition of animal interests in their own liberty. For our purposes, we only need an overlapping consensus on this point. Thus those animals that the human parties to the social contract[48] recognize as having welfare or liberty interests (for the limited political purpose of designing a just regime) may properly be included in the social contract.

This category, we should note, includes domesticated animals, even though they would seem to be closest to a creature "naturally" under human dominion. Many domesticated animals exist in their current form only because humans bred them and maintain them for human use. But domestication does not make animals "naturally" subject to humans. If it did, the same logic would have to apply to humans themselves, for what animal is more thoroughly domesticated than the human being? Rousseau is instructive on this point: He describes humans as domesticated animals but clearly did not believe this meant that any individual is naturally under the dominion of any other individual. Domestication renders us *interdependent*, not inherently unequal. This interdependence creates the *risk* of political subordination, which is precisely why we need the social contract: to authorize political relationships where no natural dominion exists.[49]

Consent

Martha Nussbaum succinctly objects to including animals in the social contract by noting that animals do not make contracts. "In a very basic way," she insists,

> the whole idea of a contract involving both humans and nonhuman animals is fantastic, suggesting no clear scenario that would assist

our thinking. . . . Because animals do not make contracts, we are
blocked . . . from imagining plausibly what a social compact would
look like. The type of intelligence that animals possess is not the sort
that we need to postulate to imagine a contractual process.[50]

Of course, even for humans the social contract is at best implicit, and usually
purely hypothetical, so the problem here is not that animals cannot in fact
consent. Rather, I take her point to be that the contract device is not useful as
a heuristic because we can't imagine what it would mean for an animal to
consent.

But that claim may be overstated. Mary Midgley argues that if consent is
taken to mean acceptance of a state of affairs, it seems that some animals are
capable of consenting. For example, animals that live in hierarchical groups
(such as dogs) may either accept or challenge the leadership of the alpha male.
Midgley suggests that popular consent may amount to little more than this
sort of tacit trust in one's leader, although admittedly most liberal theorists
require a more robust form of consent. But as Rosemary Rodd points out,
many animals do seem to have the capacity for choice. "We can often find out
what animals prefer, given a choice of several alternatives."[51] We are in the
same position with regard to animals as we are with regard to young children
or temporarily mentally disturbed persons: We simply have to engage in some
imaginative reconstruction to determine what they would prefer if they had
the capacity to reason. Of course, Rodd is referring here to narrow choices
about food or conditions of confinement, not broad schemes of social cooperation. But if the logic of social contract can be used for narrow policy
choices, it is not deeply counterintuitive to apply it to broader principles.
Indeed, as J. Baird Callicott (among others) has pointed out, relations of reciprocity between humans and nonhuman animals are virtually universal, and
the idea of the "domesticated animal contract" is a commonplace in animal
husbandry.[52] This suggests that many people have found the contract idea to
be a useful way to think through our duties toward animals.

Not everyone is convinced, though. Clare Palmer argues that applying
social contract theory to domesticated animals is particularly misguided.
The question with regard to domesticated animals, she notes, is not whether
they would choose to become domesticated (that is already an accomplished
fact). Rather, the question is whether these animals are better off living
among humans than they would be in the wild—and this question, she as-
serts, is meaningless. She does not deny that domesticated animals benefit
from the care they receive from humans. Rather, she suggests that since many

domesticated animals couldn't survive in the wild, there is no real choice for them, and therefore the social contract theory does not properly apply to them.[53] Palmer's point, of course, does not apply to those domesticated animals, like horses, goats, and pigs, that can survive in the wild. True, life in the wild may be nasty, brutish, and short for these animals, but this does not mean that social contract theory is inapposite. On the contrary, the main point of social contract theorists is that life in the wild isn't desirable for humans, either. That's why the social contract emerges as (usually) our best option.

Palmer may be thinking of domesticated animals that have completely lost the ability to survive in the wild. For them, life in the wild is not a viable option. But comparing life in the "state of nature" to life in society is not the proper way to justify the social contract. Under this reasoning, almost any social arrangement would be justified; humans and animals might agree to quite oppressive institutions, if the only alternative were no protection at all. It is better, I think, to set up the question as Rawls does: Given that one must live in some sort of society, how would a group of free and equal contractors set up that society? Social contract theory asks us to choose not between society or the state of nature but between societies governed by different conceptions of justice.[54] For domesticated animals, the question is what system of animal husbandry they would choose. That question is neither meaningless nor counterintuitive.[55]

Still, these concerns about consent lead us to a final objection from social contract theory: How can we ever know what an animal would choose or consent to? As I suggested in the introduction, I believe the difficulty of answering this question has been overstated. We can assume that animals would wish to flourish in their characteristic ways, free of unnecessary suffering. Moreover, I will argue below that membership in the social contract is limited to animals with whom we have social relationships, like pets and livestock. These are precisely the animals whose needs we understand the best and have proven able to meet. Granted, determining what promotes flourishing in particular cases can pose challenges. But that project is not necessarily any easier when we're making laws concerning humans. Humans can tell us what they want, but they can also lie or be mistaken. And, in general, human needs are more complex and extensive than those of nonhuman animals.

There is of course more to say about how we determine animals' interests, but we must postpone deeper discussion of the topic until the chapter on representation. I want to turn now to general objections to social contract theory per se, beginning with the charge that it is too individualistic. In governing animals, some would argue, we must attend to groups and ecosystems rather than focusing on individuals as the principal objects of our moral concern. This is quite true; many laws and regulations are aimed at managing whole populations of animals in order to preserve healthy ecosystems. As discussed below, not all of those animals are actually members of the social contract, so the state may not have an obligation to attend to the individual welfare of all the animals it manages. However, fulfilling our duties to members of the social contract requires us to attend to both individual *and* group welfare. Animals, both human and nonhuman, need a healthy species group in order to flourish. But it is important not to let the group perspective dominate animal welfare regulation. Humans do not relate only to species; they also have important and meaningful relationships with individual animals, and animals' welfare often depends on these relationships. Indeed, these individual human/animal relationships are the basis for animals' inclusion in the social contract. So social contract theory, as used here, is not quite as individualistic as it seems. It is aimed at protecting the welfare interests of individual animals, but it does so by protecting valuable human/animal *relationships*.

Second, some people point out that social contract theory has been used to justify illiberal practices, like race slavery and the subordination of women, by mischaracterizing the point of view of the subordinate group. We need only assume that these persons are radically different from those in the ruling class in order to convince ourselves that they would consent to their position of inequality.[56] This is a danger with respect to animals as well. Moreover, with animals we might easily make the opposite mistake: using social contract reasoning to overemphasize the similarities between humans and animals, which could also lead to inappropriate policies.

But the contract device, I think, actually makes both kinds of mistakes less likely. Social contract reasoning instructs us to look at the situation from the animal's point of view. That is a valuable piece of advice in any pluralistic society, which constantly demands that we adopt unfamiliar perspectives. Social contract theory should lead us to pursue further research into animal minds and behavior, not to show that they are exactly like us but to understand and give due respect to their differences. Social contract reasoning, at its best, promotes active, critical empathy as a political practice. Without this practice, any theory of justice is likely to be misused. So social contract theory should cultivate a habit of recognizing difference appropriately. It should promote a higher comfort level with differences among humans while at the same time making us sensitive to important moral differences between humans and animals.

A more worrisome concern is that if animals are members of the social contract, they will necessarily be second-class members. Even the more radical theories of animal rights seldom suggest that animals be given exactly the same rights as humans. Any legal rights accorded to animals must be shaped to reflect animals' capacities and characteristic modes of being. Because humans' capacities so far exceed those of nonhuman animals, human rights will generally be more extensive and weighty than animals' rights. But doesn't this make animals second-class citizens, thus working against a chief purpose of rights and social contract theory, that is, to create a more egalitarian state? In our zeal to protect animals, we may end up creating a subordinate political status—a status to which it would be all too easy to confine some humans.

This objection, however, misunderstands the nature and purpose of legal rights. The idea is not to grant legal rights to animals as a way to express a commitment to universal, equal natural rights. As discussed above, I don't think we need to link social contract theory with natural rights for animals at all. Our commitment is to the welfare of the human/animal community. Of course, in the case of humans this normally involves commitment to a set of natural rights, because the autonomy those rights protect is central to human welfare. But our aim with respect to animals is to use legal rights to support their welfare in the context of morally valuable relationships between humans and animals. So we're not creating a subordinate class of citizens by affording animals a lesser set of rights; rather, we're using legal rights and other legal devices to recognize and protect the human/animal bond. We use legal rights the same way when we care for human welfare, especially that of vulnerable and dependent humans such as children, people with disabilities, and the elderly.

IV. Members and Nonmembers

Which animals, then, are members of the social contract? This is a difficult question, because becoming a member is less a matter of philosophy than of history. It is part of the messy complexity of organic social relations on which philosophers try, but usually fail, to impose some order.

Consider the story of the iconic American pet, the dog. Dogs were not always considered proper subjects for governmental protection. Despite their usefulness, dogs during the nineteenth century were often viewed (by the non-dog-loving public) the same way wolves were—that is, as pests that could be destroyed if they became a problem.[57] But precisely because they were a nuisance to livestock breeders, they increasingly absorbed the attention of lawmakers. Complaints about dogs harassing livestock led to the widespread adoption of "dog laws" in the 1850s and 1860s.[58] By the 1860s, seventeen states had such laws.

The dog laws were aimed at controlling stray dogs and reducing their numbers, but, ironically, they also ended up giving greater legal protection to dog owners' property rights. The common law rule, still being followed by many judges in the late nineteenth century, was that dogs were not domestic animals; they were essentially wild animals and could be killed with impunity. But the dog laws overrode that rule. To be sure, these laws defined dogs as nuisances and therefore liable to be killed when they were not on their masters' land. But they also protected dogs that were under their masters' control, and they created procedures that recognized the owners' property rights. Maryland, for example, set up a summary judicial procedure for putting down marauding dogs, which including providing notice to the owner and allowing the owner to pay a fine in lieu of killing the dog. Moreover, the debates over these laws provided a forum for dog lovers to assert the value of dogs to the community. For example, one member of the Maine Board of Agriculture argued to his colleagues that "[the dog] was of great benefit in Aroostock county, in protecting the sheep from bears . . . [and the] property saved [by dogs] was greater than the value of all the sheep killed."[59] Such defenses contributed to the growing belief that dogs deserved some sort of legal protection.

Similarly, many states imposed taxes on dogs, with the aim of making it more expensive to keep dogs (and therefore reducing their numbers). But taxing dogs implied that they were property. Indeed, an 1863 US Department of Agriculture report insisted in defiance of the common law that "dogs are property, and therefore taxable."[60] Moreover, dog taxes required local officials to take a census of dogs and determine who owned them. This regulatory system further enhanced dogs' legal status. Historian Katherine Kete recounts how this process worked in France, which had a similar experience with the dog tax. Imposed in order to reduce the numbers of dogs, the tax had the unexpected effect of conferring on dogs a kind of civic personality. Dogs with licenses were, in a sense, official. They were practically citizens.[61]

In the United States, too, the civic status of dogs improved dramatically during the nineteenth and twentieth centuries. True, the law has not always kept up. Dog owners today might be surprised to learn that their property rights in their dogs are still imperfect. Tort law makes it difficult to recover damages when your dog is negligently harmed, because in most jurisdictions recovery is still limited to its market value. Compensation for loss of companionship is not generally permitted. It can also be quite difficult to create a trust to take care of one's dog after one's death.[62] On the other hand, the Animal Welfare Act was passed in large part to protect dogs—to shut down puppy mills and prohibit the sale or use of dogs stolen from their owners. The PETS Act offers dog owners some reassurance that, in the event of a natural disaster, they won't be forcibly separated from their pets. Military working dogs now have the right (if we may put it that way) to be adopted by their handlers when their service is done. Today dogs are treated, in many respects, like members of the social contract.

But the status of other animals is not so clear. Certainly our political practices do not follow the logic of Roderick Nash's moral extensionism (discussed in chapter 1). Our moral sensibilities do not gradually extend from the human community to animals as a whole, nor do they track any obvious philosophical principle. We protect the welfare of some animals more than others, just as we protect the welfare of some humans more than others. The Animal Welfare Act and other anticruelty statutes usually protect (if not in their language, in their actual enforcement) only animals with whom we have social relationships: notably, pets, livestock, and some research animals. We usually exempt wild animals from these welfare regimes. (They are protected as members of species under a different legal regime.) And we typically do not protect pests at all. Mosquitoes are notably lacking in advocates.

How, then, do we decide which animals to include in the social contract? It is difficult to adduce a set of principles from liberal theory to guide us, since liberal theory is notoriously unhelpful on the question of membership. It focuses on specifying political duties toward members of the social contract rather than specifying who should be included in the social contract. Indeed, the liberal principle of human equality tends to lead liberals to conclude that all humans should be members of the political community, and this conclusion seems to lead us toward a universal state or world government. A thoroughgoing animal rights ethic might lead us to include all animals, or at least all sentient animals, as well. Environmental theorists, taking this logic even further, sometimes argue that all beings that might be harmed by our policies (including, potentially, animals, ecosystems, and future generations) should be considered members of the political community.[63]

However, these theorists usually do not go so far as to suggest we dissolve the nation-state altogether. That hesitation to take the principle of equality to its logical conclusion is, I think, quite sound. In the first place, we must recall that political duties are not the same as moral duties, and such an extension of the political community to all beings with moral status seems entirely at odds with liberalism's commitment to limited government. Private individuals may recognize boundless obligations to all manner of creatures, but they don't have an obvious claim on other citizens' resources to satisfy those obligations. In the second place, although we do value equality, we also value community—the shared history, social ties, and sense of membership that are reflected in how we draw political boundaries. Indeed, I argue throughout this book that supporting community is very important to protecting humans *and* nonhumans, since strong communities are vital to individual flourishing. The political community is not more important than individual welfare. But in order to protect individual welfare, the political community must have some meaning. It should be something capable of informing one's identity, something to which one can feel loyal even when one disagrees with its actions. That means it should be rooted in the social ties that shape our day-to-day lives.

Equality (of humans or of all beings with moral status) is not a useful principle for defining the boundaries of the political community, because it gives us no boundaries. Probably no philosophical principle is going to do better.[64] In practice, the boundaries of the political community must be supported by a widespread consensus and deep commitment, and philosophical arguments (despite their famous analytical rigor) seldom achieve that consensus and commitment. This is why arguments about membership typically rely less on deductive logic and more on "contextual justification." As described by Don Herzog, contextual justification proceeds not by deducing conclusions from basic philosophical principles but by showing that a policy or institution is better than the alternatives, all things considered. Such justifications can draw on historical considerations, our moral and political ideals, and social theory, but they rely principally on rich descriptions of what the world might look like if we chose one course of action over another.[65] Thus a contextual argument for including the pigeons in the city park in the social contract might involve giving an account of our history with these pigeons, an explanation of how we might attend to their needs, and a glowing description of how they would benefit and our lives would be enriched by caring for them. Arguments against would no doubt make reference to the pigeon droppings all over the park benches.

Granted, some readers may find this resort to contextual justification worrisome. It suggests that determining membership in the political community is an unprincipled affair. What if we get it wrong? Surely we need some philosophically sound, metaphysically grounded criteria for deciding to whom we owe political obligations. It is a valid concern; we're looking for justifications for government regulation, and it is important in a liberal regime that such regulations have strong justifications. Of course, contextual justification does not reject principled argument altogether; moral and even metaphysical principles are among the tools people can use to critique the existing social consensus and make the case for expanding membership. But I agree with Don Herzog's response to that concern: Arguments that proceed from abstract philosophical principles may seem compelling in the classroom, but they aren't politically effective. They have a terrible track record of persuading ordinary members of the political community, and there's a good reason for that. Our political commitments—for example, our commitment to including dogs but not raccoons in the political community—have evolved over time in many vivid and concrete contexts, so we have a good sense of what they mean and require. Contextual justifications recognize that; they rely on those contexts and experiences. By contrast, our commitment to an abstract principle (like the moral equality of dogs and raccoons) is new, tentative, and untested. We have little sense of what it really means in practice and what it would require of us.[66] It also carries little emotional weight, compared to a good contextual argument. So abstract principles are not in fact a very strong basis for public policy. By comparison, contextual arguments provide much better—compelling, vivid, concrete—reasons for government regulation, and for including (or excluding) beings from the political community.

Of course, because contextual argument appeals to empirical descriptions of the way the world is and the way it could be, it is always conditional; it doesn't offer conclusions that hold for all times and places. So it doesn't promise to end political debate for good. Indeed, our ongoing debates about membership make the consensus about animal welfare I asserted above seem pretty fragile. Some subcultures, for example, practice animal sacrifice; others set great value on hunting; in some regions of the United States, dogs may still be considered little more than nuisances. These differences can lead to intense disputes over which animals are members of the social contract and deserving of state protection. But we shouldn't we treat these disagreements as a problem for our liberal democracy. On the contrary, debates about which animals should be treated as members of the social contract are prime opportunities for minority views to be aired and to influence our public philosophy—a point I shall explore in more depth in chapter 5. The very openness of such debates, unconstrained by a rigid set of principles, is part of their political value. Talking about membership is an invitation to reimagine the political community and our own ethical and political selves.

Nevertheless, despite our ongoing disagreements, I think we can identify some "rules of thumb" that may properly serve as a starting point for thinking about membership. Keeping in mind that our goal is to fashion a public philosophy suitable for a liberal community like the contemporary United States, certainly one important criterion of membership is that the animal must be recognized by humans as a subject of moral duties and as enjoying something we can call natural freedom. If an animal does not summon up in humans some sense of moral obligation—some sense that it isn't merely a resource for humans and is capable of being wronged—then it isn't a fit candidate for the social contract. The social contract, as we are using the concept here, must have a basis in humans' moral sentiments, or the idea will have no purchase on our deliberations and behavior. Many nonsentient animals, for example, do not inspire a sense of justice or moral duty, even among animal rights advocates. (Again, consider the poor mosquito.) There's little chance that we will be persuaded to recognize those animals as members of the social contract.

Still, humans do have great capacity for imagination and empathy, so this criterion might result in a very large group of potential members of our social contract. However, contract theory addresses the duties that arise out of a community's *political* relationship with the animals under its jurisdiction, so we only need to include animals with whom we have or want to have a political relationship. A political relationship may be established when the state governs animals directly (when government officials use animals to perform official functions or directly manages the animal population) and indirectly (by specifying what private individuals may do to animals). In the United States, we regulate everything from the treatment of elephants in captivity to the importation of butterflies, and similar regulatory regimes are found in most industrialized nations. Like the dog laws, these laws can confer on the affected animals a kind of civic personality that demands recognition from other civic persons. At the very least, they constitute exercises of government power that need to be legitimated.

Nevertheless, the line between member and nonmember of the political community doesn't track perfectly the line between regulated and unregulated. Some regulated animals may be pests, or may not be sufficiently sentient and aware for us to relate to them as community members. And some animals may be members of the political community even though the laws do not yet reach them; perhaps they don't need legal protection, or we haven't yet extended it to them. Animals become members of the social and political community when they become entangled in certain kinds of relationships—such as relationships of care and dependence, or family relationships—with community members, who come to realize that these animals have a good of their own that our laws and practices should respect. They become involved with our scheme of social cooperation. So we may add that animals who enjoy a generally recognized and valued social relationship with a community member are candidates for membership.

Under these guidelines, we can conclude that some animals are currently members of the social contract (understanding that the boundaries of the community are always in flux). Pets like dogs and cats are prime examples. Commensal animals, such as the birds who visit our birdfeeders, might also qualify for membership. Pests, by contrast, are not members: Their interests cannot, by definition, be harmonized with ours, and therefore they are not properly speaking engaged in a scheme of social cooperation with us.[67] Politically speaking, pests are our enemies, so our laws do not have to take their interests into account. (Of course, as individuals, we might still have moral duties toward them: not to cause them undue suffering, for example.)

Wild animals within our territory might also be members of the community, if we establish meaningful *individual* relationships with them and if their interests can reasonably be accommodated with ours. For example, wild animals in zoos and aquariums become public pets of a sort; unconfined wild animals may also achieve a special reputation and status in the community, becoming a kind of community mascot.[68] However, most wild animals are properly treated as outside the social contract. We may still be obligated to manage these populations as resources or parts of functioning ecosystems, in the interests of present or future generations of humans. But our political obligations do not extend to protecting the welfare of individual animals in the wild. (Again, as private individuals we may recognize more extensive moral duties to those animals.)

Between pets and wild animals fall two hard cases: livestock and feral animals. I have already claimed that livestock are members of the social contract. They live with us in close relations of interdependence and mutuality, and (as discussed in chapter 1) livestock have historically received the highest level of government protection. But many will find this position counterintuitive. After all, we often keep livestock in crowded, unhealthy conditions where they cannot develop physically or socially in their characteristic way. And then we slaughter them and eat them.[69] It seems inapt to call them members of the social contract, in the same way that it seemed inapt, to nineteenth-century Americans, to consider slaves members of the social contract.

The analogy between livestock and slavery isn't entirely misguided. Both groups have had deep, intimate relations of interdependence with citizens but have been treated by citizens as outside the social contract. In both cases, this contradiction has prompted calls for reform. Beyond this point, however, the

analogy breaks down. For human beings held in slavery, reform meant political autonomy and legal equality. Humans, in a modern liberal polity, need
civil and political rights to flourish as human beings: to form families, create
homes, and pursue the manifold projects appropriate to humans. Cows and
chickens do not need the same sort of autonomy to flourish; indeed, they
can't flourish without our care. I don't deny that domesticated animals enjoy
something like natural liberty, a way of life that is distinctively their own. But
that way of life is not incompatible with the practices of animal husbandry.
On the contrary, it *assumes* animal husbandry. If we "freed" livestock, most of
them would simply die off. And if we didn't eat them, we would have no reason to raise cattle, hogs, poultry, and other livestock. Some feral populations
might survive emancipation, but most domesticated species would disappear
altogether.[70]

So I think it is a mistake to say that farmers who scrupulously attend to
their livestock's physical and social needs are treating these animals as slaves or
mere resources. Bad farmers, and particularly those involved in large-scale industrial livestock production, treat their animals as mere things or commodities.[71] But good farmers treat their livestock as *livestock*. They engage in
well-developed social practices of animal husbandry, practices integral to our
development as humans and to livestock's development as domesticated animals. Nevertheless, we may still worry that the notion of a domesticated animal contract is incoherent if the point of the contract is to serve the human
desire for meat. Is killing an animal for food a violation of the relations of
mutual justification that are the point of the social contract?

Farmers usually argue that it isn't. As noted above, many of them do
understand their relations with their livestock as governed by a "domesticated
animal contract." They insist that they have meaningful and morally valuable
relations with their livestock, giving them a comfortable and happy life until
they are slaughtered. Death itself, they argue, is not a harm; it is the inevitable
price of living. What matters is the quality of one's life, which for livestock
can be quite good. Consider, for example, Wendell Berry's description of a
model dairy farmer, Elmer Lapp. Lapp's farm includes a variety of animals:
cats, dogs, chickens, cows, horses, wild ducks, bees, barn swallows, and gold-
fish who live in the drinking trough and keep the water clean. Each animal
plays a role in the economy of the farm; together they form a complex web of
interdependencies. But according to Berry, Lapp doesn't just need his animals; he *likes* them. Indeed, he needs them *because* he likes them; he brought
them into his farm because he wanted to live with them. As Berry puts it, the
farm works because the animals were liked before they were profitable. Lapp's

"delighted and affectionate understanding" is what brings the various parts of the farm together. Importantly, eating the animals is part of the order of the farm: "Eating, you feel the cycle turn, completing itself yet again. The cow eats, the hogs eat, the chickens eat, the people eat. The life of the place comes in as food, returns as fertility, comes in as energy, returns as care."[72] Michael Pollan's description of Joel Salatin's Polyface Farm in *The Omnivore's Dilemma* similarly describes a complex system in which the health of the land, animals, and humans are deeply interdependent. All of the beings on the farm share in the "sheer ecstasy of life."[73] Even Jennifer Reese's decidedly unsentimental reflection on killing chickens draws on this traditional language of reciprocity. "I've always felt there was something powerful and right in the bond between humans and animals," she reports. "The turkey and 12 laying hens that I keep in my yard wouldn't last a day without my protection. They depend on me, I on them, and it is one of the simplest, most reciprocal relationships in my life. I am not sure whether they are fond of me, but I am certainly fond of them."[74]

Some animal rights advocates would dismiss this testimony as self-serving. They do see death as a harm, so their moral intuitions tell them that raising animals for food violates our duty not to inflict unnecessary harm on sentient beings—even though acting on that intuition would mean that domesticated livestock would disappear from our communities.[75] What should we do when faced with competing moral intuitions like this, both of them plausible? I suggest that we ask ourselves, Which group seems more admirable? With whom would you like to be aligned? I'm inclined to choose the farmers over the animal rights advocates, at least in this case. People who raise livestock in this intimate, responsible, and humane manner commit themselves to a difficult and demanding job, and they make very little money from it. It doesn't make sense that they would choose this work just because they like to eat meat; they are not simply offering rationalizations for their diet. They choose this work *and* this diet because they like to raise animals. By contrast, the opposing view—that we must end livestock production altogether—does sound rather self-serving to me. Instead of preserving an ancient social practice that brings us into a deeply meaningful and demanding relationship with animals, these advocates want to get rid of that relationship *and the animals that are part of it.* True, we may be suspicious of farmers who insist that their animals are getting a fair bargain. But we should also be suspicious of people who want to avoid ethically and emotionally demanding relationships by eliminating the creatures on the other end of those relationships. Fulfilling the conditions of a reasonable domesticated animal contract asks a great deal more from us than simply ceasing to eat meat. We would have to radically reform the way we raise livestock. As citizens, we would have to take a great deal more care to find out how livestock are raised and slaughtered, to agitate for their protection, and to support farmers so that they can fulfill their obligations to their animals. More generally, we would have to see livestock as animals to whom the political community as a whole has a particularly broad and compelling set of obligations. This, I think, is the harder ethical choice. In my view, it is the more admirable one.

In sum, I don't think it is deeply inappropriate or counterintuitive to consider livestock members of the social contract. On the contrary, if we are going to raise animals for food, we *must* consider them members and accept all the responsibilities that entails. Granted, many people will find my reasoning unpersuasive and conclude that vegetarianism is the only ethically defensible choice. This is reasonable as a matter of personal ethics; as I acknowledge above, this is a matter of competing moral intuitions, both of which are plausible. But here we are concerned with fashioning a public philosophy, one that can find support broad and deep enough to justify extensive government regulation of the livestock industry. The social contract logic is, I think, our best option. It is familiar and widely shared, and it suggests a clear agenda for reform.

Whether this same logic can be extended to research animals is debatable, since animal experimentation does not have the same pedigree and in most cases does not offer the same sort of mutuality that true animal husbandry does. I discuss animal research in more depth in the final chapter, but here I will simply suggest that excluding research animals from the social contract would be problematic: If we are going to use animals for our ends, we must care for them as though we are being held to a particularly demanding contract that serves their independent interests as well as ours.

Another hard case is feral animals and strays. Many communities are faced with growing populations of unowned domestic animals, particularly cats. Some people see them as pests (spreading disease and killing wildlife) that should be captured and killed. Others would treat them as community members whose populations should be managed humanely, through capture-neuter-release programs. While much of the debate centers on the most efficient way to manage these populations, many involved in the debates insist that we (the political community) should be worried about the welfare of the animals themselves. The debate in St. Paul, Minnesota, over the city's proposed capture-neuter-release program is instructive. Online commentary about the program reveals that advocates for feral cats worry about their vulnerability to harm and consider them a public responsibility. Some comments recommended that the city remember to provide shelter, food, and water to the feral cats, even while trying to reduce their population. One praised St. Paul for caring for "the forgotten, unwanted and hopeless" cat colony. Another objected to tax dollars being spent to shoot or trap feral cats when a more humane approach is possible.[76] Commenting on a similar program in Washington, DC, one Humane Society official describes feral cats not as pests or problems but as "our neighbors."[77]

Clearly feral animals and strays occupy a liminal space; their status is indeterminate and must be decided through public deliberation, which we should expect to involve a lot of contextual justification. Advocates for feral animals may draw on principles of justice toward animals, but they will also describe new social practices that will bring us into community with these animals, explaining how such community will improve our collective life or display desirable virtues (charity, compassion, generosity). Fortunately, our legislative bodies are well suited to dealing with the issue of inclusion. Legislatures can hear from many different perspectives, devise innovative approaches, and take incremental steps toward expanding or contracting public responsibility for different categories of animals. The debate over feral animals reveals this process in action.

Even as we expand the boundaries of the political community, however, we are still leaving many animals unprotected by the social contract. What can these nonmember animals expect from us? To be sure, we may and do protect many populations of wild animals for our own benefit, to preserve endangered species and game populations. International treaty obligations lead us to extend some protections to animals that are members of other political communities, or wild animals that many nations have an interest in preserving. Beyond these obligations, we may still have moral but not political obligations to nonmember animals. For example, we have a private moral duty not to inflict unnecessary pain on wild animals, even if the law permits it. Moreover, we can reasonably ask government officials to respect and accommodate these moral sensibilities, as far as possible (to avoid inflicting unnecessary suffering on wild animals in the course of managing their population, for example). But there are limits to public responsibility for nonmember animals. A liberal government shouldn't use tax revenues to satisfy our (potentially unlimited) charitable impulses toward wild animals. Nor should it punish people for making a sport of killing nonendangered wild animals, no matter how immoral this behavior may seem to the rest of the community. But it does make sense for the government to help rescue pets and livestock from natural disasters, to prohibit cruelty to and neglect of such animals, and more generally to promote a culture supportive of healthy, positive human/animal relationships.

V. Conclusion

In sum, it appears that animal welfare laws do not pose a serious challenge to liberal principles after all. If we conceptualize the end of the social contract as the welfare of the community as a whole (rather than merely human autonomy) and recognize that animals may enjoy a kind of freedom that we cannot restrict without justification, then the social contract can include animals. These conceptual moves may be inconsistent with most contemporary social contract theories, but they do no violence to the broader liberal political tradition and the common practices of liberal regimes. We need not doubt our intuitions that Denise Okojo's dog Molly was a legitimate subject of government rescue efforts and that the legislators who voted for the PETS Act were not launching a radical departure from liberal principles.

Recognizing some animals as members of the social contract is not a major change from our current practice. On the contrary, the idea makes sense precisely because we already do it. Our public policies protect animals from cruelty, rescue them from disasters, and acknowledge that they have interests independent from those of their owners. We even justify those policies using the language of contract. Congressman Kenneth Keating, for example, defended the Humane Slaughter Act by declaring that we owe much of our "prosperity, our health, and our happiness" to livestock and are therefore obligated ("as human beings and as legislators") to protect them from unnecessary suffering.[78] Senator Jacob Javits, in support of the Animal Welfare Act, referred to our ethical obligations to the laboratory animals "that are suffering for us."[79] The language of reciprocity is a commonplace in legislative debate.

But we are not consistent in fulfilling our obligations to nonhuman members of the political community. Our legal system is still rife with anomalous doctrines that prevent pet owners from recovering damages for loss of companionship when their pets are killed, that prevent judges from considering the best interest of the pet in awarding custody in divorce proceedings, and that prevent animals from having standing to enforce laws intended for their benefit. We consistently fail to protect livestock, the animals to whom we are most heavily indebted. Many of these lapses can be corrected without working major changes in our social practices, but other practices would need radical reform under my reasoning. Most prominently, modern, large-scale livestock production methods are inconsistent with our civic duties to livestock. Of course, these production methods also create substantial environmental harms and are dangerous work environments as well. So, while reform might be expensive, failing to reform these methods may well be more expensive. But I will have more to say about animals in the stream of commerce in the next chapter.

A final point, and a major difference between my approach and the arguments of the more radical animal rights advocates, is that the social contract I describe in this chapter does not aim at protecting the autonomy of individual animals by recognizing their natural rights. Rather, it aims at protecting individual animal welfare by protecting good human/animal *relationships*. The best protection for animal welfare is to promote these relationships by supporting good practices of animal husbandry and stewardship. According animals legal rights may be a way to do that, but those legal protections will accomplish very little if they aren't supported by appropriate institutions and practices. In the end, these institutions and practices, not abstract theories about natural rights, will determine the terms of the social contract.

3

Property

Thus do the lines of owning, owning up to, possessing someone else through responsiveness to who they are, to what their particular happiness consists in, expand. . . . You cannot have interests or rights in relationship to me unless we own each other.
—VICKI HEARNE, *Animal Happiness*

PETE THE MOOSE was barely five days old when he was attacked by a dog and left in the woods to die. The couple who found him were advised by officials at the Vermont Fish and Wildlife Department that they should leave him to his fate. Instead, they took the injured moose to David Lawrence, a retired Vermont dairy farmer, who said he felt an "instant connection": "How could you refuse to take care of a baby who's gonna die if you don't care for him?" He named the moose Pete, and Pete has flourished under Lawrence's care. Boarded at an elk farm owned by Doug Nelson, Pete enjoys regular treats of fruit, bread, and jelly doughnuts. Lawrence visits him daily and has grown quite attached to the moose.

But Pete's home is under threat. According to the Vermont Fish and Wildlife Department, Nelson's elk farm is a "captive hunting facility": Hunters pay to shoot the elk, moose, and white-tailed deer that live in the six-hundred-acre fenced reserve. Vermont, like many other states, has recently imposed regulations on these hunting facilities, and they want Nelson to get rid of the wild moose and deer—including Pete. The chief rationale for these regulations is to prevent the spread of diseases, such as chronic wasting disease, that wreak havoc on populations of game animals throughout the United States. Animals confined in high densities are particularly at risk, and fences do not prevent the spread of these diseases. Opponents of hunting (like the Humane Society) also support these regulations, arguing that hunting captive populations is particularly cruel and unsporting. "Shooting animals trapped within a fenced enclosure and calling yourself a sportsman is like hiring an escort service and calling yourself a ladies' man," says Joanne Bourbeau, New England regional director of the Humane Society.[1]

Lawrence isn't interested in the issue of captive hunting facilities; he just wants to save Pete. But Wayne Laroche, the state game commissioner, is unsympathetic. "Every spring, we put out a press release telling everybody it's illegal to pick up baby animals and to possess wildlife." Lawrence, according to Laroche, clearly knew what he was doing was illegal. "Just because they named him has no bearing on the issue."[2]

Laroche may be correct as a matter of law. Vermont follows the usual common law principle that wild animals are public, not private, property. By statute, "wild animals in Vermont belong to the people in their collective and sovereign capacity, not in their private and individual capacities."[3] But as a political matter, the fact that Pete has a name, as well as a website (www.savepetethemoose.org) and a significant fan base, *is* relevant. The governor has gotten involved in the controversy, asking the commissioner to find a solution that will spare Pete's life. Lawrence insists that he'll leave the state if necessary. "It's about what's best for Peter" and the rest of the animals, he declared.[4]

It might be best for Pete the Moose if the state allowed Lawrence to establish a private property right in the animal. Liberal theory traditionally recognizes natural property rights; that is, one may establish a moral claim to property even in the absence of government authorization. Governments may restrict such rights, but only to the extent necessary to serve the common good. Liberal theorizing on this issue dates back to John Locke's *Second Treatise of Government*, which argues that working a piece of land or otherwise adding one's labor to a natural object can create a right in it that others are morally obligated to respect. Locke recognized that a wild animal is generally considered unowned until a hunter kills it, but nothing in his theory suggests that capturing and taming an animal could not also establish a property right in it.[5] Many people do capture and tame wild animals and, like Lawrence, put up fierce resistance if the government tries to take their pets away.

But recognizing property rights in animals does not necessarily ensure their welfare. Consider the story of the chimpanzee Matthew Hiasl Pan. Born in Africa, Matthew was captured in 1982 and brought to Austria to be used in experiments by the medical research company Immuno. Matthew's legal status was challenged from the moment he arrived in Austria. The Austrian government had recently signed the Convention on International Trade in Endangered Species, which made importing the chimp illegal. Matthew was accordingly removed from Immuno's custody and taken to a Viennese animal shelter. Immuno challenged the confiscation, however, and years of legal proceedings finally resulted in a judgment for the company. Animal activists offered to buy Matthew from the company, but the offer was refused. Undeterred, they physically blocked the Immuno representatives from seizing Matthew. Immuno again went to court, which again upheld its property rights in the chimp—but the shelter still refused to relinquish custody. Finally, in 1999, Immuno was bought by another company, which ended the chimpanzee experiments and officially donated Matthew to the shelter. In 2005, the Austrian parliament voted to ban experiments on Great Apes (chimpanzees, orangutans, bonobos, and gorillas).[6]

But Matthew's troubles weren't over. In 2006, the shelter had to file for bankruptcy. Legally, the chimpanzee is part of the shelter's property—and financially, it is a big liability, costing the shelter about five thousand euros each month. Animal rights groups have raised money to pay for his care, but they face a legal obstacle: If the money is given to the shelter, it will become part of the shelter's assets and go to pay its debts. They want to put the money in a trust for Matthew, but Austrian law doesn't allow nonpersons to receive gifts in this fashion. The animal rights groups accordingly petitioned the court to declare Matthew a legal person so that he could receive the money in his own name. In January 2008, the Austrian Supreme Court rejected the petition, ruling that, legally speaking, Matthew was property. He remains in the care of his friends, but clearly the ruling leaves the chimp vulnerable if the struggling shelter should close.[7]

Property rights in animals are a vexed subject. As discussed in previous chapters, the law gives fairly broad protection to property rights in livestock and somewhat less protection to property in pet animals. Property rights are protected through laws against theft, tort laws, and some aspects of family and contract law. Moreover, the duties attendant on ownership formally (if implicitly) recognize the status of the owner; you can't be held responsible for neglecting an animal if it isn't yours. But the legitimacy of all these laws has been challenged by advocates for animal rights, on grounds entirely consistent with the American liberal tradition: Owning animals, they argue, is akin to slavery.

Gary Francione is a leading critic of property rights in animals. Francione argues that treating animals as property rather than persons "facilitates their exclusion from the scope of our legal (and moral) concern."[8] Steven Wise offers further support for this view, emphasizing the difficulty of according animals status as legal persons, with legally recognized rights, as long as they are considered property—a problem that Matthew's case illustrates quite well.[9] But against this position stand theorists like Richard Epstein, who contends that human ownership can benefit animal welfare by giving humans incentives to care for them. "Because they use and value animals, owners will spend resources for their protection. . . . Ownership is not tantamount to partnership. But by the same token there is no necessary conflict between owners and their animals."[10] Epstein might argue, for example, that Pete the Moose would be better off if the state recognized David Lawrence as his owner. Of course, Francione and Wise might respond that it would be even better for Pete, and for Matthew Hiasl Pan, to have ownership of themselves, a possibility conceivable in but not currently offered by American (or Austrian) law. They suggest that we should not think of animals as property at all but should conceptualize our management of them in terms of political rule or guardianship.

This is a complicated debate, in part because property theory is not well developed with respect to animals. The following section argues that traditional property theory is decidedly unhelpful in this area. Although the classic theorists address how property rights in general may be justified, they do not give us a sufficiently nuanced approach to deciding *what sort of things can be owned*. I therefore turn to more recent work by Jeremy Waldron and Elizabeth Anderson, which addresses how different sorts of property regimes and practices affect the social meaning of animals and the human/animal relationship. Following Anderson, I argue that the chief threat to animal welfare is not their property status per se but their commodification and mass production. I conclude that these practices, even when they attempt to protect animal welfare, are inappropriate ways of valuing animals and ought to be discouraged as a matter of public policy. When they directly harm animal welfare, the state may prohibit them altogether.

I. Classical Property Theory: Is There a Natural Right to Own Animals?

Do private individuals have a natural right to own animals? More precisely, can we specify an individual natural property right in animals in sufficient detail that it can be used as a standard against which to judge conventional, legal rights? If not—if there is either no moral right to own animals at all, or at best only a right for the human community to hold them in common— then our task is easy: We simply have to consider what sort of legal regime serves the common good (including the good of animals, assuming a common right to use animals doesn't foreclose a duty to attend to their welfare). But if there is a natural right to private property in animals, then the government's ability to restrict property rights in animals may be limited, since liberal governments are expected to respect natural rights as far as possible.

To answer this question we will need to define some terms: natural right, private property, and ownership. Much can be said about the meaning of these terms, and in most theories of property it matters a great deal how they are defined. Happily, for our purposes it doesn't matter very much. We can use a nontechnical and intuitive understanding of "natural rights" as "those of our individual interests that it would be wrong or unreasonable to require us to sacrifice for the greater good."[11] These interests are important enough that we expect others (including the government) to respect them and avoid infringing them. As for "private property" and "ownership," these terms cover a wide array of different property systems. For example, in some countries, owning a piece of land means that you can sell it or bequeath it to anyone you want; in others, those freedoms are severely restricted. However, it is not hard to identify a system that recognizes private property rights in some form. I follow Jeremy Waldron in defining a system of private property as one in which material resources (and often other things) are typically divided up, with each one belonging to an individual who then has authority to decide how it will be used (subject to general laws protecting community welfare).[12] This is what we normally mean by "ownership."

In the United States, for example, individuals may own certain kinds of animals, which means those individuals have the authority (subject, again, to general laws protecting community welfare) to decide what will happen to the animal: how it will be fed, housed, trained, exercised, and even killed. Clearly no individual has complete authority over an animal, any more than she has complete control of any other piece of property. We are never free to use our property to create a health hazard or to commit a crime, for example. But in a system that recognizes private property rights in animals, private individuals—not a social group or the government—make most of the decisions that affect the lives of the animals they own. This is the system of private ownership of (domesticated) animals we are trying to justify.

Unfortunately, it turns out that it is pretty difficult to justify this sort of private property right in anything, at least as a *natural* right (an interest that it is unreasonable to ask people to sacrifice for the greater good). It is easy to see that individuals must have a right to *use* various goods in order to live a fully human life, or even to live at all. But how can one individual acquire the right to prevent others from using those goods, if the others, too, need them and perhaps could use them more effectively? Shouldn't common resources be managed collectively, to serve the good of the whole community?

John Locke is often cited as authority for the proposition that we can acquire a natural private right to property—a moral right that can trump the community's interest in the object—and we do so through our labor. As he argues in the *Second Treatise on Government*, "Every man has property in his own person.... The labour of his body and the work of his hands, we may say, are properly his. Whatsoever then he removes out of the state that nature hath provided and left it in, he hath mixed his labour with, and joined to it something that is his own, and thereby makes it his property."[13] The problems with that theory are obvious, though. First, even if we knew exactly what Locke meant by "mixing" labor with an object, why should adding something of yours to a good give you the right to the whole thing? After all, you can spill some orange juice into the ocean, but that doesn't give you the right to the ocean.[14] And Rousseau famously offered a more profound objection: "On what basis do you claim the right to be paid at our expense for work that we did not impose upon you?"[15] Why can one person unilaterally take property away from the community just by working on it, without the community's permission? Faced with these objections, it is tempting to conclude with James Tully that Locke's natural right to property is nothing more than a right to use natural goods in common with others, to support one's life and family. And, the theological context being critical to Locke's thinking, it is the right to use something that ultimately belongs to God. Under this reading, an individual's right to own animals is limited by the community's interests in the animals, and even further by the fact that God created them for his own (often inscrutable) purposes.[16]

Of course, under Tully's interpretation, we could still make the case that humans' general right to life does give them the right to kill animals for food, if they need to do so in order to live. It would be unreasonable to ask people to starve in order to preserve animal life. In such a situation, we might be able to claim a natural right to *collective* ownership of some animals. But then again, we may not: It may be that those societies highly dependent on animal protein (like arctic hunter-gatherer societies) have a duty to change their ways, perhaps even move to a more temperate climate, in order to better respect animal life. However we might resolve that ethical question, though, it is clear that Americans don't have to eat animals to have a fully human life. Other sources of protein are readily available. So our right to life does not offer a very solid foundation even for collective property rights in animals, much less private property rights.

Even if our need for protein did justify property rights in animals, however, we would still have another puzzle to resolve: Why doesn't that need justify our capturing and domesticating other humans? Clearly not everything can be owned, so why does Locke conclude that animals are among the things that can be? This is of course merely the other side of the question of animal liberty, discussed in chapter 2: Animals, according to Locke, lack the higher-order reasoning abilities that would make their subordination to humans morally problematic.[17] Remember that "ownership" here means making most of the decisions about how the property will be used. When we treat (adult, fully competent) humans this way, we call it domination or slavery. Locke is assuming that animals are not harmed by this sort of domination, because they don't have the capacity to make their own decisions about how they should live.

Of course, as Jeremy Waldron points out, if rational capacity alone determines what may be owned, some humans (of low or no rational capacity) are fair game, and some animals may be much closer to persons than Locke realized.[18] Indeed, this was precisely the argument made by Matthew Hiasl Pan's defenders. They insisted that the intellectual, social, and even moral capacities of the Great Apes are so close to those of humans that we cannot justify treating them as mere things.[19] But as I discussed in chapter 2, even if most animals don't have humans' intellectual capacity, they may have something like natural freedom: minds and intentions deserving of respect. If so, then from a Lockean perspective, humans' right to own them is in question, no matter how much labor we have expended in the project.

Unfortunately, Locke doesn't give us much help in answering that question. Locke's theory of property assumes a world inhabited by humans (who have natural liberty) and things (which can be owned). It has no place for fellow-creatures: beings that have moral status, enjoy a kind of freedom different from the sort of rational autonomy humans have, and are capable of living in various kinds of meaningful, dependent relationships with humans. Locke simply doesn't give us much guidance in deciding what to do with these creatures.

We reach the same impasse under alternative theories of property. For example, some theorists, following John Stuart Mill, would base a right to private property on the notion of desert.[20] It is a plausible approach: If your labor adds value to an object, then no one else has a better moral claim to that value than you do. However, Alan Carter points out that others still may suffer some loss—some diminishment in freedom and equality—by virtue of your unilateral appropriation of a common resource. It is hard to see why you have a right to take the good in the first place, even if you do add value to it.[21]

But more to the point, this theory offers no satisfying approach to property rights in animals. True, if we had no moral duties to animals, then we would not be committing any moral wrong in taking possession of them. Our labor, then, might be deserving of reward. But if we accept the position that animals may be wronged, then we need to establish that treating them as property is not morally wrong *before* we conclude that we deserve property rights in them.

Others arguments for a right to private property contend such a right is essential to achieving rational independence, political autonomy, and other kinds of individual moral goods. None of these theories, however, establish that it is important to own particular *kinds* of property, like animals. Hegel's theory of property is the most fully developed and probably the most influential of these theories.[22] Hegel argues that the institution of private property is essential to human freedom, because individuals express personality and become self-aware largely through controlling things. More specifically, humans give purpose to things by taking control of them, by embodying human intentions in them. Through this activity, we make the nonhuman world less alien and more human; we make it a place where we can feel at home. Even more importantly, we express ourselves through this taking of possession; we make our will concrete and public so that others can recognize it. This process of taking control of things is therefore a key avenue to developing our personality.

Why this development of personality through private ownership is an essential step on the path to a fully ethical community is a long story, but we needn't explore it here. This truncated account of his theory is sufficient to explain its appeal; it elucidates why we might develop strong psychological attachments to the things we control, including animals, even in the absence of legal property rights.[23] But it doesn't explain whether we *should* control animals in this way. For Hegel, what makes something capable of being owned is that it has no rational intentions or goals, no free will of its own; it is "empty" of intention. Under Hegel's view, humans should not be owned because they do clearly have wills of their own. Animals, by contrast, lack intentions; that is, they lack the capacity to formulate goals and think critically about what to do. But if we disagree with Hegel that animals lack ends and intentions of their own that deserve respect, what then?[24] Animals are not humans and don't need to express their personality by owning things, but they aren't mere things, either. They may not have long-term aims, and their minds may be in some sense alien to us, but their purposes are not completely incomprehensible. They don't fit neatly into Hegel's theory. Again, we are hampered by too simplistic a model of the political world—one that recognizes only persons and things, not fellow-creatures.

When we turn away from natural rights to utilitarian justifications for private property rights, we find they are no more helpful. Under a utilitarian analysis, if property rights on balance serve to maximize a community's happiness, then they are justified. But again we confront the problem of deciding whose happiness we are trying to maximize. Are the animals themselves to be included in our calculations? If so, we will probably be left with, at best, highly qualified and limited property rights in animals, and certainly nothing like a *natural* right—a right that would limit the government's ability to pursue other ends, like animal welfare.

In sum, none of the classical approaches to property give us much help in deciding how a regime of property rights ought to deal with animals. They tell us that a being's rational nature, free will, and happiness may be relevant to the question of ownership, but how relevant? Does the fact that some animals have something like free will and intentions mean we shouldn't own them at all? But those capacities are an important basis for our ability to form meaningful relationships with them—and surely those relationships are among the things we want to protect with property rights. Moreover, it is entirely possible, as Epstein argues, that some animals (especially domesticated animals) are happiest when they are owned by humans; this sort of relationship may be most conducive to their welfare. If we are going to recognize property in animals, we need a theory that is sensitive to the distinctive qualities of animals: their moral status, their biological and social natures, and their role in the mixed human/animal community.

Waldron provides a starting point for such a theory. He notes that things capable of being owned vary dramatically, and it is unlikely that the same concept of ownership could apply to all of them. Most property rules are concerned with control and access to material resources, so they apply most easily to things we conceive of as material resources. When we try to apply them to other sorts of things—ideas, air, sunlight—we find ourselves in difficulty and have to devise new legal regimes.[25] It makes sense, for example, to distinguish between personal items and means of production, to treat nonmaterial things (like ideas) differently from material objects, and to have special rules for large-scale natural resources, like oceans, the atmosphere, and Antarctica. Legal scholar Eric Freyfogle agrees, arguing that we should discard the idea that property rights can be defined without reference to the thing being owned. Land parcels, for example, differ greatly, so private landowners have different rights and responsibilities depending on whether they own beachfronts, wetlands, or critical wildlife habitat. The problem with natural rights theories is that they are not sensitive to these differences.[26]

We can, however, take one important point from natural rights theories of property: They reflect the intuition that property rights are not simply created by law. The state is not free to define property rights any way it wishes, without reference to social practice. Property rights depend on a fairly high degree of social support—and so do state efforts to reject property rights claims. Immuno could get all the court judgments it wanted, but enforcing those orders would have been a public relations nightmare. The state of Vermont will face a similar public relations problem if it tries to take Pete the Moose from David Lawrence's custody. To be sure, social practice is also affected by the laws. But social practices concerning property are often deeply rooted and hard to change simply by changing the laws. We have already noted that people get very attached to animals. So the state's room to maneuver here may be quite limited. Even if we do not acquire natural property rights in animals, we do—in the absence of and sometimes in defiance of the state—establish relationships with them that we then expect the state to recognize. Property rights in animals must capture this social and moral reality.

II. The Social Meaning of Ownership

Animals, it seems, are a distinctive sort of good. On one hand, they are in some respects like the sort of things we own, physically speaking: They are material and we can exercise control over them. Morally and socially, though, they are different. Animals have moral standing and a will of their own. They have interests, feelings, and a kind of natural liberty. And we have more extensive social relationships with animals than we do with inanimate objects. We don't conceive of them purely as material resources all the time; their social meaning is more complex than that. Finally, the community has a distinct interest in the welfare of at least some animals (those that are members of the social contract). That welfare interest must receive appropriate protection.

We need a theory of property that is sensitive to these sorts of differences among goods, and Elizabeth Anderson's pluralist-expressivist theory of value is an excellent place to start. Anderson's theory resonates with Waldron's and Freyfogle's insights about property and accords as well with Joseph Raz's emphasis on the role of social practices and institutions in supporting liberal freedom (an emphasis I discussed and endorsed in chapter 2 and will return to in the final chapter). Because it rejects the simple person/thing dichotomy that governs classical liberal theory, Anderson's theory is a better foundation for liberal property theory than Lockean, Hegelian, or utilitarian approaches.

Anderson begins with the idea of value. Goods may vary not only in how much we should value them, she argues, but also in *how* we should value them. That in turn is a function of what *kind* of good it is and its relationship to the valuer.[27] She thus departs dramatically from the traditional liberal world of persons who must be respected and things that can be used. She recognizes respect, awe, love, admiration, and many other modes of valuation that are appropriate to different kinds of goods and beings. While humans in general should be respected, for example, one's children should be loved. Similarly, some natural objects may be treated as commodities that can be owned, bought, and sold. But the Grand Canyon should be treated differently, with admiration or awe.[28]

Importantly, however, these different modes of valuation are not a matter of purely subjective, individual preference. Anderson emphasizes the *social* dimension of rational valuation; an individual's ability to value something rationally depends on the existence of appropriate norms, institutions, and practices. Valuing a good properly, under this view, is not just a feeling; it involves conduct and expression. "To adequately care about something requires that one express one's valuations in the world, to embody them in some social reality." And being rational, for Anderson, is "a matter of intelligibly expressing our varied concerns to others."[29] A rational person governs her conduct by shared norms established in dialogue with others, including norms that express different ways of valuing people and things. These norms in turn constitute different spheres of social life, governed by different ideals.[30] For example, in our society, going to church and praying is a rational, understandable way to value your deity appropriately, with reverence. But this mode of valuation is possible because we have the social practice of going to church and praying. If we didn't have this or some other set of practices around the value of spiritual reverence, it would be very difficult to express that value at all. In short, one is capable of valuing something in a particular way, and thus of acting consistently with one's ideals in a way that makes sense to others, only in a social setting that upholds norms for that mode of valuation.

Under this view, one could not express respect or affection for an animal in a rational way (in a way that is intelligible to oneself and others) in a society in which animals are viewed *only* as commodities or resources. The proper mode of valuation for commodities is *use*, or subordinating the good to one's own ends.[31] Showing consideration or love to a mere commodity is a moral mistake and would be viewed by others as irrational. It would be like petting and cooing over your refrigerator; no one would understand what you were doing or why. So if one came to such a society bearing an ideal of friendship with animals, one would find it difficult to realize that ideal.

Anderson thus endorses Joseph Raz's argument (discussed in chapter 2) that individual autonomy can flourish only in a public culture that supports it and offers many opportunities for individuals to develop their capacities. We need shared norms and practices that give meaning to our choices; without this rich social background, autonomy is meaningless. And as Raz noted, the government may have a role to play in promoting this public culture. Policies that respect and allow us to express the various social meaning of animals will create a richer public culture that expands the options for living in community with animals.

On the other hand, Anderson's analysis also clarifies why the legal status of animals is so controversial: Members of the same culture may disagree about the social meaning of a good, leading to conflict about what sort of behavior is rational. Is it rational, for example, for David Lawrence to treat a stray moose as a pet? Clearly there is room for debate on that point. Such disagreements might reflect different understandings about how to realize a shared ideal, or simply different ideals. As Anderson acknowledges, "There is a great diversity of worthwhile ideals, not all of which can be combined in a single life."[32] Some people may believe that the ideal of animal friendship means that wild animals should never be subjected to human domination by being turned into pets. Others may regard taking care of an injured wild animal as a good expression of that ideal. Still others may wonder why anyone would care about a moose; they don't share the animal friendship ideal at all.

These differences are not necessarily intractable, but resolving them is a matter more of contextual justification (as described in chapter 2) than of deductive logic. Political argument on this terrain will consist largely of appeals to imagination and sympathy, and to rich descriptions of what the world would be like if we pursue one ideal (or one conception of an ideal) over another. As Anderson puts it, to justify one's ideal, "one must be able to tell a story that makes sense of the ideal, that gives it some compelling point, that shows how the evaluative perspective it defines reveals defects, limitations, or insensitivities in the perspectives that reject these valuings."[33] For example, in order to defend an ideal of animal friendship, I would refer to our considerable stock of stories about friendship between humans and animals, including wild animals, showing that this relationship offers emotional satisfactions unavailable to the non–animal lover. Further, I might criticize those who don't share this ideal as cold, hard, and narrow, and offer empirical evidence for those interpretations.[34]

It is more difficult, of course, to resolve the dispute between those who show friendship for wild animals by taking care of them and those who show friendship by leaving them alone. The defenders of the "hands-off" policy have a strong case, even if it means leaving Pete the Moose to die. Respecting the social meaning of animals, after all, is more complicated than merely shielding them from harm. Harm is often an important consideration in the proper treatment of sentient creatures, but harming a creature is not the only way to violate its social meaning. In fact, actions that end up benefiting an animal in some material way (like causing it to come into existence, a common result of creating markets in animals) may nevertheless be objectionable because they express an inappropriate valuation of the animal (for example, breeding Dalmatians in order to harvest their hides for a fur coat). Nor is harming animals always inappropriate. Indeed, killing a wild animal for food may be consistent with its social meaning and our best ideals of human/animal relationships—even though certain forms of hunting, such as baiting, trapping, and Internet hunting, might be criticized for the attitudes they show toward the prey animal.

At this point, we may encounter, again, the objection first raised in chapter 2: This theory depends too heavily on social attitudes rather than some secure, philosophically justified moral principles. How can a consensus on social meaning provide a strong justification for government regulation? What if the society as a whole is wrong? Surely we need to correct mistaken social valuations by going back to basic philosophical principles. My answer, again, is that of course we can draw on philosophical principles to critique the existing social consensus—that is part of the process for resolving disagreement that Anderson describes. But I would also reiterate my argument in chapter 2, that contextual justifications aimed at imagining how our social practices could be improved *do* offer good reasons for policies, and they are likely to be more politically effective than simply relying on deductive arguments aimed at proving why those practices are morally wrong.

Moreover, Anderson's theory does in fact help us think critically about what sort of goods may be owned and how they should be owned. For example, Anderson has argued against the commodification of various kinds of goods, including women's reproductive labor and some environmental goods. She acknowledges that many goods ("economic goods") are properly treated as commodities and subject to market norms, which are impersonal, egoistic, and want-regarding. In other words, the market responds to desires backed by the ability to pay, without regard to the buyer's personal characteristics or her reasons for wanting something.[35] These norms are appropriate to the exchange of many ordinary goods, and they help to realize freedom of exchange, an important element of autonomy. But not all goods should be exchanged in this way. For example, she points out that many people resist treating *all* natural phenomena as mere commodities; when asked how much they would be willing to pay for an environmental amenity like a scenic view or a sunset, some people simply refuse to answer, treating the question itself as irrational. She interprets this refusal as expressing (quite rationally) the idea that certain natural phenomena should be subject to a different mode of valuation: admiration or awe, not mere use.[36]

Animals are among those things that should not be treated simply as commodities. Given our general recognition (expressed in animal welfare laws, among other things) that animals have moral status and we have a duty not to subject them to unnecessary harm, Anderson is certainly on solid ground in asserting that, according to our social norms, animals deserve "consideration," or attention to their welfare. Pets deserve even more: affection or family love.[37] But our relations with animals may in fact be more complicated than that; some animals may be "mixed goods." Anderson recognizes that we may often rationally treat natural phenomena and other kinds of goods as commodities *in part*. She allows for "hybrid" practices and institutions that allow a good to be partially commodified. Medical treatment is an example: We do treat a physician's labor as a commodity in some ways, and this is practical and socially beneficial. However, our medical institutions and codes of professional practice require that market norms do not wholly govern the exchange of this "mixed" good. Nonmarket norms (in this case the professional norms of care) will sometimes demand that doctors forget market considerations and simply act in the patient's best interest.[38] Animals, too, may be bought and sold, as long as the norms of consideration are allowed to trump market norms, where necessary. Of course, that would require substantial reform of markets in animals, a point I will turn to below.

In sum, under this theory, social practice and public policy—including property rights regimes—should respect (or at least allow citizens to respect) the social meaning of different kinds of goods, in order to protect our ability to realize different ideals in different spheres of social life. One could argue even further that failing to value an animal appropriately is a kind of injustice that governments should prevent, particularly with respect to members of the social contract. Misvaluation is an example of what David Schlosberg (drawing on the work of Nancy Fraser and Iris Young) calls the injustice of "misrecognition." Misrecognition commonly takes the form of insults, degradation, and devaluation, which constitute harms even where they don't directly affect one's rights.[39] But, according to Schlosberg, misrecognition can be a problem of justice even if its victim is not capable of understanding the insult. Indeed, the most troubling sort of misrecognition is structural, not psychological: social and political structures that routinely fail to accord a subject the appropriate status. Schlosberg points out that animals can be and often are subjected to this sort of institutionalized subordination.[40]

Whether or not we agree with Schlosberg that misrecognition constitutes an injustice toward animals, however, we can at least agree with Anderson that it constitutes an ethical mistake that the government should try to avoid. Under this theory, then, property rights in animals can be justified only if they allow us to express the social value of animals in appropriate ways. So the key question is what kind of ownership (if any) is consistent with an animal's best, most justifiable social meanings?

III. What Should It Mean to Own an Animal?

Wise and Francione suggest that property rights in animals are wholly inconsistent with animals' social meaning, that owning an animal amounts to treating it as a thing, a mere object or commodity. I think that conclusion is too hasty. True, our historical experience with human slavery has taught us to be wary of treating beings with moral status as property. But even Francione recognizes that slaves, while treated as property for some purposes, could also hold certain rights and enjoy legal protections.[41] Slaves had what Ariela Gross calls a "double character" as commodities and moral actors. This double character necessarily created tensions that could be resolved only by emancipation.[42] But treating moral beings as property doesn't have to create such problems. As argued in the previous chapter, for example, dogs became members of the social contract in the United States in part through regulations that created property rights in them, which then served to justify further protections for their welfare—including limiting what an owner may do to her dog. Recognizing an owner's property rights in an animal can be a way to improve its civic status by giving the human/animal relationship formal protection. Conversely, commodification of animals can take place even in the absence of strong property rights; as mentioned in chapter 1, in the United States, markets in pet animals flourished even in the absence of many legal protections for the owner's property interest. So property status itself does not necessarily turn animals into mere commodities or things; other social forces are also at work.

But this doesn't mean that property rights in animal as they currently stand are in no need of reform. Francione and Wise are right that our legal system often fails to protect animals' interests, making it difficult for the political community to guarantee to them the consideration and affection they are due. According to Francione, where human and animal welfare conflict, the law typically "balances" human interests in animals against the animals' own welfare, but the fact that humans have property rights in animals consistently tips the balance in favor of humans. As far as the law is concerned, we are balancing the human's interest in her property against the property's interest in itself—an absurd exercise in which the human usually wins. As a result, "regulation of animal use does not, as a general rule, transcend that level of protection that facilitates the most economically efficient exploitation of the animal." In particular, industry-standard methods of livestock raising and animal training and breeding are typically not viewed as imposing *unnecessary* pain on animals (even if more humane methods are available). Their suffering serves a human economic goal, and that is usually sufficient to justify the practice to lawmakers.[43] Thus Francione and Wise have a point: When the law and policy makers treat animals as mere economic resources, animal welfare usually suffers.

But there is an alternative to banning property rights in animals altogether. Private ownership of domestic animals is best understood as a custodial arrangement, in which the owners' rights in the animal are subject to a general duty to care for its welfare. David Favre in fact suggests that the law should recognize that animals can have "equitable self-ownership." His proposal takes advantage of the fact that our legal system allows the title to property to be divided into two elements: legal and equitable title. The person with legal title has control of the property, but the person with equitable title is meant to receive the benefits of it. Legal title is thus qualified by the title-holder's duty to serve the interests of the beneficiary. Under this model, an animal's guardian (holding legal title) would have property rights in the animal against the rest of the world, but would be bound to make decisions with animal's best interest in mind.[44] Importantly, under this custodial model, the individual guardian/owner may legitimately be concerned not only with the animal's welfare but also with preserving her particular *relationship* with the animal. For example, she may legitimately refuse to sell her dog to a wealthy dog-lover who would provide it with higher-quality dog food. The dog's individual interests are to be served within the context of the owner's interest in the relationship.

This model of equitable self-ownership seems to respect the social meaning of animals and their role in the mixed community. Moreover, it can be used for animals without doing violence to our traditional legal concepts; it fits neatly into the structure of American property law. We should not underestimate the problems it could create for our court system, of course. Some judges do make use of this custodial model when deciding, for example, who should get the family pet in a divorce proceeding. They may award shared custody and visitation rights that serve the "best interest of the pet" and recognize both owners' interest in the relationship. But that approach may require considerably more court resources to administer; it might involve supervised visitations, for example. Understandably, many judges do not want to further complicate what is already an immensely complicated business of dissolving a family.[45] On the other hand, Favre points out that under this model, an abused animal would not have to wait for the state to bring criminal charges against its owner. A private citizen (for example, a court-appointed guardian ad litem) could bring a civil suit on behalf of the animal, challenging the legal owner's actions.[46] The custodial model could thus improve enforcement of animal welfare laws. Whether we want to devote more resources to this end is, I think, a separate issue. We can at least put in place the legal tools we need to protect animals' welfare adequately and respect their social meaning, even if, in the end, we choose to prioritize other public goals.

A final objection to this model is that using property rights to protect the human/animal bond may seem to disadvantage the poor. How can people with few resources acquire property rights in an animal? And if owning an animal comes with a heavy set of responsibilities, are we making animal companionship a privilege of the wealthy? The first question, I think, is not particularly difficult. Under our existing property laws, one can acquire property not only through contract and gift, but simply by finding it. Pets are commonly acquired in this fashion, and shelters are full of free dogs and cats. But there's no doubt that the costs of pet ownership can be high, and imposing further duties on pet owners could increase that cost. Some form of public support (such as subsidized medical care) may be required to make the option of animal companionship available to more citizens. Remaking workplaces to accommodate pet owners, discouraging landlords from prohibiting pets, and other practices (not all of which necessarily require government regulation) would further expand our options in this area. Such policies and practices serve animal welfare but are also entirely in keeping with our concern for human autonomy, which is furthered by social practices that increase the range of good options people may choose.

This approach would provide an easy solution to the dilemma of Matthew Hiasl Pan: As a being with equitable self-ownership, he ought not to be treated as a mere asset of the shelter. Moreover, he could be the beneficiary of a trust set up on his behalf. The problem of Pete the Moose is less easy to resolve, but I think this approach does help to explain our intuitions about the case. Both sides of that conflict have embraced the custodial model of animal ownership: On one hand, David Lawrence has established a custodial relationship with Pete, of the sort we usually recognize by respecting a pet owner's property right in the animal. Since Lawrence seems to be a good guardian, we are inclined to let him continue to take care of Pete. On the other hand, the state of Vermont has good reason to bar individuals from owning wild animals, because most people are not in a position to take care of them. Vermont's policy values wild animals appropriately by showing them consideration and respect. It is not in the best interests of the wild animal populations or the mixed human/animal community to start making pets of these undomesticated creatures, and it shows a lack of respect for wild animals to turn them into pets in this fashion if (unlike Pete) they are perfectly capable of surviving on their own. The difficulty is that it is hard to enforce this "hands-off" rule for sick or injured wildlife. Taking care of an injured animal, even a wild animal, also shows proper consideration for its welfare. One reasonably successful way to deal with this conflict is for the state to allow wildlife rescue and rehabilitation organizations to deliver this care. There is such an organization in Vermont, and David Lawrence probably should have sought its services rather than making a pet of the moose. Since he didn't, resolving Pete's situation will now require a great deal of discretion, judgment, and tact on the part of the government officials. Such a resolution, I think, could be facilitated by the nuanced, sophisticated approach to property rights offered by Anderson's theory.

IV. Problem of Commodification

The key test of Anderson's theory, however, is not how well it deals with the atypical situations of Pete the Moose and Matthew Hiasl Pan. I endorse her theory of value because it provides a strong basis for criticizing the greatest threat to animal welfare in the contemporary United States: commodification and mass production of animals for the market. Anderson's theory pinpoints precisely the ethical problem with commodification: When animals are treated as consumer goods and subject to the norms of the marketplace, economic efficiency supersedes consideration, and animal welfare suffers.

Not all animal production results in the commodification of animals. Consider, for example, a small hog operation on the Peterson farm, in Northfield, Minnesota. The Peterson family has been raising hogs for three generations, and they are now teaching their fourteen-year-old son Shane the family business. Shane's methods are similar to those that his great-grandfather probably used: His sows farrow in roomy, straw-bedded pens with plenty of exposure to natural light. Their piglets roam in and out of their mothers' pens until they are weaned, at about five weeks. Shane then moves the older pigs to his uncle's barn, on the neighboring farm, where they can range inside a large straw-bedded room or go outside to a fenced yard. His hogs are healthy; he spends little on antibiotics and loses very few pigs to disease.

Shane is raising his pigs for market, and it pays well enough. The operation involves more labor than large-scale, intensive production does, but Shane's labor is cheap and his overhead is low. The main point of the operation, however, is for Shane to learn how to raise hogs in case he wants to go into the business. As for Shane, he likes pigs. "They have a lot of personality," he says, "and it's never boring." He says he doesn't get too attached to the individual pigs, but he's clearly fond of the herd as a whole. The Petersons select their breeding sows for their temperament, and they seem to like Shane in return. He will climb into the pen with a six-hundred-pound sow to feed her a can of soda and scratch her back while the piglets frolic around him.

This is what Anderson would call a hybrid practice. Shane can treat his pigs with consideration for their welfare because he doesn't have to make much of a profit. Market norms don't predominate in his operation; he's learning not how to make a fortune but how to raise pigs. This sort of hybrid operation was once the norm on American farms, where pigs were traditionally raised as a relatively profitable sideline to growing crops. To understand what happened to this production method, let us look at the transformation of hog production in North Carolina from the 1970s to the 1990s.

This story is a familiar one in the annals of American business. North Carolina's emergence as a leading pork producer was largely the work of entrepreneur Wendell Murphy, the "Ray Kroc of pigsties."[47] Murphy first got into hog production in the 1960s. He soon had an impressive stock of three thousand pigs, but a cholera epidemic hit the farm in 1969, and the US Department of Agriculture destroyed the entire herd. Unable to raise hogs on his own land, he had the bright idea to contract with his neighbors to raise them: Murphy supplied the fences, food, and piglets, and paid the contractors one dollar for every market-ready pig.

Contract farming was already common in the poultry business. Murphy successfully adapted it to hog raising, and over the next two decades he expanded his operations across North Carolina, Oklahoma, Missouri, Kansas, and Illinois. But his innovations weren't limited to franchising. The cholera episode motivated him to find ways to reduce the threat of disease, and, consulting with agricultural scientists, he adopted a new production process: Instead of raising his pigs from birth to market weight (250 pounds) on the same farm, he segregated them at different stages of their life cycle. Young pigs were weaned when they were fifteen days old and sent to a clean, disease-free facility. When they reached fifty pounds, they were sent to a finishing farm, to be prepared for market. This system, he reasoned, prevented older hogs from passing on diseases to younger ones. This change and other scientifically based innovations allowed him both to reduce the amount of feed necessary to grow a hog to market weight and to increase the productivity of his sows. The contract system allowed him to standardize these production practices throughout the state. By 1997, his company owned 6 million hogs. In 1999, in a deal reportedly worth $460 million, Murphy Family Farms was bought by Smithfield Foods, the nation's largest vertically integrated producer of fresh pork.[48]

This is not, however, a simple American success story. Murphy's career was controversial. In 1982, for example, Murphy was elected to the state's General Assembly, where he served for ten years. During that time, he sponsored or supported laws that gave tax breaks to hog producers and exempted them from environmental and local zoning regulations.[49] In 1995, reporters from the *Raleigh News and Observer* ran a multipart exposé on the growth of hog farming in North Carolina, for which they won a Pulitzer prize. Soon Murphy was facing substantial public criticism. Most of the controversy focused on his legislative self-dealing and on the risk of water pollution from the lagoons used to hold the manure produced by thousands of hogs. The reporters also questioned whether the contract farmers were getting fair compensation for their labor. The welfare of the hogs themselves received less public attention. But the state legislature responded by placing a two-year moratorium on new hog farms (an act that limited Murphy's growth in the state but also protected him from competitors). Intensive hog farming now faces legislative challenges in several states.[50]

Wendell Murphy's story is just one example of the revolution in American livestock production—a revolution encouraged and actively supported by state and federal government. The intensification of hog production in fact began shortly after World War II, promoted by the US Department of Agriculture's policies aimed at lowering the cost of food while increasing farm revenue. The key to this change was to make farms bigger and more mechanized; the department's chief message to farmers was "Get big or get out." For hog producers, the major change was moving the hogs indoors, into containment buildings, and confining pregnant sows in individual pens or "gestation crates" (to better control the farrowing process and protect newborns from being crushed by the sows). To lower costs, hog producers gradually made the gestation crates smaller, enclosed larger numbers of hogs in the buildings, and replaced straw bedding with hard concrete or slatted floors.

These changes led to a new set of pig welfare problems. Although hog producers insist that the clean, sheltered environment makes for happy pigs, the
animals are still subject to a number of stressors. For example, Murphy's
practice of weaning pigs after two weeks and segregating them away from
their mothers may shield them from disease, but it also distresses them and
prevents them from developing antibodies to those diseases. Crowding
increases aggressive behavior by the pigs, and when they are deprived of straw
to browse, they are more likely chew on one another's tails. Pregnant sows are
isolated and have easy access to food and water, but they get stressed when
they can't move freely and engage in nest making. And confinement of large
numbers of animals has led to the emergence of a new set of diseases, especially
enteric and respiratory diseases that are hard to treat.[51]

Having created this challenging set of problems, hog producers attempt to
manage them—not by creating more natural environments but by trying to
make their pigs less piglike. Since tail biting has become a problem, tails are
docked. Young pigs have their teeth clipped and are castrated, making them
more manageable. These practices also increase the risk of disease, which have
to be managed by costly antibiotics.[52] In general, intensive production methods
make the hogs' distinctive biology, behavioral instincts, and sociality into
management problems. Under this system, the ideal animal would do nothing
but reproduce and grow meat. It would be a self-replicating commodity.

I do not want to create the impression that large-scale producers don't
care about the welfare of their animals. They have economic incentives to
keep their pigs healthy, and presumably the same humane sympathies as the
rest of us. But agricultural economists and industry experts encourage them
to view animal welfare as a cost—a cost that is under constant pressure
from market competition. Unlike Shane Peterson's operation, it is a system
governed almost entirely by market norms.[53] Despite our history of strong
state interest in livestock (discussed in chapter 1), modern animal welfare
regulations typically exempt livestock from their protections. The only
federal law governing their treatment on the farm is the Humane Slaughter
Act, which regulates only the method of slaughter. Thus under Anderson's
theory, the whole system is based on an ethical mistake: It treats animals as,
first and foremost, a commodity. They are merely used, subordinated to the
economic ends of the humans involved in these commercial transactions.
To be sure, even if the mass production of livestock expresses a misvaluation, it may not always result in an animal's physical suffering. But we must
bear in mind that for Anderson, misvaluation is a matter not merely of
taking the wrong attitude toward a good but of treating it inappropriately;

our values are expressed in our conduct.[54] Therefore, we may expect that someone who values an animal merely as a commodity will attend only minimally to its physical and social needs—specifically, only to the extent necessary to preserve its market value. Indeed, we should view such conduct as not just caused by but partly constitutive of "valuing an animal as a mere commodity."

This problem of commodification and mass production is not confined to large-scale livestock operations. We see some of the same trends, and the same animal welfare issues, in the production of pet animals. Pet animals have been produced for markets since the mid-nineteenth century, which is when we first see advertising, brand identification, and breeding standards developed for dogs and cats.[55] But as with other forms of commercial animal production, the commodification process intensified after World War II. In the 1950s the market for pets expanded, and farmers looking for additional sources of revenue were encouraged by the US Department of Agriculture to raise dogs for sale. Thus the rise of mass marketing of pets coincided with the rise of breeding factories (or "puppy mills").[56] As mentioned in chapter 1, these large-scale breeding operations quickly became notorious for their unhealthy conditions, and a 1965 *Life* magazine investigative article on "dog farms" was an important impetus for the nation's first federal Animal Welfare Act.[57] But regulation has not eliminated puppy mills, and the treatment of animals by breeders and retail pet shops continues to be a major focus of animal protection groups like the Humane Society of the United States, the American Society for the Prevention of Cruelty to Animals, the Companion Animal Protection Society, and the Animal Protection Institute.

The pet trade is now a big industry. According to the American Pet Products Association (APPA), 39 percent of U.S. households include at least one dog, and 35 percent include at least one cat. Only about 10 percent of dogs and 18 percent of cats are adopted from animal shelters; most pet animals are purchased from retailers. Sixty-two percent of pet shops sell live animals, and according the APPA, these sales generated $1.6 billion in 2004.[58] But they have generated a great deal of controversy. For example, in 2005 the Animal Protection Institute conducted an investigation of California pet shops, producing a graphic report entitled "Little Shops of Sorrows." The investigation documented sick and neglected animals in 44 percent of shops visited and large percentages of animals confined in unhealthy, cramped, or crowded conditions (32 percent), often without adequate food or water (25 percent).[59] According to a constant stream of exposés, conditions in "puppy mills" are much worse.[60] In addition, animal welfare advocates complain that the pet trade increases the numbers of abandoned or euthanized animals by creating an oversupply and by selling to people who don't appreciate the responsibilities involved in caring for pets.[61] Indeed, many of them recommend that pet owners acquire animals only from animal shelters, with a view toward abolishing the mass marketing of pets altogether.[62]

To be sure, pet animals receive more government protection than livestock. The federal Animal Welfare Act outlines minimum standards of care for dogs, cats, and some other kinds of animals bred for commercial resale. Large-scale commercial facilities that breed or broker animals for resale—to pet stores, for example—are required to be licensed and inspected by the US Department of Agriculture, to ensure that they comply with these standards. Enforcement tends to be lax, however, and operations making less than five hundred dollars per year and most retail pet stores are exempt from federal humane care standards.

Pet stores are also subject to state anticruelty laws, but (as of 2010) only twenty-seven states and the District of Columbia impose any specific humane care standards on pet shops. Such standards generally require that pet shops provide adequate food, water, and sanitation; only some specify that animals receive veterinary care, ventilation, appropriate temperature and housing, and diurnal lighting. Nebraska alone requires pet store employees to receive training, and California is the only state to require that animals be socialized.[63] Enforcement of these laws is also lax by the standards of animal protection advocates.[64] To be sure, the Pet Industry Joint Advisory Council, an industry lobbying group, has tried to defend the pet trade by promoting the conception of pet retailers as "caretakers" whose primary interest lies in their animals' welfare, in their humane treatment and happiness.[65] But there are few institutional means—no codes of professional ethics, no long periods of professional socialization—to limit the influence of the profit motive on pet retailers. They are subject only to occasional public exposés, rare state inspections, and their own humane sympathies. The continuing concern among animal welfare advocates about poor conditions in pet shops suggests that these are not enough to counterbalance the profit motive in the pet trade.

To the extent that the pet trade is governed by standard market norms, it is morally objectionable under Anderson's theory; like livestock production, commodification of pet animals constitutes a misvaluation that undermines the norms of care and consideration they deserve. Nevertheless, I am not advocating (as some animal rights advocates do) that we should terminate commerce in animals altogether.[66] Commerce in animals is morally problematic only when it is institutionalized in such a way that such market norms are allowed to *predominate*. Many families raise and sell pets on a small scale, treating these animals as pets first and commodities only secondarily. Like Peterson's hog operation, this is a hybrid practice. Rather than behaving like ideal market actors, these families may refuse to sell animals to people they think will not make good owners, or may become attached to animals they've sold and try to maintain a relationship with them. This sort of pet trade does not necessarily violate the norm of consideration or even the more demanding norms of family love. Similarly, Petco and PetSmart, two of the largest pet product retailers in the country, have pioneered a different hybrid practice: Instead of selling dogs and cats, they work with local animal shelters to sponsor animal "adoption" on their stores' premises. This approach also seems to respect the social meaning of pets adequately—the animals themselves are not treated as consumer goods, merely as the occasion for buying consumer goods. It has won widespread approval by animal welfare advocates and the general public.[67]

There are signs that similar changes are coming to the livestock industry. Following the European Union's lead, some states have banned the use of gestation crates or battery cages for hens.[68] Smithfield Foods, in response to consumer concerns, announced in 2007 that it was planning to phase out the use of gestation crates.[69] The Animal Welfare Institute and other organizations have gone further, promoting humane animal husbandry standards by developing guidelines and a certification system. For example, in 1989 the AWI conducted a pilot program, selling pork raised according to AWI's standards under a USDA-approved label (called "Pastureland Farms"). The program was short-lived, but the AWI standards have been formally adopted by a growing number of pig farmers since 1997.[70] (Not coincidentally, Shane Peterson's uncle was the first hog producer to be certified under this system.)

Of course, the chief obstacle to such changes is economic. Industry representatives may insist that standardizing the Petersons' level of attention to livestock welfare raises the cost of meat more than consumers are willing to pay. Whether this is true is a contentious question and a difficult one to answer. It is natural to assume that because intensive methods were adopted as a way to increase production and decrease the costs of food, abandoning those methods would lead to decreased production and increased costs. But, as mentioned above, intensive methods create their own costs—higher overhead, greater reliance on antibiotics, more deaths. And regulation might motivate the industry to come up with less expensive methods of production that still protect animal welfare.

To be fair, the economists are right that we must consider the costs of animal welfare protections in shaping public policy. But they are wrong to frame the central question as "How much is the consumer willing to pay for animal welfare?" This question entirely misses the point: We should not think of animal welfare as just another cost that can be quantified and weighed against other goods I could be purchasing with my money—as though my saving twenty cents on a carton of eggs compensates (whom?) for the suffering of the chickens that produced the eggs. This is just the wrong way to think about our duties toward livestock. Valuing livestock appropriately means attending to their welfare, whatever the cost. If it turns out that consumers (or taxpayers, through subsidies) aren't willing to pay that cost, then raising livestock for market will no longer be a viable career choice. That isn't a plausible scenario, of course; no one seriously argues that humane methods would drive up the price of meat so far as to end the demand for meat altogether. Such methods would, at most, make meat and other animal products somewhat more expensive, leading us to eat less of it—perhaps with greater appreciation for its true value.

V. The Limits of State Action

If I am right that the commodification of animals violates their social meaning, we must still consider whether we are justified in using the coercive power of the state to counter such practices. It is one thing for animal welfare organizations to criticize the commodification of animals as a serious moral mistake; it is quite another thing for the state to prohibit people from making this mistake. As argued in chapter 2, the liberal state respects individual autonomy and therefore does not seek to make its citizens live up to the highest standards of ethical conduct. It may enforce minimal levels of virtuous conduct necessary for civic order, but it confines itself to promoting such virtues as lawfulness, tolerance, respect for others, and a basic level of patriotism. The primary responsibility for promoting higher standards of behavior lies with the institutions of civil society. Humane societies, animal welfare advocacy, the animal-training profession, traditions of humane animal husbandry, and family traditions of pet-keeping develop, promote, and principally enforce our cultural traditions of animal care. The business community also has an important role to play; professional societies and professional socialization can reinforce good animal husbandry practices. But may the state support these efforts, using its coercive power in preserving the social meaning of animals?

Anderson considers the proper sphere of state power in her discussion of whether the state should enforce surrogate motherhood contracts (which in her view violate the norms of family love). She suggests two reasons the state should prohibit such contracts: First, she contends that by enforcing surrogacy contracts the state becomes implicated in the valuations expressed in those contracts.[71] Under this reasoning, the state should also prohibit (or refuse to enforce) contracts that commodify animals, lest it make the moral error of misvaluing those animals. This argument is quite weak, however. Normally we do not attribute to the state the values expressed in a contract. For example, the fact that the state of New York enforces a contract to pay a star baseball player a high six-figure salary does not mean that the state of New York considers that player to be so valuable, or even that the state endorses the commodification of athletic talent. It simply allows others to do so. In the sort of pluralist society that Anderson describes—where social groups may pursue different ideals and conceptions of the good life—the state must be allowed to enforce contracts expressing these different ideals without being considered to endorse them.[72]

Anderson's second argument is stronger, but still inadequate to justify a strong state role in regulating commerce in animals: She contends that the state is legitimately concerned with the failures of respect and consideration that can affect the welfare, freedom, and autonomy of its *human* citizens. This principle is consistent with conventional social contract theory, which teaches that the state is properly concerned with protecting human freedom (defined by Anderson as access to a wide range of significant options through which one may express one's diverse valuations) and autonomy (for Anderson, the ability confidently to govern oneself by principles and valuations one reflectively endorses).[73] One might argue that state intervention in livestock production and the pet trade furthers the freedom of human citizens. We may worry that if market norms are allowed to supersede the norms of consideration, we could end up in a world that offers no opportunities to develop the kind of positive, enriching animal relations that our current practices make possible. Humane methods of animal husbandry—the practices that the Petersons are trying to teach to Shane—would no longer be possible, because we would no longer know how to view animals as anything other than commodities. This would constitute a constriction of human freedom, under Anderson's definition of freedom. Anderson's critique of commodification is in fact animated by the concern that it is difficult to prevent market norms from invading other spheres in this way, especially when so many people hold up market norms as the epitome of rational action. There seems to be something particularly imperialistic about the market in our consumer-oriented capitalist society. So, we may be concerned that if animals are widely bought and sold as commodities, it may become impossible to view them in anything other than those terms: as fashion accessories, status symbols, or investments.

But I am not sure market norms are quite as imperialistic as this argument assumes. For example, I see no evidence that this problem is particularly acute with respect to pets. On the contrary, over the past century we have seen the proliferation of new practices and products that allow us better to express affection and consideration for our pets. I hardly need mention the vast range of goods and services available for pets. Historian Katherine Grier notes that veterinary medicine is evolving at an extraordinary pace as owners are willing to spend money on procedures like organ transplants.[74] The mass marketing of pets may actually encourage these practices by expanding markets for new pet-related goods and services. Indeed, even while it contributes to the commodification of animals, the pet industry publicly promotes the family-member ideal of pet ownership in order to create more demand for pets and their accoutrements.[75] Pet retailers' behavior may be cynical and self-serving, and we may worry that their marketing practices tend to reduce the quality of relationships with family members to a matter of buying them things. Nevertheless, the proliferation of pet-related commodities does not on the whole seem to be bad for human-pet relations. So restricting the pet trade, at least, is not strongly justified by an interesting in preserving for humans a wide range of significant options for expressing our valuation of animals.

The case of livestock is harder, because farmers need to make a profit off their livestock operations; market forces make it difficult for them to pursue alternative animal husbandry practices. Even so, we have seen the persistence of free-range husbandry and a growing market for animals raised humanely, despite competition from intensive operations. Intensive production has not completely eliminated other options for exercising human autonomy. And in its favor, industrialized production methods arguably give us access to inexpensive meat, which frees us to spend our income on other things—this, certainly, is also a boon to human liberty and autonomy. Perhaps this meat is of lower quality, but keeping it on the market does provide consumers with a choice.

On what grounds, then, could the state regulate the commodification of animals? Of course, it may be the case that the environmental costs (to humans) of intensive livestock production will ultimately justify banning it altogether, regardless of animal welfare concerns.[76] But quite apart from environmental concerns, I think that the welfare of the animals themselves constitutes a fully adequate reason for (limited) state intervention in pet and livestock production, even at some cost to human liberty and autonomy. As I argued in chapter 2, state power extends to all members of the social contract—and of all animals, pets and livestock are most obviously members of our social contract. Under this view, the state should intervene in animal production and commerce to the extent necessary to protect their welfare. Of course, being treated as a commodity does not harm their welfare in the way humans are harmed psychologically, simply by being misvalued. But that misvaluation, I have argued, can be expected to result in animals' biological and social needs remaining unmet while they are in the stream of commerce. Animals, and particularly domesticated animals, are acutely vulnerable to mistreatment and are therefore particularly dependent on strong norms of good care. Any practice that systematically treats them as commodities is likely to undermine those norms and will probably lead to poor care. This rationale justifies government regulation aimed at enforcing minimum levels of animal welfare in the pet and livestock trades. It can also support using some government resources to promote a culture of good animal husbandry—at least where there is already a broad social consensus about what the culture entails. But, as I will argue in greater depth in chapter 5, the primary responsibility for embodying better ideals of animal friendship and respect in our social practices does not lie with the state. This is a job better left to civil society.

VI. Conclusion

We began this chapter with the question of whether the state should recognize property rights in animals. Answering that question, it turns out, requires us to develop a new theory of property—a theory that is sensitive to their moral status, biological and social natures, and role in the mixed human/animal community. Accordingly, I have drawn on Anderson's value theory, arguing that humans may enjoy property rights in animals if such rights are designed to allow us to express the social value of animals in appropriate ways. The general aim of the property regime should be to protect beneficial human/animal relationships, not merely to protect individual human autonomy or economic freedom. But I have also warned that using state power to end the widespread commodification of animals would constitute a problematic intrusion on human freedom. Indeed, it might well be impossible anyway. There are not only theoretical but also practical limits on the liberal state, as the state of Vermont discovered in dealing with David

Lawrence's relationship with Pete the Moose. Fortunately, Anderson's theory directs our attention beyond the state—and beyond the question of property rights—to the other institutions and practices that can play a critical role in raising the social status of animals and creating the conditions under which they can thrive.

For example, the production of research animals (standardized, genetically identical mice, for example), genetic modification, and patenting of animals are extremely worrisome developments under my analysis. Even if these practices result in concrete benefits to human welfare and don't physically harm the animals in question, they still represent an attitude toward animal life that is not consistent with its best, most justifiable social meanings. While it may be difficult to justify state action prohibiting such practices, the public can ask that scientists defend them. To do so, scientists would have to tell a compelling story about the quality and meaning of their relationships with these animals—a story that would make laboratory research on animals look like a valid, choiceworthy way of showing fellowship with animals. I don't think this is impossible; some forms of laboratory research (like behavioral research) can be seen as a high-quality form of animal husbandry. But much of this research looks, at least to outsiders, like reducing animals to objects that exist only for human purposes. Indeed, many researchers have reported that it is virtually taboo in the scientific community to talk about their relationships with and feelings toward lab animals[77]—a taboo that, under this analysis, is probably doing nothing to help legitimize the practice or protect the welfare of the animals. What we need is more imaginative exploration by the scientists themselves of their relationships with the animals under their care, along the lines we see among pet owners and livestock producers, and more public critical reflection on those relationships. It is impossible to predict where such reflection will lead, but it is not too much to hope that it will help us to develop more humane, respectful, and enriching relationships with animals—relationships deserving of legal protection.

4

Representation

The animals can remember. . . . But our language they will never speak; not from lack of intelligence, but from the different construction of their speaking apparatus. In the world of man, someone must speak for them. And that is why, in a nutshell . . . goddesses and witches exist.
—ALICE WALKER, *The Temple of My Familiar*

We are their voice.
—ASPCA MOTTO

AS ALICE WALKER points out in the quote above, it doesn't take any special magic to speak *to* animals. The real challenge lies in speaking *for* animals. If there is anything mysterious and magical about governing animals, we will confront it here, in our discussion of how they can be represented in the political process.

Democratic government of a mixed human/animal community seems to require that nonhuman animals receive political representation. Indeed, representation is central to the legitimacy of modern liberal regimes. But representation is a complex concept, and its practice even more so. The concept of representation is related to the concepts of political agency, authority, and accountability; its practice can take place in both political and legal institutions, and it can be regarded as both a formal institution and an informal, creative performance. Indeed, this is a topic on which artists, writers, and other culture workers have a great deal to contribute. Not all politically relevant representation takes place in political or legal arenas.

Consider, for example, the work of Joanna Macy. A scholar and practitioner of Buddhism, Macy approaches animal representation not as a political practice but as a spiritual practice, a creative performance that may heal one's relationship to the nonhuman world. Macy's workshops are used in classrooms, churches, and grassroots organizing; they focus on helping people "transform despair and apathy, in the face of overwhelming social and ecological crises, into constructive, collaborative action."[1] One of her most popular workshops, the Council of All Beings, centers on the transformative potential of speaking for animals.

This is how the workshop goes: The council opens with a ritual, perhaps using incense or rattles, drumming, or chanting. The participants don masks of the various animals or other nonhuman entities that they will speak for in the council (their "allies"). They then enter the council one by one, each participant inviting her ally into her body. In the council area, participants may begin to make noises and to move around like animals. Slowly they form a circle. When the circle is fully formed, the facilitator welcomes everyone, introduces himself, and (speaking from the perspective of his animal ally) tells the council how he sees life on planet Earth at the present time. Participants take up this conversation, offering their allies' own perspectives on the planet's condition. For example, a bird might complain, "The shells of my eggs are so thin and brittle now, they break before my young are ready to hatch." A cow might offer, "I'm tightly crowded in a dark place. . . . My calves are taken from me, and instead cold machines are clamped to my teats." The council is not just a place to register complaints, however. The participants may also suggest ways that animals can help humans to better care for the planet, naming the gifts, skills, and teachings that animals can pass on to humans. ("I, Condor, give you my keen, far-seeing eye. Use that power to look ahead beyond your daily distractions, to heed what you see and plan.")[2] Toward the end, participants take off their masks, moving back into human form. The council is closed with another ritual.[3]

Clearly, the main point of representing animals in the Council of All Beings is not political but spiritual. In Macy's words, the council "aims to heighten awareness of our interdependence in the living body of Earth, and to strengthen our commitment to defend it. The ritual serves to help us acknowledge and give voice to the suffering of our world. It also serves, in equal measure, to help us experience the beauty and power of our interconnectedness with all life." But even an intensely personal spiritual practice may have political impacts. As Macy herself explains, "The beings that co-exist with us in the web of life are profoundly affected by our actions, yet they have no hearing in our human deliberations and policies, no voice to call us to account. The Council of All Beings gives them a voice—and because it is our own as well, it can change the ways we see and think."[4] People who engage in this sort of creative performance might enter the political arena thinking and experiencing the world differently.

In fact, this practice of donning masks and claiming to speak for a nonhuman animal fits easily into our traditions of political street theater. For example, David Schlosberg's book *Defining Environmental Justice* refers to an incident at a public hearing in Eugene, Oregon, on a proposal by Hyundai

Corporation to build a semiconductor chip plant in a wetland. At the Army Corps of Engineers hearing, one citizen testified dressed up as a Fender's blue butterfly, an endangered species that would be affected by the project, and spoke from the butterfly's point of view. Her statement focused on the impact the proposed facility would have on its daily life. She was followed by another citizen (not in costume) who read testimony from the perspective of a western pond turtle, another endangered species, again speaking about the project's effect on the turtle's daily life. Both speakers noted that the proposed mitigation measures would not prevent the destruction of habitat or travel corridors, matters that would of course be of great concern to the butterflies and the turtles. Schlosberg, who observed this hearing, noted that these testimonies left the army colonel "literally squirming in his seat." (Happily for the colonel, the speakers did not identify any particular law that was being violated, so the corps was able to delete their testimony from the record.)[5]

Army colonels are not the only ones who might be unsettled by such performances. There is undoubtedly something uncanny, even eldritch, about the idea of speaking for animals. As Walker points out in her novel *The Temple of My Familiar*, in Western cultures the ability to communicate with animals has traditionally been a feminine power, closely associated with witchcraft.[6] It is a power wielded by the oppressed, a way of turning their subordinate position into a source of strength and superior understanding. Perhaps it is not mere coincidence that most of the people claiming to speak for animals referenced in this chapter are women. Women have always been prominent in moral reform movements in the United States, of course. But if Walker is right, their leadership in the animal welfare movement may have deeper roots in folk traditions surrounding witchcraft and familiars.

Those traditions may also explain the broad public interest in the story of animal management expert Temple Grandin. Grandin is a professor of animal science at Colorado State University, a designer of facilities for livestock processing, and a leader in the animal welfare movement. Through her teaching, consulting, and writing, she has worked for decades to improve standards in slaughter plants and livestock farms. Such efforts have earned her a "Proggy award" from People for the Ethical Treatment of Animals (PETA), which claims that "Dr. Grandin's improvements to animal-handling systems found in slaughterhouses have decreased the amount of fear and pain that animals experience in their final hours, and she is widely considered the world's leading expert on the welfare of cattle and pigs."[7] But Grandin is also, famously, a person with Asperger's syndrome, a variety of autism. She has written perceptively and eloquently about how this condition—a condition that often isolates and disempowers its subjects—has given her a unique insight into how animals experience the world.

The mind of an autistic person, according to Grandin, has some interesting parallels to the minds of nonhuman animals. For example, animals, like autistic persons, think in pictures rather than abstractions. Like autistic persons, they are hyperattentive to small details of sight, sound, and odor, and experience fear as a primary emotion.[8] She draws on her superior understanding of animal minds to imagine how a slaughterhouse, for example, is experienced by a cow:

> When I put myself in a cow's place, I really have to be that cow and not a person in a cow costume. I use my visual thinking skills to simulate what an animal would see and hear in a given situation. I place myself inside its body and imagine what it experiences. It is the ultimate virtual reality system, but I also draw on the empathetic feelings of gentleness and kindness I have developed so that my simulation is more than a robotic computer model. Add to the equation all of my scientific knowledge of cattle behavior patterns and instincts. I have to follow the cattle's rules of behavior. I also have to imagine what experiencing the world through the cow's sensory system is like. Cattle have a very wide, panoramic visual field, because they are a prey species, ever wary and watchful for signs of danger. Similarly, some people with autism are like fearful animals in a world full of dangerous predators.[9]

Most twenty-first-century Americans won't suspect Grandin of witchcraft; they would call her extraordinary empathy and insight by the ordinary name of "scientific expertise." But it is still uncanny, this power to enter into an animal's perspective, to give voice to it, and, by so doing, to transform our collective understanding of both animals and ourselves.

If representing animals seems mysterious, though, perhaps it is no more mysterious than the business of representing human beings. Representation, in Hannah Pitkin's oft-quoted words, means "the making present in some sense of something which is nevertheless not present literally or in fact"—a feat of legerdemain, at least, if not magic.[10] And political representation is particularly powerful and mysterious: It is supposed to make present in our legislative assemblies the nation itself, or the "will of the people." Political representation invokes the political community. In doing so, it gives voice to the voiceless and makes present those who are absent.

None of this requires supernatural powers, of course. Like any good magic trick, political representation is achieved through artifice; it takes clever institutional design, a rich tradition of political practices, and some imagination and creativity. This chapter considers whether and how this sort of everyday magic can be invoked on behalf of animals. I argue that political representation of animals does pose some challenges for liberal regimes; it requires us to develop novel ways to authorize representatives and to hold them accountable. But representation of animals is possible, and not only in theory. It is already being accomplished in a variety of creative practices, in both political and legal arenas, and in ways that do no violence to our liberal institutions and values. On the contrary, better representation of animals, along with other vulnerable members of our community, could help us better to realize *human* freedom.

I. The Problem of Political Agency

If some animals are members of the political community, then democratic principles and ordinary prudence demand that their interests be represented in the policy process, in some way. Indeed, many environmental theorists insist that representation of nonhuman nature (animals, species, and even ecosystems) is an essential element of a properly constituted democracy. Robyn Eckersley, for example, argues that representation of nonhuman interests (along with those of future generations and noncitizens) will lead to better decision making by encouraging more wide-ranging public deliberation about the potential risks of our decisions. It could also encourage us to internalize the perspectives of a broader range of beings. Our decisions would thus be better informed and, she hopes, more just toward all those affected by them.[11] Although I argued in chapter 2 for a more limited political community than Eckersley envisions—in my view, the political community is confined to those with whom we have meaningful individual social relationships—her argument certainly applies to the nonhuman members of it. Surely all members of the political community who may be affected by political decisions ought to be represented in the decision-making process.

Unfortunately, political representation of nonhumans raises some difficulties for liberal political theory. No less an authority than Pitkin, author of the most influential account of representation in the liberal canon, gives us reason to think nonhumans cannot be given political representation. The problem is not, as we might believe, that it is impossible to know what animals' interests in public policy are. On the contrary, as a number of scholars have pointed out, in some ways animal interests may be easier to discover than human interests are. Humans' needs may be more complicated than those of animals, and humans often don't know themselves what they want, much less what's good for them. Moreover, humans often want conflicting things. With animals, we don't have to wrestle with conflicts between what they want and what's good for them; we can assume that they want what is conducive to their welfare. Grandin demonstrates quite effectively that scientific investigation informed by empathy can help us discover what is conducive to their welfare. Indeed, there is a broad consensus among animal welfare experts about how to conceptualize animal welfare and what conditions are conducive to it. They look, for example, to mortality, morbidity, risk of injury, good body condition (sustaining production and reproduction), the ability to perform species-specific activities (including social interaction, exploration, and play), and the absence of abnormal behaviors and physiological signs of stress.[12] To be sure, we know more about domesticated animals than wild ones, and are better able to evaluate their welfare. But as I argued in chapter 2, it is domesticated animals to whom we owe the greatest duties as citizens. And even if our knowledge of their interests is uncertain, surely it is better to rely on this uncertain knowledge than to plead ignorance as an excuse to deny animals representation altogether.[13]

The problem with representing animals is not that we lack adequate knowledge of their interests. The problem is that they cannot participate, as it were, in their own defense. Pitkin insists that political representation cannot take place unless the represented "can . . . be (conceived as) capable of independent action and judgment, not merely being taken care of." She is referring here to how we ordinarily use the word "represent" in political contexts. "A true expert taking care of a helpless child is no representative," she points out.[14] Nor do we call a government "representative" merely because its citizens are well cared for; if we did, a benevolent dictatorship would be representative. "Representative government" generally means that the citizens have some control over what government does. That is, in fact, the main point of representation.[15]

This is why it seems wrong to talk about the political representation of nonhuman animals. Animals do have agency of a kind, of course: They can do things, affect their surroundings, express themselves, and form relationships. But they don't have the capacity for exercising political agency or judgment in the ways with which we are familiar. Specifically, we can't ask them to participate in debates about public policy and express their grievances. Nor can we ask them to choose representatives and to hold those representatives accountable through elections (and associated practices, like making campaign contributions). Given the inability of animals to influence the policy process through the usual mechanisms of representative government, it would appear that we can at best be as benevolent dictators toward the animals we govern.

But this conclusion doesn't seem quite right. Indeed, the logical result of that line of argument is that the most vulnerable human members of our community—those lacking power and voice—cannot be represented either. But surely this conflicts with our ordinary understandings; responsible politicians *do* try to represent the interests of the powerless. In fact, that is often the justification for expanding representation: because the represented cannot speak for themselves. And if (like Pitkin) we're going to rely on the ordinary use of the word "represent," we must acknowledge that people do talk about representing the interests of animals in the policy process. The American Society for the Prevention of Cruelty to Animals (ASPCA), for example, claims not simply to take care of animals but to "speak for" them, and we have no difficulty understanding what they mean by that. They try to represent animals' interests, to act on their behalf. Such claims are echoed by animal advocates in many liberal democracies. We may debate whether they represent animals adequately or appropriately, but we're not confused about what they're trying to do.

Indeed, as Pitkin herself recognizes, the concept of political representation can carry a wide range of meanings. On one end of the spectrum, we can think of a representative as a mere delegate for her constituents, acting rather like a lawyer carrying out instructions from a client. This concept does assume that the constituents (the voters) are actively controlling the representative: instructing her, monitoring her, and punishing her if they dislike her actions. But a competing model (famously associated with Edmund Burke) deemphasizes the independent action and judgment of the voters, focusing instead on the notion that a representative is someone who acts for or in the interests of the represented. This model sees the representative as more of a trustee: someone who uses her independent and informed judgment to discover the true interests of her constituents and to align them with the national interest. This "trustee" model seems suitable for animals, as it is for anyone else who cannot participate in electoral politics.[16]

Traditionally, liberal theorists have been somewhat ambivalent about the trustee model of representation. On one hand, some of them have embraced the trustee model as a way to put some limits on the will of the majority. This is the view famously expressed by James Madison in *The Federalist Papers*, where he defended a representative over direct democracy because representation could "refine and enlarge the public views by passing them through the medium of a chosen body of citizens, whose wisdom may best discern the true interest of their country and whose patriotism and love of justice will be least likely to sacrifice it to temporary or partial considerations." He recognized, of course, that we might instead end up with representatives "of factious tempers, of local prejudices, or of sinister designs," but he thought that danger less likely in a large republic, where the clash of conflicting interests would make it difficult for any faction to secure a majority and thereby control the representative.[17] This desire to keep representatives relatively independent of the voters is not uncommon in liberal thought. If one is worried that the masses will not respect the rights of minorities, it might seem a good idea to empower the political classes to rely on their own judgment. Defenders of animal rights might be particularly anxious to encourage representatives to use their own judgment rather than following the (often unenlightened) views of the majority.

On the other hand, most liberal theorists are wary of the trustee model because of its implications for the idea of government by consent. As discussed in chapter 2, the consent of the people is an important foundation for political authority in liberal regimes, and representation is a primary way of making such consent meaningful. A system of political representation gives ordinary citizens a chance to participate (indirectly) in the policy process, to show their consent by allowing them to choose their governors. Specifically, the citizens are supposed to *authorize* the representative by voting for her, and then (through another election) hold the representative *accountable*. These acts of authorization and accountability give citizens some control over the government; if they dislike their leaders' decisions, they can choose new ones. Elections are in fact so important to political legitimacy that voting is enshrined in liberal democracies as a political right, a key expression of the citizens' subjective will to which the representative must pay attention. But the trustee model of representation, by emphasizing the independent judgment of the representative, makes elections much less meaningful. After all, if the representative has better political judgment than the constituents, then we shouldn't expect the constituents to scrutinize her positions, to second-guess her decisions, or to punish her by voting her out of office. If we embrace the trustee model, we seem to be embracing a much-restricted sphere for citizens' political agency. "Consent of the people" is reduced to mere unthinking deference to the political class.

But this analysis suggests that our original formulation of the problem, that animals naturally lack the political agency that humans naturally enjoy, was misleading. It now appears that humans' political agency is not a natural fact either; it is *constituted* by the electoral system. In other words, even for humans, political agency doesn't really exist until we create institutions like elections and so on, institutions that allow us to act politically. Indeed, to experience voting in contemporary mass democracies as a meaningful expression of political agency requires a well-developed social context, imagination, and interpretation—not to mention a wild leap of faith that one's vote might somehow make a difference someday. If human political agency is socially constructed (not to say wholly fictional), why can't we create some sort of meaningful political agency for animals as well? Wouldn't it simply involve designing other methods for animals' interests to be represented in the political process in a meaningful way?

In fact, we can take this line of reasoning even further, as Michael Saward has. Saward argues that representatives actually *construct their constituents*. They don't create the individual voters, of course. But representatives make claims about who their constituents are, what their interests are, and what they want. In other words, "at the heart of the act of representing is the depicting of a constituency *as* this or that, as requiring this or that, as having this or that set of interests." So "to speak for others—as elected representatives do, of course—is to make representations which render those others visible and readable."[18] Representatives make their constituents "visible," painting a mental image of who the constituents are—an image that in turn becomes the basis for political action and policy decisions. In this way, their "representative claims" help to constitute the political community.

Such claims are, of course, part of the process I discussed in chapter 2 of determining the boundaries of the political community: Representing animals is one way to establish their membership in the social contract. Under this view, those who speak for animals in the political process constitute the political community as including animals. In other words, they make animals visible in the political arena. More prosaically, they encourage human citizens and policy makers to think about animal interests, to consider themselves responsible for animal welfare, and to conceptualize the political community as including animals. Theorist Jennifer Rubenstein calls this "democratic representation," as opposed to "preference representation." The aim of democratic representation is not simply to transmit constituents' preferences to the legislature, but to enhance the functioning and overall representativeness of democratic institutions by making them more inclusive and responsive.[19] Representing animals can enhance the overall quality of democratic decision making by making animal interests visible or readable to policy makers.

Even under this analysis, however, we should not conclude that representatives are free to represent any animals in any way they please. Determining the boundaries of the political community is, after all, a complex business.

Political representation, like state regulation, can play an important role in that process, but other kinds of social practices and relationships are also quite important in determining who we consider members of our community. So just because a citizen chooses to speak for a Fender's blue butterfly does not mean the community is ready to establish political relations with butterflies.

And just as social practices can constrain representatives, so can animals themselves. Our fellow creatures are not wholly passive in this process: They think and have experiences, they behave in certain ways, they suffer or flourish, and they form relationships. True, the representative makes animals' activities appear in the political arena, where they take on political meaning, so representatives do play a central role in creating or expanding (or contracting) animals' political agency and determining which animals we will recognize as members of our political community. But, as Saward points out, a representative "can't simply conjure claims out of the air."[20] Claims that are persuasive and politically effective must resonate with the audience; they must be made from existing terms and understandings. So these claims about animals' interests cannot be wholly divorced from our everyday relationships with animals, our experiences of taking care of them and watching them suffer or flourish. For example, when a radical animal rights advocate claims that pets are oppressed, that claim generally fails to resonate with the experiences of pet-owners—experiences that are shaped by the behavior of pets themselves. On the other hand, when people who operate dogfights claim that their dogs are well cared for, that claim also fails to generally resonate with people who have seen how fighting dogs fail to thrive. It is not improper to say that these animals are exercising a very limited but still critical form of agency. It is not the sort of rational agency we attribute to humans, but it is nevertheless a kind of agency—"the ability to *be*"[21]—that can and does take on political meaning when represented in the political arena.

I am suggesting, in short, that instead of concluding that we can't represent animals because they lack political agency, we should view political representation as a way to create a distinctive kind of political agency for animals. It may not be as extensive as human political agency, but it is meaningful to the extent that it is rooted in and grows out of our daily experiences of communicating with and taking care of animals. And, just as it does for humans, representation of animals gives substance to the idea of government by consent: Although animals cannot give actual consent, political representatives can insist that we act *as though* we needed to secure animals' consent to our policies. By creating a kind of political agency for animals, they also help to create something like government by consent. Under this view, political representation is an important means of *constructing* a social contract that includes animals.

Even if we reject this whole line of reasoning, however, we are still left with the basic problem: If we agree that some animals have interests we must respect, how do we ensure that our policy making takes account of those interests? Whether we call it true representation or "quasi representation," someone must speak for the animals. After all, political representation isn't just a device to ensure that citizens can participate in their own governance; it is also a means of creating a good deliberative body, one that will engage in effective deliberation and be likely to discover the best interests of the community. Our aim, ultimately, is to ensure that the political system is responsive to animal interests along with the interests of human community members. How do we achieve that?

II. Authorization and Accountability

Once again, liberal practice is ahead of liberal theory on the question of how to represent animals. Los Angeles has had animal representatives for several years, thanks to animal rights activist Charlotte Laws. In 2004, Laws ran for the Greater Valley Glen neighborhood council on the promise to represent both humans and nonhumans.[22] She won the election handily and immediately set out to fulfill her campaign promise. On her suggestion, the neighborhood council created a new position called Director of Animal Welfare (DAW). Not surprisingly, they appointed Charlotte Laws to the position, where she has worked to put animal welfare issues on the neighborhood council's agenda. The program has received favorable press and public support; the city government has endorsed the DAW program, and about fifty Los Angeles neighborhoods now have them. Most are appointed by the neighborhood council, but the DAW bylaws allow the general membership of the program (the other DAWs) to appoint a DAW where there is no neighborhood council, or where the council doesn't want to make the appointment. Any DAW can be removed by the neighborhood council.

Charlotte Laws describes the DAW program as an effort to increase the representation of animals in policy making. Indeed, the bylaws for the program are explicit: "The DAWS provide a voice and a form of political representation for nonhuman animals."[23] It is, to be sure, a limited form of representation. The neighborhood councils themselves do not have much policy-making authority. Created by the city of Los Angeles in 1999, the councils are "quasi city entities" intended to advise government officials. They are representative bodies, elected by neighborhood residents, and they do have control of a limited budget. But their primary role is to help the city council respond to local concerns and to foster greater grassroots participation in city government. Toward that end, they hold hearings, advise the city council, and facilitate communication between the neighborhood and city agencies. Directors of Animal Welfare, in turn, consult with the neighborhood councils on matters relevant to animal welfare. They can bring policy proposals to the councils, which in turn can recommend these proposals to the city council. In addition to this agenda-setting role, they advise the city's Department of Animal Services and sometimes organize public events like pet adoptions.

The DAW program may sound somewhat idiosyncratic, but it is part of an international trend toward institutionalizing the political representation of animal interests. Such efforts, we should note, go beyond the traditional animal welfare goal of improving the quality of public policy. As suggested in the previous section, these activists are seeking representation as a way of renegotiating the terms of the social contract itself. Their goal is not simply more humane policies but political inclusion; they are trying to expand the prevailing *conception* of the political community.

Leading the way is the Dutch Party for the Animals, which was founded in 2002 with the aim of providing representation for nonhuman animals. As explained on their website:

> We want the legal position of animals to be laid down in our legislation. In this way, we can prevent animals from continually being the victims of political whims. At present, animal welfare still hardly plays a role in our legislation. This should change as soon as possible.
>
> Naturally, we also believe that people are also important. However, the political world is exclusively made up of representatives of human interests. This is why a political party, which primarily focuses on animal welfare, is so important. It is the most effective way of getting animal interests on to the political agenda.[24]

The party's aim is to ensure that "each kind of interaction with and use of animals . . . be continually subject to a careful weighing-up of the gravity of human interests and the consequences for the animal."[25] More specifically, the party wants to put animal welfare issues on the legislative agenda and to pressure other legislators to honor what is often mere lip service paid to animal welfare. And it has been quite successful. Led by the charismatic Marianne Thieme, by 2006 the party had garnered enough votes to win two seats in the

Dutch parliament. Those seats were retained in the 2010 election, and it has also won several municipal elections. These electoral successes have helped the party to increase the amount of media attention and parliamentary debate paid to animal welfare in the Netherlands.[26]

The Dutch party has inspired similar efforts in other countries. For example, the British Animals Count Party was established in 2006 to provide "a voice for the animals" through a party dedicated to "respect and compassion for all living beings."[27] It complements the British Protecting Animals in Democracy (PAD) campaign, an effort to "achieve political representation for non-human animals" by lobbying, rating the political parties on their animal welfare records, and encouraging tactical voting on this issue.[28] And the recently founded American Humane Party, "the first American political party committed to the rights of all animals, not just the human kind," hopes to run a candidate for the US Senate in 2012.[29]

Representing animals need not be institutionalized through electoral politics, however. Some theorists have suggested that we increase representation of nonhuman interests in other ways. For example, legislatures could adopt the practice of routinely consulting an animal representative on policies that might affect animal welfare. Or they could require the government to promote and fund representatives of nonhumans just as, in some systems, political parties receive government support. Similarly, legislatures could require regulatory agencies to include animal representatives and direct them to consider nonhuman interests.[30]

Of course, these approaches to political representation do seem to depart from our standard representative practices to some extent. Most notably, they don't create a direct electoral tie between the representative and the constituent. Elections usually serve as the chief mechanisms by which constituents authorize representatives and then hold them accountable. Obviously, Directors of Animal Welfare and members of the Party for Animals are not elected by animals themselves, nor do they answer directly to animals through elections. This is Pitkin's point: without an electoral connection, "speaking for animals" looks less like representation and more like simply "taking care of animals."

But elections are not the only way to authorize representatives or to hold them accountable. As most liberal theorists recognize, focusing on elections is really too narrow an approach to understanding political representation, even for humans. Representativeness is a feature of the system as a whole, and it is achieved through many institutional mechanisms and social practices. Many unelected persons, from advocates to experts to government officials, perform representative roles at various times and places. Even elected representatives do not follow the simple electoral model; they often consider themselves bound to represent people who did not vote for them but with whom they have cultural ties or common concerns. So a black congressman might regard himself as representing not just his own constituents but black citizens generally, just as a representative supported principally by the mining industry might consider herself bound to represent its interests in addition to her constituents' interests.[31] The mechanisms that authorize such representatives and hold them accountable extend well beyond elections.

In fact, coming up with ways to authorize representatives for animals isn't particularly difficult. Animals themselves don't have to do the authorizing; the power to appoint representatives is often lodged elsewhere, in deliberative or legislative bodies. Neighborhood councils, city councils, legislatures, and agencies can all appoint representatives when appropriate. Of course, the major problem with letting the deliberative body appoint the representative is that they might choose people who reflect the body's own views, rather than the true interests of the represented. There are, however, ways to avoid this problem. For example, the DAWs program offers an interesting alternative, allowing the DAWs themselves (operating according to standard parliamentary procedure) to appoint a DAW to a neighborhood that asks for one. And theorist Andrew Dobson suggests a rather ingenious system in which members of the electorate are selected (at random or by some other criteria) to vote for representatives of nonhuman interests.[32] A less radical approach is simply to rely on the general electorate to vote for people (like Charlotte Laws) who promise to represent both humans and nonhumans.

Similarly, a variety of methods are available to hold representatives accountable. These methods have evolved out of necessity because elections are extremely blunt tools for this purpose, especially in the United States. Our representatives have very high rates of incumbency, and even when one loses an election, it is difficult to know exactly why. Voters' decisions are determined only partially by the individual representative's performance; party affiliation, larger social and economic forces, and even name recognition can all lead to results that can hardly be interpreted as holding representatives accountable for their actions. So we have developed other ways of holding representatives to account. Most prominently, elected representatives might lose important staff members or campaign contributions from key constituencies, or they may be subject to public shaming in the press if they betray the people they are supposed to represent.

Such practices are examples what Jennifer Rubenstein calls "surrogate accountability." This term refers to situations in which a third party sanctions the representative on behalf of those they are supposed to represent. She cites the example of donors to nongovernmental organizations; such donors might stop contributing if the organizations fail to serve the interests of those they are supposed to help.[33] In the same way, animal welfare organizations and other human animal lovers might refuse to support or might publicly shame a purported animal representative who fails to pursue animal welfare. In effect, we can rely on multiple layers and overlapping spheres of representation, with each group claiming to represent animals' interests holding the others to account, making them justify their decisions before a critical audience of animal lovers.

Finally, beyond surrogate accountability, we can also rely on what theorist Jane Mansbridge calls "gyroscopic" representation. This unlovely term attempts to capture the notion that representatives may act according to internalized commitments and consider themselves accountable only to their own principles.[34] For example, when I asked Charlotte Laws to whom she was accountable, she did not refer to campaign contributors or to the neighborhood council that appointed her; she cited her own commitment to animal rights. In other words, she holds herself accountable to the principles that have guided her public career.[35]

These may all seem like "second-best" forms of representation, but to say that animals are represented imperfectly is not to say they cannot be represented at all. Still, we may be somewhat reluctant to embrace the idea of institutionalizing animal representation quite yet. One concern has to do with priorities: After all, there are human groups that may not yet be adequately represented in our political processes. Why focus on creating animal representatives instead of representatives for children or the mentally impaired, for example? In response to this point I would simply suggest that by creating a model of representing groups with limited political agency, we are making it easier to represent all such groups. Whether we begin with children or animals, we should expand our institutional capacity to represent the voiceless—and their capacity to influence the political process.

On the other hand, we may worry that expanding representation may in fact make our system less democratic. One of the few critics of Los Angeles's DAW program, for example, is John Yates, writing for the American Sporting Dog Alliance. He complains that these programs are generally filled with animal rights activists who have ties to "radical" organizations like the Humane Society and PETA. His chief concern seems to be that such programs *overrepresent* a minority view regarding animal policy—a view that is hostile to human ownership and use of animals.[36] His critique suggests that representing animals really amounts to representing the views of animal rights activists, or even double-counting the votes of animal lovers. If he's right, then representing animals creates a less representative, and therefore less democratic, system.

Happily, this also is not a particularly difficult concern to answer. First, with regard to elected representatives like members of the Party for the Animals, no one's vote is being double-counted. Arguably, it is *non*–animal lovers who end up overrepresented. When an animal welfare party appears on the electoral landscape, animal lovers may be forced to vote either for that party or for someone who represents other interests they care about, thereby effectively splitting their votes. Of course, that is a problem with most electoral systems. Every voter has to decide which of the various causes she cares about will receive her vote; she will seldom find a candidate whose issue profile lines up exactly with hers. Having a party for the animals offers those most passionate about the issue the chance to register their preferences, but in order to do so they may have to give up the opportunity to vote for immigration liberalization, increased spending on education, or some other important cause. In any case, their votes are not being counted twice.

As for appointed representatives, most of these proposals amount to appointing someone simply to advise the policy makers. DAWs, for example, don't have a vote themselves. And even if they did, it would not necessarily give them greater influence in the policy process than other better-funded and more established interests. Voting on a policy, after all, is only one step in a very complex process in which various interests exercise influence in many different ways: setting the agenda, shaping the options, affecting how policies are interpreted and enforced. The rationale for creating institutionalized representation for animals is that (1) animals have independent welfare interests, interests that are not identical to and can't be reduced to the preferences of human animal lovers. And (2) because they can't participate in electoral politics, these interests are systematically underrepresented. If that analysis is not plausible, then we needn't pursue these reforms. But if it is plausible, then we ought to address it. The fact that many humans would approve of and also benefit from these reforms is just an additional reason to do it. The only question is how and by whom animal interests should be represented, which is the subject of the next section.

III. Evaluating the Representative Claim

If the representation of animals is to be meaningful, surely we need some criteria to determine who really *is* representing them, in a substantive sense. In other words, we need to consider how to evaluate representative claims. This inquiry takes us beyond institutional design to issues requiring more nuanced political judgments. As theorist Andrew Rehfeld points out, becoming a representative isn't just a matter of following the rules; you don't become a representative by winning an election. You become a representative because the relevant audience has decided that winning the election, or some other procedure or criterion, gives you a *valid claim* to be a representative. But making a claim to represent a group is, at its heart, a rhetorical act, a performance. Charlotte Laws, Marianne Thieme, and Temple Grandin have this in common: They have all had to face an audience and win it over. And as any artist knows, a successful performance cannot be reduced to fulfilling any given set of criteria. There is always a creative element involved in performing, an opportunity for interpretation or even reinvention. Just as we can't reduce a great musical performance to simply hitting the notes properly, we can't reduce great political representation to just following the rules. One must make the representative claim in a way that the relevant audience accepts as compelling and true.

Importantly, the "relevant audience" here does not mean the people (or entities) being represented. Their views are usually important, but ultimately the representative claim must be accepted or rejected by the deliberative or policy-making body in which the representing takes place: the neighborhood council, city council, or legislature, for example.[37] These bodies may look initially to the results of an election, but once the election is over, the representative still has to convince the policy makers that he really does, consistently and reliably, represent his constituents' true interests. This is abundantly clear where there is no formal electoral process—for example, when a legislature is appointing someone to represent an interest or group. In such cases, the legislature must consider other criteria to decide what, exactly, makes this person representative. Is it his knowledge of the issues, his commitment to the group, a shared history or identity with the group? What exactly makes his representative claim persuasive?

There's no simple answer to this question. Which criteria the legislature or council pays attention will depend on the nature of the body, the function of representation, and a host of other considerations.[38] Of course, there are some general criteria that commonly come into play with all forms of political representation. Particularly relevant to the representation of animals are *knowledge of* and *commitment to* the interests of the represented. But these criteria can be interpreted and fulfilled in different and not always predictable ways.

It is tempting, for example, to assume that animal rights or animal welfare advocates best fulfill the knowledge and commitment criteria and therefore have the strongest claim to be representing animals. But Jennifer Rubenstein reminds us that representation and advocacy are not the same activities, and advocates don't always make the best representatives.[39] Advocates themselves often insist that they are *not* representatives, in part because they don't want to displace other, better representatives. For example, the ASPCA presumably would not want the fact that they try to "speak for animals" to become a reason *not* to institutionalize more formal and accountable animal representatives in the policy process. And advocates might also resist being described as representatives because representation isn't always the best description of what they're doing. Advocates may prefer to speak for a broad policy approach or general ideological position, rather than defending the interests of a particular set of individuals. So an animal rights activist might try to end the practice of raising animals for food altogether, a cause that is undoubtedly relevant to animal welfare but doesn't translate readily into "serving the interests" of those animals (because if they weren't raised for food, they probably wouldn't exist at all). Similarly, an advocate for preserving biodiversity might speak to the preservation of species without taking the interests of any particular animals as her primary concern. Indeed, if her goal is preserving biodiversity in general, she might wish to be free to advocate reducing the population of some species.

Furthermore, representatives often have a formal, institutional position that gives them duties toward the institution itself—a duty to facilitate good deliberation, to promote democratic participation, or to observe rules and regulations that could impair strong, impassioned advocacy. Although when asked, Charlotte Laws described her role as Director of Animal Welfare as basically the same as her role as advocate, it is clear that she behaves somewhat differently as a representative. She agrees that she is more willing to compromise, to listen to all sides of an issue, and to think like a policy maker rather than an advocate.[40] This different role is reinforced by the different sort of accountability to which she is subject: As an advocate, she was accountable principally to the people who supported her cause; as a representative, she is accountable to the neighborhood council, which has the power to remove her.

Nor should we view institutionalized representation as simply a compromised, less effective form of advocacy. On the contrary, one of Laws's reasons for suggesting the DAW program was to create a formal, institutional, and respectable position that animal rights advocates might be willing to occupy, which would give them greater legitimacy and authority in policy making.[41] Laws's intuition is that, as DAWs, they would be seen as representatives rather than advocates: more responsible, more committed to institutional values and to larger democratic values. This goal would not be met if representation of animals was seen (as Yates described it) as simply another form of animal rights advocacy.

To be sure, the fact that Laws had a long and consistent history of animal rights advocacy probably did help the neighborhood council accept her claim to be a reliable representative. If she showed too passionate a commitment to the cause, however, her audience might question the reliability of her knowledge; we might worry that such intense commitment could lead a representative to discount information that doesn't support her agenda. Along the same lines, certain kinds of expert knowledge may either bolster or undermine one's claim to be committed to animal welfare. Grandin, for example, cites her scientific expertise in animal neurology and behavior as an important basis for her representative claim, and such expertise is particularly compelling where the representative must speak to animals' physical welfare. Less academic forms of knowledge—experience as an animal trainer, livestock manager, or game manager—can also be the basis of a representative claim. In emphasizing such expert or practical knowledge, however, representatives could bring into question their commitment to animals' interests. First, this sort of scientific knowledge of animal welfare may seem abstract and objectifying. Scientific discourse about animal physiology often seems to reduce the animal to a mere pain- and pleasure-registering machine. Second, and even more problematically, such scientific knowledge of animals may mark someone as one of the exploiters. Grandin, after all, has spent a career working for the livestock industry, whose interests may lie in seeing less regulation on behalf of animal welfare. Game managers and animal trainers could be considered similarly compromised.

This potential tension between knowledge and commitment means that an animal representative's claim must rest on much more than paper credentials. Grandin's ability to be taken seriously as an animal welfare advocate is a testament not only to her scientific expertise but also to her ability to "come across" as unbiased, as having special insight into animal behavior, and as genuinely committed to animals. This is a matter of public performance, of finely tuned self-presentation. For example, a large part of Grandin's legitimacy as a representative of animals comes from her claim to be able to think like animals. If she took that claim too far, however (if, for example, she dressed up like a Fender's blue butterfly or summoned a Council of All Beings) she might lose that credibility altogether. This is precisely the problem that Charlotte Laws was grappling with when she proposed the DAW program: how to help people who "speak for animals" avoid the movement's associations with mysticism, witchcraft, and New Age spiritualism. In her view, and clearly in the view of other politicians like Marianne Thieme, animal representatives need to emphasize their professionalism, their willingness to work within the system and to speak the common policy language of bureaucratic efficiency and scientific rationality. They may feel a spiritual kinship with animals, but that isn't what they talk about when they face a group of policy makers.

Still, we shouldn't assume that the animal welfare movement's associations with spirituality, mysticism, and feminine power must always be a liability. As I insisted above, representation is a creative performance; as such, it is not a static or predictable affair.[42] If someone like the pop music deity Bono can make a plausible claim to be representing the global poor, someone like Joanna Macy could emerge as a plausible representative for animals, based on her empathy and spiritual insight. Democratic representation is a dynamic process; its form and meaning is always in flux, like the boundaries of the political community itself. In the 1960s, political representation of animals was hardly thinkable. Today, thanks to rhetorical and institutional innovation—the everyday magic of representation—it is becoming routine.

Representing animals in our legislatures is not enough, however. Effective implementation of animal welfare policies requires that animals be represented in the legal system as well, in the courts and agencies that enforce these policies. No theory of representation is complete if it neglects this legal arena; after all, it hardly matters what our policies are if they are implemented without regard to the interests they are intended to protect. But providing legal representation for animals raises a different set of issues than those involved in providing political representation. A court is a different kind of forum than a legislative body, so we must address a different set of institutional and political constraints.

IV. Legal Representation

Antoine Goetschel probably didn't expect his legal career to include representing a dead fish, but being the official "animal advocate" for the Swiss canton of Zurich undoubtedly holds many surprises. Switzerland has some of the toughest animal welfare laws in the world, and Goetschel's position was created in 2007 to help enforce them. Appointed and paid by the canton, he is a kind of public prosecutor dedicated to animal welfare cases. Although he doesn't prosecute cases himself, he is charged with making sure judges take animal welfare cases seriously. He explains the animal protection code, reviews files, and suggests fines, and he can also appeal verdicts. In early 2010,

Goetschel's responsibilities included urging the conviction of fisherman Patrick Giger for animal cruelty.

Giger's alleged crime was not killing the twenty-two-pound pike he pulled out of Lake Zurich, but taking ten minutes to do it. The proud angler boasted of the struggle to the local newspaper, which published the story. Unfortunately for Giger, this minor celebrity brought his battle with the fish to the attention of an animal welfare group, which urged the state prosecutor to file charges against him. Goetschel took up the fish welfare cause as well—and not for the first time.[43] In 2008, Goetschel represented a collection of fish that were used in a game show. The contestants were supposed to catch the fish by hand, and Goetschel argued that this treatment violated the Swiss law that animals be treated with dignity. But the defendants in game show case escaped conviction, and so in the end did Giger. Goetschel did find a German precedent holding that even one minute was too long to keep a fish on the line, but the court wasn't convinced. It acquitted Giger, leaving Swiss anglers free to tell their fish stories.

The Giger case attracted considerable attention because it coincided with a national referendum on a law to require all Swiss cantons to appoint animal representatives like Goetschel. Advocates for the law argued that statutory protections for animals often go unenforced. Fines are low, and in most cantons, prosecutors see animal welfare as a low priority. In 2008, 224 animal cruelty cases (one-third of all such cases in Switzerland) were prosecuted in Zurich. This suggests that the animal advocate position does improve enforcement. Nevertheless, the Swiss voters were not prepared to endorse Zurich's approach, and they defeated the proposal by a large margin.[44] Goetschel continues to defend the animals of Zurich, but his position remains exceptional.

There is nothing about the American legal system that would prevent us from empowering someone like Goetschel to provide legal representation for animals. While American courts have held that a nonhuman animal lacks the standing to bring suit in its own name, that rule can be changed by statute. As discussed in chapter 1, the laws regarding what sort of entity can be named as a plaintiff in a lawsuit is largely a policy judgment. Like the people of Zurich, we might decide that animal welfare laws could be better enforced if someone were empowered to bring suits on the animals' behalf. But legal representation of animals raises some concerns about institutional capacity.

To summarize the discussion in chapter 1, American courts currently allow groups or individuals to bring suit under animal welfare or environmental laws in order to protect their own aesthetic, recreational, financial, or even, possibly, emotional interests in an animal. But they do not have standing to defend the animal's own interests. Even the owner of a pet may have only limited ability to defend her animal's welfare, since her legal interest in the animal is usually limited to its market value. Government agencies are usually charged with enforcing animal welfare statutes, but they are often overburdened with other responsibilities. As a result, there may be no person with the standing and incentive to bring suit to defend statutorily protected animal interests. The courts, for their part, have been unwilling to give the rules of standing a broader interpretation, primarily because they're concerned about their capacity to resolve the kind of cases that might be brought by animal welfare advocates—cases aimed at setting or changing public policy. Judges are supposed to resolve disputes about the legal rights of the parties, disputes that take the form of adversarial contests in which the parties have actual knowledge of the specific controversy and a concrete stake in its resolution. As Supreme Court Justice Antonin Scalia has argued, courts should not engage in policy making that isn't rooted in such a dispute; they are not legislatures, tasked with the job of making policy that serves the general interest.[45]

Thus while political representatives are supposed to survey the broad policy landscape, bringing to light the range of interests involved in policy decisions, define and redefine these interests, and keep all of them in play during debate, the job of the legal representative is very different: to identify and focus the court's attention on the particular interests of the party implicated by a specific action. A judicial forum aims at narrowing the conflict rather than broadening it. The court tries to make the dispute fit into existing legal categories and resolve it using existing legal rules, rather than trying to create new categories, rules, or rights. So our problem is this: How can we arrange for humans to represent animal interests in court in a way that respects the nature and function of such a forum? The legal representative must defend the interests of one particular animal, not a species of animals or animals in general. How do we create that particular, one-on-one representative relationship?

Some scholars suggest that such lawsuits could be modeled on *in rem* actions or on actions on behalf of corporations.[46] But these, I think, are misleading analogies. An *in rem* action is a lawsuit in which a piece of property (like a ship or a book) rather than a person is the subject of the dispute. The action is aimed at settling the legal status of the item—for example, determining which parties have a claim to how much of a ship, or whether a book may be banned as obscene. In such cases, the parties involved are representing their own interests; the property itself has no independent interest. Similarly, American law allows corporations to be parties to lawsuits, and corporations are treated like persons for such purposes. But in such cases the corporation is represented by its officers, who in turn represent the owners (the shareholders). This is simply a way to represent the interests of many human parties in one action, rather like a class action lawsuit. There is no interest of the corporation that is independent of the interests of all these human actors.

A better analogy is the guardian ad litem. The guardian ad litem is a person appointed by the court to represent the interests of a party (usually a child) who cannot choose or instruct his own attorney. The person being represented is the ward. The guardian ad litem is supposed to represent the independent interest of the ward, but because the ward is presumed to lack the ability to determine his best interest, the guardian must rely on her own judgment to make those decisions. This seems like a workable model for representing animal interests. Guardian ad litem programs are a familiar feature of the American legal system and are used routinely in tort and family law cases involving child welfare. Guardians ad litem needn't even be lawyers; they are usually volunteers who receive special training and supervision provided by the state judicial system. And in the absence of a formal guardian ad litem program, American civil procedure rules typically allow the court to appoint a "next friend," a self-nominated representative of a party to a lawsuit who is unable to represent herself. The next friend need only convince the court that she is dedicated to the party's best interests.[47] These approaches are easily adaptable to animal welfare cases. Moreover, they are fully compatible with the proposal discussed in chapter 3 of recognizing animals' "equitable self-ownership," a proposal that allows humans to have a custodial or guardian relationship with animals.

Zurich's animal advocate position is also fully compatible with the American legal system. The advantage of this approach is that the animal advocate would be appointed by, answerable to, and presumably funded by elected officials, which would give her additional democratic legitimacy and make her responsive to the public. That advantage, of course, can also be a political liability: Public support for the position may be lacking. By contrast, a guardian ad litem or next friend can be appointed by a judge—and American judges are often unelected with very weak public accountability. Judges could ensure that animal interests get some representation even if the public has other priorities. The key point, however, is that all three of these options are consistent with the role and capacity of American courts. They all create an institutional position, a legal advocate for animals, that corrects for the underenforcement of animal welfare laws but differs from the position of advocacy groups. Because the animal advocate or guardian ad litem represents a specific animal, she is not acting as a policy maker or as an advocate for broad policy positions.

Her primary duty is to seek justice for the animal *within* the existing legal framework, rather than seeking sweeping changes in the law. Of course, an animal advocate like Goetschel would, like any public prosecutor, be obligated to consider the public interest in deciding which cases to take on and how to prosecute them. That would give her a somewhat larger policy role than a guardian ad litem enjoys. Nevertheless, her primary responsibility would remain vindicating the legal rights of particular individuals as defined under current law.

In short, we already have available institutional forms that could be adapted to create legal representation for animals. The more challenging issue, I think, is deciding *when* an animal's interest must be represented. For example, we might require that an animal advocate be appointed in any court proceeding in which an animal's interest is substantially affected. This is probably a workable standard, but it covers just a tiny fraction of legal transactions, most of which never end up in court. A broader rule—requiring representation in *all* legal transactions affecting animals, for example—is probably unworkable. Home sales, bankruptcy proceedings, estate planning, marriages, and all manner of routine legal transactions could have some impact on animal welfare. It is hardly feasible or necessary to require an advocate at every one.

Again, the analogy to child welfare is helpful. Most legal transactions affecting children go forward under the assumption that parent or guardian will look after the child's interest. By analogy, we expect animals' owner to defend its interests in most legal transactions. Indeed, as discussed in chapter 3, that is one of the great advantages of allowing private ownership of animals—to ensure that someone is legally responsible for its welfare. So we would need to appoint legal representatives only for unowned animals, or when the owner is incompetent or has an adverse interest (when, for example, an owner is charged with animal cruelty). Of course, most unowned animals are not members of the social contract, so (as discussed in chapter 2) we have no political obligation to represent their interests in the legal system. Indeed, trying to represent the interests of all wild animals would impose an insupportable burden on the legal system. Even Goetschel's attempt to represent the interests of a wild pike in Lake Zurich was probably misguided; this is the sort of intrusive state action that Americans probably would not tolerate (and the Swiss apparently do not either). Only those few wild animals who have become members of the community through social custom would need special representation. Animal advocates could probably focus on these and on cases in which an owner mistreats her own animal.

But what about adoption—or, more precisely, transfer of custody? Should animals have their own representative when they are sold or given away? I suspect this would not be the most efficient way to protect animal welfare. Normally we expect animal owners to ensure that animals go to good homes. Establishing and promoting norms of good care should ensure that there are good homes for them to go to. Beyond that, I would simply reiterate the point made in chapter 3, that the best way to protect animals in the stream of commerce is to discourage the mass production and marketing of animals altogether.

V. Conclusion

I have argued that there are no insuperable theoretical or practical difficulties to representing animal interests in a liberal regime. Doing so is consistent with our ordinary understanding of the word "represent," and it would not unduly strain our deliberative and judicial bodies to appoint someone to speak for the animals. If we agree that some animals (those that are members of the social contract) have interests that we are politically obligated to consider, then it is perfectly consistent with liberal values to represent them in the political and legal process. To be sure, there is a creative, dynamic element to representation; representing animals in politics does not merely confirm the existing boundaries of the political community but may help to expand them. Speaking for animals in the political sphere may be part of the process of redrawing the lines, of bringing new groups of animals into the social contract. As liberals committed to limited government, we might worry that such expansion will also expand the boundaries of legitimate state power. Indeed, extending representation too far—to wild animals, species, or ecosystems—might well lead to overly intrusive state regulation. But pets, livestock, and other domestic animals are already widely accepted as proper subjects for state action. Representing their interests in policy making and in legal proceedings merely ensures a better, more informed basis for government action.

I wish to argue, however, that extending representation to animals is not only consistent with human freedom but can also further it. My guide here is the novelist, essayist, and theorist Alice Walker. One of the themes animating Walker's work is the way oppression separates humans from each other and from the animals they love and care for. Such separation, she argues, serves to isolate oppressed people and to break down the empowering bonds of community. Representing animals, in her view, can help to restore community and empower the oppressed.

Walker develops this argument in her short essay "Am I Blue." Blue is the name of horse owned by a neighbor and pastured near Walker's house. As she became acquainted with the horse, she discovered to her delight that she had no trouble communicating with him. She says, "I was shocked that I had forgotten that human animals and nonhuman animals can communicate quite well; if we are brought up around animals as children we take this for granted. By the time we are adults we no longer remember." The animals don't stop expressing themselves, of course; it is just that adults learn to ignore them. Walker suggests that we are able to learn this kind of indifference or deafness because we have power over them; we don't *have* to listen to them. In other words, animals' "inability" to communicate with us is not a natural fact; it is an artifact of our domination over them. Blue's owner, for example, was able to ignore the very clear indications that the horse was lonely. The horse was allowed the company of a mate for a few months, but as soon as the mare was successfully impregnated, she was taken away and Blue was left alone again.[48] The owner never had to consider Blue's feelings in this matter.

The owner's insensitivity clearly disrupted any chance of community between himself and the horse, and between Blue and Blue's mate. But, importantly, he also disrupted Walker's relationship with the horse. After his mate was taken away, "Blue was like a crazed person. . . . He galloped furiously, as if he were being ridden, around and around his five beautiful acres. He whinnied until he couldn't. He tore at the ground with his hooves." She reports that he gave her "a look so piercing, so full of grief, I almost laughed (I felt too sad to cry) to think there are people who do not know that animals suffer."[49] Walker's companionship was clearly not enough for Blue; he needed another horse to whom he could relate in a species-specific way. And Walker, as a human herself, felt implicated in the owner's treatment of Blue. He was suffering, she says, because of "people like me who have forgotten, and daily forget, all that animals try to tell us."[50] Walker concludes that there could be no peace between her and the horse until this injustice was corrected and the horse's own small community was intact.

This, then, was Walker's stake in the situation: The poor treatment of Blue denied Walker a source of companionship, a relationship that could be important to her own self-development and flourishing. As a black woman growing up in the American South in the 1960s, she was a victim of oppression herself. In order to recover from the damage she had suffered from racism and sexism over the years, she needed the support that even a small community could provide. The owner's treatment of Blue deprived her of what might have been a healing friendship with the horse.

Walker's point, of course, is a more general one. She saw in the horse's treatment something that resonated with that of her own enslaved ancestors, who were also denied the opportunity to form normal attachments, to marry and raise children—and, not coincidentally, the opportunity to own pets and raise their own livestock. It is an insight as old as Aristotle, who also explained in vivid detail how tyrants try to destroy trust and community among those they wish to dominate.[51] The lesson of Walker's essay takes that point further: Injustice works to separate people from each other, but it can even disrupt the human/animal bond—which may be the only bond left to the poor and disempowered. Injustice breaks down all kinds of community, isolating its victims and rendering them all mute and powerless.

Walker's analysis suggests that resistance to this sort of injustice can begin with learning (or relearning) how to represent animals—how to speak to and for them. In an essay on a Balinese chicken, she reflects on how creative writers can perform this representative function: "A writer's pen is a microphone.... Once given permission by the writer ... horses, dogs, rivers, and, yes, chickens can step forward and expound on their lives." The magic of this, she suggests, "is not so much in the power of the microphone as in the ability of the non-human object or animal to *be* and the human animal to *perceive its being*."[52] According to Walker, attending to animals, listening to them and speaking for them, can help to repair the bonds disrupted by oppression. It can help disempowered, isolated humans to develop a sense of self, the beginnings of community, and a foundation for political action.

Walker's analysis helps to make sense of Macy's intuition that an exercise like the Council of All Beings can "transform despair and apathy ... into constructive, collaborative action." It explains how Grandin's autism, by giving her a unique understanding of animal minds, could be an unexpected source of empowerment. It explains, in sum, how the magic of representation can work to enhance community and, in doing so, serve human freedom. Representing animals is part of forming and maintaining healthy mixed human/animal communities—communities where all sorts of human and nonhumans can flourish together, and where everyone's voice can be heard.

5

Reform

IN THE DECEMBER 6, 2010, edition of *Time* magazine, futurist Ray Kurzweil happily predicted that in the coming decades, "we'll grow in vitro cloned meats in factories that are computerized and run by artificial intelligence. You can just grow the part of the animal that you're eating." According to Kurzweil, this would be a great improvement over factory farms. Getting meat from living animals, he pointed out, "is yucky."[1]

Kurzweil's vision is one conception of progress; producing meat by cloning would certainly inflict less suffering on animals. But it would also mean the end of traditional practices of animal husbandry and the virtual disappearance of most livestock. Perhaps a better future would involve small-scale, sustainable operations that respect the cultural meaning of livestock and maintain, in improved form, traditional practices of animal husbandry. Grass-fed bison ranches, urban livestock production, or even hunting could also figure in a defensible vision of a better, more fully realized animal welfare society. In fact, we can imagine several different versions of that society. That's the problem, and the beauty, of liberal pluralism. In a liberal society, citizens are expected to have different values and to pursue differing visions of the good life—for humans and for animals. Kurzweil's vision may be a defensible choice, but it is not our only defensible choice.

But maybe Kurzweil's point was that these different choices are irrelevant: The irresistible force of the market, combined with the direction of technological development, make cloned meat inevitable. There's really no point arguing about which utopian system of livestock production we'd prefer; the future is already written. Under this view, a liberal government is too limited to exercise any effective control over the direction of animal husbandry. Liberal governments are mostly concerned with respecting individual autonomy, and that means respecting the freedom of the market and technological development. Trying to move us toward any particular vision of the animal welfare society would involve some very illiberal restrictions on individual freedom. It is merely ironic (and not evidence of creeping totalitarianism) that our individual freedom is going to lead us all to choose Kurzweil's cloned meat.

Fortunately, political theorists aren't in the business of predicting the future of meat production. But we are in the business of explaining how liberal citizens should pursue social reforms aimed at realizing such visions. These reform movements pose two problems for the liberals. The first is pluralism: A mixed human/animal society could legitimately take many different forms, and there is no obvious way to choose among them. So whose vision of the future, if any, should the state endorse? I'll address this problem in its most challenging manifestation: How should a liberal society that is moving toward greater protection for animal welfare deal with the practices of minority groups that are inconsistent with the majority's vision? Should the state suppress minority practices in the name of protecting animal welfare, or should our zeal for reform sometimes give way to the value of respecting cultural diversity?

The second problem is the liberal state's limited capacity to achieve social change: Even if we did agree on a specific vision of the animal welfare society, it seems that the state can't do much to achieve that vision without violating liberal values—not, at least, if it must rely on its coercive powers, such as criminal prohibitions. Trying to enforce a particular vision of human/animal relations seems guaranteed to infringe more deeply on individual autonomy and equality than liberal citizens should tolerate.

These two problems, it turns out, are deeply interrelated; both will require us to turn our attention to the noncoercive, creative powers of the state and to the central role played by civil society in achieving more harmonious relations between humans and animals. I argue below that there are limits to liberal toleration of minority practices, but a liberal state interested in progressive reform ought to welcome and try to accommodate cultural diversity as far as possible. Therefore, liberal governments should use the coercive power of the state sparingly and judiciously to avoid extinguishing the creative energy generated by the free play of cultural differences.

In particular, I will sound a note of caution against pursuing animal welfare reform by relying heavily on criminal law. Regulations that impose severe criminal penalties on people who abuse animals, violate regulations intended to ensure animal welfare, or engage in activities that endanger animals are the most common kinds of animal welfare laws, and they are the sort of regulations that spring to mind most readily when we think about protecting animal welfare. Indeed, chapter 2 was devoted to arguing that such criminal prohibitions of animal cruelty can be justified under liberal principles. But using that power as our *chief* means of changing social practices is problematic. Criminal laws tend to put human and animal interests into conflict and to raise the stakes so high that compromise becomes difficult. Even worse, expanding the reach of the criminal justice system may deepen long-standing racial and class inequalities. A reform movement that relies too heavily on criminalizing animal abuse will simply fuel the perception that we can protect animals only at the expense of humans.

Therefore, I argue that criminalizing animal abuse should be the last and least important element of any reform agenda. Creating a more fully realized animal welfare state requires more constructive work than simply enacting prohibitions and penalties. It requires us to develop social practices and build institutions that align human and animal interests and empower humans to care for animals better. The state's wide array of creative, noncoercive powers can contribute to this project. But the central sphere of this sort of activity is civil society, from animal welfare organizations to churches, schools, and professional associations. And this point takes us back to the importance of cultural diversity: Improving animal/human relations is a creative endeavor, requiring imagination, judgment, and a wide array of social skills. We will thus need the participation of a diverse array of civic associations and social groups, including minority racial, ethnic, and religious groups. Such groups may offer new insights and a wealth of creative ideas about how to transform both dominant and minority practices. Harnessing their energy and imagination is the best way to realize the aims of the social contract for both humans and nonhumans.

I. Animal Sacrifice and Liberal Toleration

In 2004, the city of Euless, Texas, sent police officers to the home of Jose Merced to stop him from killing a goat in his garage. The killing, according to the city, was in violation of a long-standing ordinance that regulated animal slaughter within the city limits. It should have been a routine exercise of the city's police power, its authority to protect the health and safety of the city residents.

But this case was far from routine. Merced is an oba, a priest of the Santeria religion, and he claimed that sacrificing a goat was an essential part of the ritual to initiate a new priest. According to the expert on Santeria who testified at Merced's trial, animal sacrifice plays an important role in the faith.

> Santeria's practice centers around spirits called *orishas*, which are divine representatives of Olodumare, the supreme deity. Santeria rituals seek to engage these *orishas*, honor them, and encourage their involvement in the material world. Doing so requires the use of life energy, or *ashé*, the highest concentration of which is found in animal blood. Thus many Santeria rituals involve the sacrifice of live animals to transfer *ashé* to the *orishas*.[2]

Such rituals are performed at important events, such as the initiation of a new priest. So enforcing the Euless ordinance potentially violated Merced's freedom of religion—or so he argued in *Merced v. Kasson*, which came before US Court of Appeals for the Fifth Circuit in 2009.

Specifically, Merced argued that the city had no legitimate grounds to prevent him from killing goats in his garage. The sacrifices, he insisted, posed no health risk, nor did they constitute animal cruelty. He would purchase the animals from local markets and have them delivered to his house about fifteen minutes before the ceremony. The sacrifice itself involved slitting the animal's carotid artery with a short knife. The animal is typically cooked and eaten after the ceremony. He had been conducting such sacrifices, about one per year, for the past sixteen years, without interference, when police officers suddenly showed up at his house in September 2004 to inform him that the rituals were illegal.[3]

The city, on the other hand, insisted that it was just enforcing a standard zoning ordinance, common to many cities. Passed in 1974, the ordinance provides that "it shall be unlawful to slaughter or to maintain any property for the purpose of slaughtering any animal in the city." It also prohibits keeping any four-legged animal on lots smaller than one-half acre, even if only for a very short time.[4] There's no question that Merced's animal sacrifices violated these ordinances. But Merced claimed that the ordinance should not be enforced in a way that infringes his constitutional right to the free exercise of religion.

Merced had good grounds for his complaint; this was not the first time the constitutionality of a prohibition on animal sacrifice had been challenged in federal court. In 1987, practitioners of a variety of Santeria opened the

Church of Lukumi Babalu Aye in the city of Hialeah, Florida. Predictably, the church caused great consternation among many other residents of the city. Objections focused on the practice of animal sacrifice, which was described by its opponents as "mutilating animals," an "indefensible and repugnant" practice not consistent with "civilized behavior." A lawyer representing several neighborhood organizations clarified their position: "Santeria," he said, "is not a religion. It is a cannibalistic, Voodoo-like sect which attracts the worst elements of society, people who mutilate animals in a crude and most inhumane manner." Reverend Dias of the Joreb Baptist Church was more restrained, but complained, "That there are still people in this era, in our civilized society of the United States, still sacrificing animals in religious rituals is indefensible and repugnant."[5] Many animal rights organizations, including the American Society for the Prevention of Cruelty to Animals and the Humane Society, are opposed to animal sacrifice, and there had already been a number of confrontations around the country between practitioners of Santeria and animal rights advocates. Indeed, when the *Hialeah* case arose, the Humane Society was lobbying city councils around the country to adopt a model ordinance proposing up to six months in jail and a thousand-dollar fine for anyone convicted of ritual animal sacrifice.[6] The city of Hialeah didn't go that far, but after a raucous meeting in which participants denounced Santeria as barbaric devil-worship, the city did adopt an ordinance banning animal sacrifice under penalty of a five-hundred-dollar fine or imprisonment for up to sixty days.[7]

The church promptly challenged the ordinance in court as a violation of their freedom of religion, but the trial judge disagreed. He was persuaded that the practice did constitute a potential health hazard to humans and was also influenced by testimony from the vice president of the Humane Society (Dr. Michael Fox) that cutting the carotid arteries was not necessarily a humane and painless way to slaughter animals. Fox testified that if both arteries aren't severed cleanly at the same time, the animal might linger in considerable pain. And chickens, which have four carotid arteries, are particularly difficult to kill quickly and cleanly.[8] The trial judge also accepted the city's argument that banning the practice was necessary to prevent psychological harm to children who might be exposed to it.[9] In short, the judge concluded that the ordinance did infringe religious freedom but that the infringement was justified by the government's strong interests in preventing animal cruelty and protecting human health.[10]

That ruling, however, did not stand; although the appellate court affirmed it, the Supreme Court disagreed. In fact, the Supreme Court issued a unanimous opinion striking down the ordinance—a rare show of solidarity by nine justices who are usually deeply at odds over the separation of church and state. Although several animal rights and animal welfare organizations filed amicus briefs in support of the city, the Supreme Court did not think protecting animal welfare was the real issue.[11] Justice Kennedy's opinion for the Court focused instead on religious discrimination. Although he acknowledged that health hazards and animal welfare were legitimate subjects of government regulation, he concluded that the true motive behind the ordinance was hostility to the Santeria religion. He pointed to evidence like statements from the city council meeting that Santeria was "devil-worship" and noted that other kinds of ritual slaughter, like kosher procedures, were not prohibited. In fact, the ordinance was carefully drawn to protect every way of killing animals normally practiced in the city, except for ritual sacrifice by practitioners of Santeria. The ordinance was, according to the Court, a clear attempt to discriminate against a minority religious practice and therefore violated the church's free exercise of religion.[12]

The *Hialeah* decision was welcomed by practitioners of Santeria as proclaiming a general right to practice animal sacrifice, but that isn't precisely what the Court held. It did not reject the lower court's rule that a religious practice may be prohibited when it conflicts with the government's interest in preventing animal cruelty or protecting human health; it simply concluded that these were not the true motives behind this particular ordinance. Under the Court's reasoning, a generally applicable law that is actually intended to protect animals from cruelty and not motivated by hostility toward any particular religion could be enforced against someone who was practicing animal sacrifice. So the *Hialeah* decision didn't necessarily dispose of the issue in Merced's case. There's no evidence that the Euless ordinance, which was enacted long before Merced came to town, was motivated by a desire to suppress Santeria. True, its enforcement may have been; the police were apparently responding to a complaint about Merced, which may have been motivated by prejudice against Santeria. We can't be sure, however, since the court never actually reached that issue.

Instead of addressing the constitutional issue, the judges upheld Merced's other claim, that the ordinance violated the Texas Religious Freedom and Restoration Act. This statute prohibits a local government, such as the city of Euless, from enacting a land use regulation that imposes a "substantial burden" on religious practice, unless the regulation serves a "compelling government interest" and is the "least restrictive means" of serving that interest.[13] The statute is designed to give protection to religious minorities who might be unduly affected by a generally applicable law. It represents a commitment to religious freedom and diversity, and that commitment worked in Merced's favor. The Euless ordinance clearly did place a substantial burden on Merced's religious practice, so the court had to decide whether the city's reasons for forbidding animal slaughter in the city limits were "compelling" and whether there was another way to serve that interest without interfering with Merced's religious practices. To be sure, the city's purposes in enacting the ordinances were compelling: to protect human health and to protect animal welfare. But Merced's animal sacrifices, in the court's view, did not pose a threat to public health, nor were they (in the court's judgment) inhumane. It certainly wasn't necessary to ban all animal slaughter in order to serve the city's legitimate interest in protecting the health and welfare of its human and nonhuman inhabitants. Under the Texas law, Merced must be allowed to perform his rituals.

Of course, not all states follow Texas's practice of allowing exemptions from general laws to accommodate religious practice. Nevertheless, the *Hialeah* and *Euless* decisions bode ill for animal rights activists who hope to end the practice of animal sacrifice through legal prohibition. True, both decisions took for granted that protecting animal welfare is a strong, even a compelling, government interest. So a carefully drafted law prohibiting animal slaughter, supported by good public health and animal welfare concerns and not motivated by hostility to animal sacrifice per se, probably would pass judicial scrutiny even if it were applied against someone practicing animal sacrifice. But banning animal sacrifice itself—that is, allowing the humane slaughter of animals for any reason *except* a religious one—probably would not be allowed. According to these cases, such a ban conflicts with our liberal constitutional values of toleration and religious freedom.

But is that the right result, under liberal theory? How far should our animal welfare laws accommodate the diverse religious, moral, and cultural differences we find in our pluralist society?[14] It is a familiar but tricky problem for liberal regimes: Should the political community insist that everyone follow general moral norms, or must we, in the name of respecting cultural diversity and religious freedom, tolerate social practices that violate those norms? For some philosophers, the answer to this question rests on one's position on moral relativism, or the view that there are no universally valid moral truths—that moral judgments derive from and only make sense within the context of a particular culture. Presumably a moral relativist would find it more difficult to justify condemning divergent cultural practices than would a nonrelativist. However, following my usual practice of avoiding metaphysical questions whenever possible, I'm not going to address this issue here. Whether or not universal moral truths exist on some metaphysical plane, such moral uniformity clearly doesn't exist in the political world. Our problem isn't moral relativism but cultural pluralism: the fact that people within the same political community may ascribe to deeply divergent world-views. This diversity poses a political problem, one that is particularly acute with respect to cultural minorities. We can expect, in a majoritarian political system, that the dominant cultural perspective will usually be reflected in our laws. (I am assuming there is a dominant cultural consensus; a political community composed entirely of deep and conflicting subcultures probably would not be governable by liberal means.) The question is how a liberal regime, committed to ruling with the consent of the governed, should deal with minority groups—groups like practitioners of Santeria, whose world-view and practices are very much at odds with those of the majority.

My answer to that question is going to turn, in large part, on which moral norms are being challenged, so it is important to clarify that the case against animal sacrifice involves two different kinds of claims. Animal welfare advocates in the *Hialeah* case, for example, put a great deal of emphasis on the claim that the specific practice (severing the carotid artery) might inflict unnecessary pain and suffering on the animal (if, for example, the artery isn't severed cleanly). The objection is not that killing an animal for purely spiritual reasons is necessarily immoral but that this particular method of slaughter is unnecessarily cruel, and that the general animal welfare laws should be interpreted (or rewritten) to prohibit it. Proponents of animal sacrifice, in turn, usually defend their practice by arguing that it is humane when performed properly and that the people conducting the ritual know how to do it correctly. They don't disagree with the moral norm that animals should not be subjected to needless suffering. They merely wish the laws to recognize their method of ritual sacrifice as one of the humane ways to kill animals. It may look like they're asking for an exemption from the generally applicable laws, but in fact they're really asking that the general laws be drafted carefully to avoid prohibiting a practice that is actually (in their view) perfectly consis-tent with the general moral norm of avoiding cruelty to animals.

This debate over the method of slaughter may be distinguished from a deeper kind of value conflict also at play here: Some opponents of animal sacrifice seem to believe that it is wrong to kill an animal except to fulfill a "real" human need, like our need for food or medicine. Under this view, the religious reason for killing the animal simply isn't valid; it isn't a reason that a civilized, rational person should take seriously. This objection is not just a dispute about the facts of animal suffering; it is a conflict between radically different religious beliefs and worldviews. The dominant religious groups in the United States do not practice animal sacrifice. Christians take great pains to distance themselves from the practice. Nor do Muslims and Jews practice animal sacrifice; kosher slaughter as practiced by some orthodox Muslims and Jews is best understood as a ritualized way to slaughter animals for meat rather than a true sacrifice. Very few Americans can be expected to understand the theological premises and worldview that make sense of the Santeria ritual.

Of course, one might argue that kosher slaughter and even nonkosher slaughter isn't that different, morally, from animal sacrifice. They're all just different (but equally humane) ways to produce meat for the table. Some of the defenders of animal sacrifice take this position, but I think it misses the point of the moral objection. Surely the *reason* one kills the animal is relevant to the moral significance of the act (just as the *reason* the city is banning the practice also matters to whether the law is just). Jose Merced's primary purpose in killing animals is not to eat them. He sacrifices animals in order to release the spiritual energy concentrated in animal blood and to transfer it to the *orisha*. If one believes that this reason is just a lot of mystical nonsense, then it does look like Merced is killing animals for no good reason; he looks like someone who drowns cats just for fun. On the other hand, if one considers Merced's beliefs reasonable and worthy of respect, then his actions look more justified. Indeed, Merced may seem to be treating animals with greater dignity and a more profound appreciation of their spiritual value than do those of us who eat mass-produced, store-bought chickens.

The animal sacrifice controversy therefore involves a deep conflict between competing and possibly irreconcilable worldviews. Of course, as Claire Jean Kim perceptively argues, characterizing such conflicts as a "clash of cultures" oversimplifies matters quite a bit. Cultures, after all, are not homogeneous or stable, and people involved in these conflicts are often doing more than defending or attacking an established practice; they're trying to define who they are and who the "other" is.[15] For example, there is a good deal of conflict among practitioners of Santeria over the nature and meaning of their faith. Santeria appeared first in Cuba, where it seemed to be a folk version of Catholicism combined with some elements of traditional African beliefs. But the founder of the Church of Lukumi Babalu Aye, Ernesto Pichardo, rejects any association with Catholicism. His aim in establishing the church is to purify the faith and return to the beliefs of its ancient African practitioners.[16] Thus the *Hialeah* case wasn't merely a clash of two differing worldviews; it was also part of an intrafaith effort to work out what Santeria is and what relation it has to African identity and to Catholicism. Animal sacrifice is important to the Church of Lukumi Babalu Aye in part because it helps to differentiate the faith from more Christianized versions of Santeria.

On the other side, there appears to be more at stake for the opponents of animal sacrifice than just animal welfare concerns. For example, the Catholic Church is uneasy about the fact that many Santeria practitioners identify themselves as Catholic. In 1986, the US Conference of Catholic Bishops was sufficiently concerned about the rise of Santeria to make a strong statement that animal sacrifice violates the Catholic liturgy and is not consistent with Catholic teachings. So resistance to animal sacrifice has also been, in part, a matter of defining Catholic identity. And, more problematically, most of Santeria's practitioners today are dark-skinned, working-class Cubans who flooded into south Florida during the 1980s. The religion has become associated in the media and among the white majority with drug dealing, crime, and poorly educated immigrants.[17] Criticizing animal sacrifice as barbaric is one way to identify these recent immigrants as outsiders, to reinforce an ethnically and racially exclusive concept of American identity. Indeed, Claire Jean Kim points out that this "othering" language—characterizing a group as barbaric and uncivilized because of its treatment of animals—is a common trope in American culture, constituting a chief means of distinguishing "real" Americans from racial or ethnic outsiders.[18]

Clearly, one important lesson to take from this conflict is that there are ways of defending animal welfare that undermine human welfare by reinforcing racial divisions and exclusions—a problem I will discuss in greater depth below. But the point I want to acknowledge here is more limited: Subcultures and faith traditions are not homogenous, coherent, integrated wholes. Rather, they are fluid, ill-defined, overlapping, and contested. Respecting someone's cultural or religious practices begs the very difficult question of what exactly that culture or religion is. Unfortunately, however, that fact doesn't negate the problem posed by cultural pluralism. If anything, it deepens the problem, since it means that subcultures themselves are pluralistic. The fluid and contested nature of culture ensures that even within an apparently homogeneous cultural group, we can expect to find a great deal of individual value conflict. As a result, we can't expect everyone to agree on any set of fundamental values as a basis for public policy. Governing by consent is quite challenging in the face of this diversity.

One way to deal with this challenge is the approach suggested by John Rawls that we adopted in chapter 2: We decided to seek only an overlapping consensus of reasonable comprehensive moral doctrines, rather than complete, deep unanimity, to support our public (or governing) philosophy. As long as there is broad support for a norm of protecting animal welfare (as there is among Santeria practitioners as well as other Americans), it doesn't matter much what deeper metaphysical commitments that norm is based on. Another move is to insist on a fairly limited scope for state power. Liberals' respect for individual autonomy—their insistence on protecting a sphere of individual freedom that the state may not infringe—is a good strategy for preventing the state from being drawn into these inevitable cultural and religious conflicts among different social groups. The state has no business, for example, getting involved in the religious sphere by deciding whether animal sacrifice is a legitimate spiritual practice or just "voodoo."

But working against this laudable desire to keep out of cultural and religious conflicts is a competing liberal impulse, a desire to use the power of the state to change social practices, to better realize the ends of the social contract for humans and nonhumans alike. This progressive agenda seems to be what is driving the conflict over animal sacrifice. Groups like the Humane Society and the ASPCA would like to *extend* protections for animals beyond the status quo—to cultivate more respectful and humane attitudes toward animals across the board, among all groups in American society. Banning animal sacrifice is only one part of a larger program that might involve discouraging more widespread practices like hunting and factory farming. This is a perfectly reasonable agenda, under any number of moral philosophies. But it may not be reasonable to use the power of the liberal state to realize it, at least not if doing so would illegitimately infringe individual liberty and suppress cultural differences that ought to be allowed to flourish.

Admittedly, it is hard to draw a bright line telling us exactly how far the liberal state should be willing to protect or infringe on cultural differences. It is a matter of finding a workable balance between competing values. On one hand, some liberals (let's call them pluralists) put a great deal of value on cultural goods—that is, collective goods, like language and religious traditions, that can be made available to individuals only through participation in a vital, living culture. These pluralists would like for the liberal state and its citizens not just to tolerate but to celebrate and promote the flourishing of cultural differences. Will Kymlicka, for example, points out that the liberal idea of freedom centers on the importance of individuals' choosing their own life plan, and one can't do that without a societal culture that offers such choices and makes them meaningful. Kymlicka thus values cultural membership in itself, as an "anchor" for identity and a basis of self-respect, a vital foundation for self-development.[19] But most pluralists celebrate not just cultural integrity but cultural *differences*: Being exposed to many different cultures makes it easier to get critical distance on your own culture, and therefore to revise your vision of the good in light of insights from other cultures. Under this view, the condition of cultural pluralism is a rich source of new insights and ideas, contributing to individual rational autonomy and personal and social development.[20] Pluralists would therefore allow conflicting values to flourish (peacefully) with minimal state interference, and even with state accommodation and support—for example, the kind of support offered by Texas's Religious Freedom and Restoration Act, requiring general laws to accommodate minority religious practices.

On the other hand, many liberal theorists (call them the antipluralists) worry that celebrating cultural differences might undermine the liberal commitment to liberty and equality. After all, many subcultures endorse inegalitarian values, promote restrictions on individual liberty, and even violate human rights. On what basis could they claim any special treatment from a liberal state? Brian Barry, a leading spokesman for this position, argues that a liberal state is seldom justified in accommodating *any* deviations from our general laws to accommodate minority religious or other cultural practices. He argues that a central value of liberalism is that all citizens have a common set of legal rights and duties, and this commitment to equality trumps any argument for giving a group (religious, cultural, or otherwise) a special exemption from those rights and duties.[21] Stephen Macedo also insists that a liberal state must promote and enforce certain general moral norms, even if they conflict with a group's traditional culture or religious beliefs.[22] In fact, it may not be sufficient for the state to guarantee equal civil rights; the state may need to reach deep into the institutions of civil society—into churches, families, and other civic associations—to make sure they aren't promoting illiberal values that would undermine our public commitment to equality, individual liberty or, in our case, animal welfare.

One can see why someone committed to a progressive agenda of extending animal welfare protections might favor the antipluralist view. Reforming widespread social practices regarding animals would involve reaching deep into the institutions of civil society; it might involve changing our diets, recreational activities, and family relationships. It is tempting to resort to the state's coercive power to accomplish these changes, and the antipluralist position seems to offer a strong justification for doing so. But in fact, I don't think the antipluralist view supports such an agenda. I suspect even a thoroughgoing antipluralist like Brian Barry would hesitate to expand state power so deeply into our private lives. His commitment to equality is matched by his commitment to individual liberty: Returning to the principle of limited government, he points out that a good way to ensure that the state is not treating citizens differently is to *limit* its interference in their daily lives—which would also allow for the flourishing of (a reasonable amount of) cultural diversity.[23]

In practice, no one wants to stamp out all cultural differences. But neither is anyone willing to tolerate all cultural practices no matter how illiberal those practices are. Pluralist William Galston, for example, argues that there are some "core evils" that the government can and must prevent. These are harms to human welfare that reason and historical experience have taught us to abhor, universal "bads" that must be avoided if we are to have minimally decent lives. Galston lists tyranny, genocide, cruelty and humiliation, starvation, and epidemics as examples.[24] Kymlicka, another pluralist standard-bearer, would go further, insisting that a liberal society needn't endorse any cultural practices that violate basic civil and political liberties.[25] These judgments may rest in part on our Rawlsian consensus of reasonably comprehensive moral doctrines: If virtually all moral theories condemn a practice as evil, we can confidently outlaw it. But Galston's reference to experience gestures, also, toward what I called in chapter 2 "contextual justification": One can justify outlawing a practice not only by referring to basic moral principles but also by showing that this prohibition is better than the alternatives, drawing on historical considerations and rich descriptions of what the world might look like if we chose one course of action over another. Drawing on these kinds of arguments, even committed pluralists can say with confidence that a liberal state may outlaw practices that violate the liberal value of respect for individual human dignity and autonomy. And if our argument in chapter 2 was persuasive, we should also be able to prohibit the wanton infliction of pain and suffering on animals. The liberal state is obligated to ensure decent lives for *all* members of the social contract, and that includes animal members.

But "decent" is a pretty low standard, and it is also clearly a malleable one. What counts as a "decent" life for both humans and nonhumans has changed dramatically over the past two hundred years, largely as the result of progressive reform movements like the animal welfare/animal rights movement. Better understanding of animal physiology and psychology has led to improvements in the basic standard of care for livestock and other domesticated animals. Reformers are certainly justified in seeking to raise that standard even further—to improve methods of handling livestock, for example, to better realize the end of humane treatment already widely accepted and codified in existing animal welfare laws. My argument is simply that they should be wary of relying on coercive state power to achieve their more ambitious ideals for social reform.

As argued in chapter 2, the use of coercive state power needs strong justification in a liberal state, and it is hard to find that justification for a program aimed at radical social change. It is not too difficult to come up with a reasonable consensus on a set of practices that clearly fall below the standard of minimal decency—Galston's list of "bads." But it is far more difficult to achieve a rationally defensible consensus on which set of social practices we should be aiming for. As Galston would put it, there's a wide range of individual and communal ways of life that are rationally defensible, and there's no way to come up with a rank ordering of them that everyone should agree on.[26] So there's no universally valid conception of the good life that the state is justified in imposing on its citizens. As applied to animal welfare, this means that even though all of us (well, let's say most of us) may agree that torturing animals is wrong and can be prohibited (at least with respect to animals that are members of the social contract), there's no universally valid conception of the *best* relations between humans and animals that the state is justified in requiring all of its citizens to follow. Under this view, the state can legitimately use its coercive power only to outlaw the "bads" (and I would add the caveat, developed below, that even here coercion should be used with caution and restraint). But it should not coerce its citizens into adopting a certain conception of "best practices."

This moderate, limited pluralism, I think, is practical and well suited to the moral and political world we twenty-first-century Americans live in. To be sure, we have a pluralistic society characterized by a great deal of value conflict. Nevertheless, very few people try to mount a defense in favor of torturing animals, and certain kinds of cruelty are uncontroversially banned. As I pointed out above, proponents of animal sacrifice usually don't ask to be exempted from these bans. Rather, they insist (quite plausibly) that ritual slaughter is no more cruel than other legal methods of slaughter. They're asking for equal treatment, not a special exemption from the general rules protecting animal welfare. True, there is plenty of room for factual debate over which practices do inflict pain and suffering, but those debates assume and even reinforce the shared value of preventing cruelty to animals.

The debate over whether humane slaughter laws should permit kosher slaughter also follows this pattern. Most such laws require that animals be stunned by an electric current or captive-bolt pistol before being killed, so that they are unconscious when their throats are cut. Kosher slaughter, by contrast, requires that the animal be conscious when the throat is cut, and the federal Humane Slaughter Act allows the use of this method as well ("whereby the animal suffers loss of consciousness by anemia of the brain caused by the simultaneous and instantaneous severance of the carotid arteries with a sharp instrument and handling in connection with such slaughtering").[27] Brian Barry argues, persuasively I think, that there is no justification for allowing orthodox Jews and Muslims to practice kosher slaughter if the legislature has determined it isn't humane. But that's not what the legislature has determined.[28] Rather, the Humane Slaughter Act explicitly declares that both of these methods—electric shock and severing the carotid artery—are humane and may be used (by persons of any religious faith) to slaughter livestock. Again, what looks like an exemption is not; it is simply a more careful or detailed statement of the general rule of humane treatment.

In sum, we needn't fear that a commitment to cultural pluralism means we must tolerate *any* sort of treatment of animals, or riddle our laws with exceptions to the basic standard of humane treatment. It does, however, require us to be tolerant of practices that, while not obviously cruel, don't make sense to us. Tolerating a practice does not mean simply ignoring it or pretending that it is none of our business, of course. Liberal pluralists argue, rightly, that liberal citizens (on both sides of the debate) must be willing to engage one another in discussion of serious moral issues. They must listen seriously to members of different cultures, take the time to understand their arguments, and make sincere efforts to find common ground and make reasonable accommodations of minority practices where such accommodations are practical and justified. As Galston puts it, tolerance does not imply or require "an easy relativism about the human good; indeed, it is compatible with engaged moral criticism with whom one differs." But it does mean "the principled refusal to use coercive state power to impose one's views on others, and therefore a commitment to moral competition through recruitment and persuasion alone."[29] In short, a commitment to cultural pluralism implies a commitment to maintaining social spaces free of state coercion, where citizens may debate with each other about the meaning and ethics of their practices and learn from one another without fear of being fined or jailed.

Under this view, animal rights advocates should not attempt to criminalize animal sacrifice. Instead, they should approach the issue as an opportunity to enter into conversation with a group of fellow citizens whose cultural practices look strange or different. And practitioners of animal sacrifice should be equally willing to engage the arguments of animal rights advocates, to take their moral arguments seriously. After all, much of the value of living in a pluralist society is the opportunity to learn from people with a different worldview. By resisting the impulse to use state power to stop practices one abhors, one opens up a space for such conversations—conversations in which varying views of the moral and spiritual status of animals can be explored with a view toward developing richer, more meaningful relations with animals and with other human beings.

For example, many critics of animal sacrifice characterize the practice as an example of human arrogance and dominance, describing its practitioners as callously using animals for their own ends. Practitioners of Santeria see animal sacrifice very differently. For them, sacrifice is the essence of humans' relationship to the divine. While prayers merely express what people want from their relationship with the gods, sacrifice, as an act of communion, actually constitutes that relationship, making real the reciprocal bond between humans and the gods.[30] Indeed, far from expressing human dominance of nature, the sacrifice recognizes the physical and spiritual *interdependence* of living things:

> Animals die so that human beings may live.... All are related by delicate exchanges and balances of nature that make human life possible. . . . [Animal] blood is offered to the *orishas* to show human beings their dependence on the world outside them and to give back to the invisible world something of what it gives to the visible.[31]

This practice is grounded on a view of the entire material world as sacred, as an expression of spiritual reality whose wholeness depends on making such exchanges. This perspective thus reinforces humans' dependence on and unity with the whole material and spiritual world.

Animals are particularly powerful and important in this worldview; even the *orishas* depend on the vitality of animal life. Some practitioners insist that the animal offers itself during the ritual, just as a human possessed by a spirit may be said to offer or sacrifice himself to that spirit. But whether or not the animal can be seen as a voluntary participant, the sacrifice itself is meant to be an act of profound humility and gratitude on the part of humans for this gift of life. From this perspective, our factory farms must look obscene, if not positively blasphemous. Indeed, perhaps a more spiritual and ritualized approach to animal slaughter would benefit our livestock. Recall the point made in chapter 3: Social practices that respect and allow us to express the various social meanings of animals can create a richer public culture that expands the options for living in community with animals. It is arguable, at least, that the Santeria ritual expresses a spiritual reverence for animals that the rest of us might learn from, if we are willing to approach their practices with respect and understanding.

Admittedly, this program of respectful dialogue may sound utopian—particularly given that Roger Caras, president of the American Society for the

Prevention of Cruelty to Animals, reacted to the *Hialeah* decision by calling Santeria a "voodoo-like religion" that "is not legitimate in the context of modern America."[32] But utopian ideals have a legitimate place in political discourse, and there are good pragmatic reasons to embrace this one. The alternative to dialogue and persuasion is the use of state power to coerce social change. That's a much riskier program, as the next section argues.

II. The Limits of Criminal Law

In August 2007, Michael Vick, the African American starting quarterback for the Atlanta Falcons, pled guilty to federal charges of dogfighting. He was sentenced to twenty-three months in prison and agreed to pay $928,000 for the care of some fifty-four dogs that were found on his property.[33] Professional dogfighting is a lucrative industry, attracting fans from a broad cross-section of American society, and it also seems to have become part of a subculture among professional athletes. Vick had ties with that subculture and was running a large dogfighting operation from his Virginia property. The Humane Society, which helped to build the case against Vick, saw the conviction of a star athlete as a way to draw attention to this growing industry's particularly brutal mistreatment of dogs.[34]

Predictably, public reaction to the case divided along racial lines. People for the Ethical Treatment of Animals (PETA) was among the most outspoken critics of Vick. The organization publicly called for a harsh prison sentence and suggested that a lifetime ban on all contact with animals would be an appropriate punishment—even after Vick successfully completed PETA's own course on preventing animal cruelty. According to the PETA blog discussion of Vick's case, "PETA believes that almost anyone can come to understand that animals are capable of suffering and deserve respect." But "given the crimes Vick has admitted to, he needs to serve hard time and be banned from any contact with animals." The blog item goes on to insist, "This is not a race issue. We don't care if he's orange. This is not a race issue. White people who fight dogs need to fry."[35]

PETA's attempt to bracket the issue of race was doomed to fail. As I pointed out above, the charge of animal cruelty is an all-too-common way to establish a minority group as barbaric and un-American; it is one of the central practices by which we constitute racial difference. And the dogfighting controversy seemed to invite Vick's critics to draw on a standard racist trope, the association of black men with bestiality. Claire Jean Kim describes several cartoons drawing on this tactic: "In one cartoon, Michael Vick is pictured next to a fighting dog and the caption reads, 'Pop Quiz: Find the True Animal.' Many cartoons reversed the status of dogs and Vick. In one, a dog sitting curbside gives Vick the finger as the latter is driven away in a van labeled 'Animal Control.'"[36] As Kim notes, the animalization of black people is a venerable Western tradition dating back to the 1500s and has served as one of the central strategies in establishing white supremacy. Given this history, it is naive at best to say that this issue doesn't involve race.

African American leaders, sensitive to both the legitimate outrage over dogfighting and the racial dimension of the conflict, were ambivalent in their response. African American actor Whoopi Goldberg offered a hesitant defense of Vick, calling dogfighting "part of his cultural upbringing." "Instead of just saying he is a beast and he's a monster, this is a kid who comes from a culture where this is not questioned."[37] (Indeed, PETA spokesman Dan Shannon said that before taking the PETA course, Vick seemed to be unaware of the scientific and biblical arguments against animal mistreatment.)[38] Michael Dyson argued that dogs are given greater respect than black men.[39] Dennis Hayes, interim president of the NAACP, would not exonerate Vick but sympathized with those who expressed support for him: "What we have to understand is the backdrop. We have to understand that what we're hearing expressed by some African-Americans is their anger and their hurt, distrust, in a criminal justice system that they feel treats them as animals."[40]

The backdrop Hayes is referring to is not simply a subculture whose values differ from those of the majority. To be sure, this case does seem to involve real value conflict. Dogfighters often defend their practice by insisting that aggressive behavior is good and natural for dogs. This is partly a factual claim that can be argued on empirical grounds, but it also, arguably, is part of a larger set of beliefs about the nature of animals, the naturalness of cruelty and violence, and indeed about the meaning of "nature" itself. But, unlike the animal sacrifice case, in this case there are strong grounds for insisting that dogfighting violates the standards of decency embodied in our general animal welfare laws. Dogfighting involves the infliction of severe pain and suffering on dogs for no better reason than entertainment, and dogs subjected to this treatment do not flourish or live even minimally decent lives. A commitment to cultural pluralism does not require us to condone dogfighting.

But there is another backdrop that we have to consider before urging resort to criminal law to suppress this practice: a criminal justice system that is at best seriously compromised, and at worst hopelessly dysfunctional. The most striking feature of the American criminal justice system is that we incarcerate vastly more people than any other industrialized nation, with the exception of Russia. Since 1973 (when the prison population was so low that experts were considering eliminating prisons altogether), the prison population has grown dramatically—increasing by 8 percent each year, to a rate of 648 persons per 100,000. By contrast, Finland incarcerates 56 persons per 100,000, and Italy is at 86 persons. Germany is on the high side, imprisoning 90 persons per 100,000. All of these countries have crime rates similar to ours, but we keep far more of our citizens in prison.[41] In 2000, 6.47 million Americans were under penal oversight—in prison or on probation or parole.

But the rates for African Americans are far higher than those for whites. In 1993, the incarceration rate for African Americans was 1,895 per 100,000, compared to 293 per 100,000 for whites. By 2007, that rate had grown to 2,290 per 100,000 for African Americans, compared to 412 per 100,000 for whites.[42] Although African Americans make up only 12 percent of the population, they supply over 50 percent of the prison population. Strikingly, 30 percent of African American men who do not attend college can expect to face jail time at some point. (The comparable figure for white noncollege men is 10 percent.)[43] These disparities cannot be explained by higher crime rates in African American communities. Although violent crime rates are higher among African Americans than they are among white Americans, convictions for violent crime have not been increasing dramatically. The disparity in incarceration is due largely to drug convictions: People of color are convicted of drug offenses at rates out of all proportion to their drug activity, which is roughly equal to that of other ethnic groups.[44] Such stark racial disparities have led one researcher to conclude that our criminal justice system is a "stunningly comprehensive and well-designed system of racialized social control that functions in a manner strikingly similar to Jim Crow."[45]

The growth in the prison population is largely due to changes in sentencing policy that were part of the federal "war on drugs," which began in the 1980s. These changes included imposing mandatory prison sentences and longer sentences for relatively minor crimes—especially drug-related offenses.[46] The purpose of harsher sentences, one assumes, is to deter crime; presumably that is the principal rationale behind calls to increase penalties for animal abuse. But most of the social scientific evidence suggests that harsher sentences do not reduce crime rates. On the contrary, a recent study, after reviewing several decades of research on the subject, concluded that variation in sentence severity has *no effect* on levels of crime.[47]

Increased sentencing severity does, however, have a dramatic effect on communities. Harsher sentences for animal abuse, for example, would likely fall the hardest on the same low-income minority communities that are currently suffering disproportionate rates of imprisonment for drug crimes—not because they're more likely to abuse animals but because these communities are heavily policed and people in them are less likely to have lawyers. Currently, 80 percent of criminal defendants are indigent, but funding for public defenders is extremely limited, and many defendants never meet with a lawyer at all. Moreover, nearly all criminal cases are resolved through plea bargains, and persons facing severe penalties are much more likely to accept a plea bargain even if they are innocent (and they certainly are more likely to do so if they cannot afford a lawyer!)[48] And accepting a plea bargain, even with limited jail time, can have serious consequences: Persons convicted of felonies often cannot vote, receive public benefits (including public housing), or get a license for a wide variety of professions. Parolees and probationers face a complex set of rules, violations of which can get them rearrested.[49] All of this makes it difficult for people convicted of felonies to be reintegrated into the community. The community often suffers from these inequities as well, as high rates of incarceration disrupt families and other social organizations. Whole communities can be destabilized by increases in incarceration rates.[50] There is little reason to believe that animal welfare would be better protected in such destabilized communities.

For these reasons, animal welfare advocates should be wary of expanding the reach of the criminal justice system in their quest to suppress practices like dogfighting. But there may be a deeper problem with relying on criminal penalties to create a culture conducive to animal welfare. Although, as I suggested above, there is real value conflict between the dog-fighters and their opponents, the conflict also involves problematic *shared* values: It is not hard to see the same notions of masculinity at play in both the practice of dogfighting and the PETA spokespersons' savage denunciations of dogfighters. Both groups seem to be enacting an ideal that associates manliness with ritualized violence (dogfighting; trial and imprisonment). These rituals of violence may help to create communal bonds within their respective groups; perhaps some PETA members enjoy the same sense of bonding and group solidarity when facing off against dogfighters that dogfighters enjoy when watching a fight. But such rituals undermine broader communal bonds. Specifically, threatening dogfighters with imprisonment undermines communication and trust between animal welfare advocates and dogfighters, and it also threatens to disrupt the communities in which dogfighting goes on—the very communities that must be persuaded to adopt new and better practices. Animal welfare advocates may believe that calling for harsher criminal enforcement is the best way to express our social abhorrence of animal abuse and so express the proper level of respect for animals' moral status.[51] But resorting to the criminal justice system is divisive and threatens to weaken the very communal bonds that are the best protection for animal welfare.

If calling for increased criminal enforcement isn't the best response to a social practice like dogfighting, what is a better alternative? To begin, we must try to resist the frenzy of denunciation and take a clearer view of the practice and the people who engage in it. As Whoopi Goldberg was trying to suggest, we must at least aim for understanding before judgment. To be sure, dogfighting involves unjustified violence toward animals, but it isn't equivalent to the isolated, sadistic torture of animals. It is best understood as a form of poor, misguided animal husbandry. Michael Vick, for example, was raised in a community where dogfighting was common. (He witnessed his first fight when he was seven years old.) He became a licensed breeder and reportedly loved his dogs, even though he also admitted to some horrible acts of brutality. Such oddly mixed expressions of affection and pride for the dogs they are abusing are fairly common among dogfighters. My point is not to defend the practice but to suggest that it can contain the seeds of something worth preserving and building on. It appears, in Vick's case, to involve a desire on the part of this young African American man to be a member of a mixed human/animal community in the only way that seemed to be open to him.

This desire shouldn't be treated lightly; it has survived against remarkable odds. African Americans have a long and difficult history with dogs, which were used by members of the white ruling class before and after Emancipation to hunt down, torture, and kill fugitive slaves and other "troublemakers." Bloodhounds were, of course, bred for precisely that purpose. Indeed, Orlando Patterson suggests that blood sports were engrained in southern culture both because they were part of the Celtic culture of honor transmitted by the Scottish/Irish settlers and because they became an integral part of the culture of slavery.[52] Dogfighting is undoubtedly a part of that troubled legacy.

But Alice Walker's perspective, as discussed in chapter 4, invites us to explore African American traditions more deeply and to consider how community with animals survived under such unfavorable conditions. She reports, for example, that she and her husband bought a dog when they moved to Mississippi to do civil rights work, in order to help protect their home from white violence. She also tells a story about civil rights activist Mrs. Hudson, who relied on a German shepherd as her sole protection against the Klan.[53] Dogs were not only members of southern rural African American communities; it seems the human/dog bond was part of the protective shield that *defended* those communities. And that devotion was returned—for example, by victims of Katrina who refused to leave their dogs behind to drown in the flooding of New Orleans. This tradition of mutual care and protection is worth naming and reclaiming.

A defense of animal welfare that is sensitive to this history would sound very different from PETA's rhetoric of crime and punishment. It might instead go like this: Freedom includes the freedom to create and maintain healthy relationships with animals, although not the right to abuse them. These positive relationships are important in a mixed human/animal community not only because they enrich and protect our human lives but because they help to protect animals, who are among the most vulnerable members of the community. So our social policies should support, or at least not undermine, good practices of animal care and companionship as they arise in every subculture. Certainly in evaluating these practices, we must give due weight to the universalistic moral arguments offered by groups like PETA concerning the proper, respectful treatment of animals. But we must also attend to the social and political context in which these arguments are deployed, and avoid using them to undermine a social group's right to or capacity for animal husbandry. There is an indigenous tradition of animal husbandry, especially dog-keeping, in the African American community. If it overemphasizes violence as a result of our troubled history of race relations, that emphasis should be corrected. With proper attention placed on the social needs of dogs and their nonaggressive virtues, this tradition can serve as an important defense of the rights and welfare of our animal fellow-citizens and their human companions.

What would this defense of animal welfare mean for the Michael Vick case? At a minimum, it suggests that the proper law enforcement goal is Vick's rehabilitation as a dog owner.[54] Unfortunately for its proponents, the criminal justice system doesn't have a very good track record at rehabilitating offenders. A 2009 study suggests that being arrested and prosecuted merely increases the offenders' distrust of the criminal justice system. It does not typically lead them to take responsibility for their behavior or resolve to change it.[55] Thus far, the best rehabilitative model seems to be the drug court, a special court that promotes rehabilitation through court-ordered substance abuse treatment paired with intense judicial oversight, in which the judge can administer a range of sanctions short of incarceration. There is some evidence that this model does reduce recidivism in drug cases.[56] However, what works with drug offenders may not work with other kinds of offenders.

There are of course other alternatives to incarceration, and animal rights/welfare activists should fully explore them before urging imprisonment. Some kinds of animal abuse (like animal hoarding and many cases of neglect) stem from mental health issues; offenders need treatment rather than imprisonment. People involved in dogfighting purely for profit shouldn't be treated as violent offenders, nor should the compulsive gambler. For these, too, probation under community-based supervision, involving treatment and community service, may be more appropriate than imprisonment.[57] The Humane Society and PETA, in their more reasonable moments, seem confident that education programs can help rehabilitate the casual or ignorant abuser. For the habitual violent offender, incarceration may remain the only alternative for the foreseeable future. But a truly effective response to animal abuse requires us to look beyond the criminal justice system. Instead, reformers are better advised to focus on programs aimed at public education, economic development, and community development—programs that can serve animal welfare *and* race and class relations simultaneously, rather than putting them into conflict. I discuss that approach in more detail below.

Unfortunately, the Vick case suggests that leading animal rights organizations like PETA are currently ill equipped to appreciate the racial dimension of animal welfare policy. That's not surprising; African Americans are underrepresented in all animal welfare organizations. A 2005 study found that of the thirteen organizations responding to the survey, eight had no African American employees, and African Americans made up only 4 percent of the total number of employees, with only 0.8 percent at the level of officers or managers. In no organization were more than 7 percent of the employees African American.[58] Under these circumstances, African Americans and other minorities concerned about their relationships with animals should consider creating their own animal welfare/animal rights organizations, with the aim of defending, elaborating, and publicizing their distinctive traditions of animal husbandry.

None of this is intended to suggest dogfighting should be legal or that Michael Vick should not have been prosecuted for his role in the dogfighting operation (although I don't think jail time was necessarily the right response). Nor am I arguing that we should decriminalize animal abuse altogether. My point here is more limited: When we rely too heavily on the criminal justice system to deal with a widespread practice like dogfighting, we risk deepening racial and class inequalities and disrupting communities without accomplishing any positive gains for animal welfare. A better response to the growth of the dogfighting industry is a creative, community-building approach that focuses on education, organization, and reforming existing practices. I doubt any experienced animal welfare/rights advocate would disagree with that conclusion, of course; most of these organizations are heavily invested in such programs. But many of these organizations are also enthusiastically pursuing more extensive and severe criminal penalties. For example, the Humane Society, in addition to urging increasing the severity of penalties for dogfighting and trying to criminalize animal sacrifice, has sponsored campaigns to criminalize Internet and captive-animal hunting, the slaughter of horses for human consumption, and "crush" videos (videos of small animals being tortured—an appalling form of entertainment but one that is probably protected by the First Amendment). These practices may well be morally objectionable, but the punitive approach to ending them can have negative consequences for civil liberties and racial and class equality—and, consequently, for animal welfare. Instead, reformers should favor an agenda that brings human and nonhuman interests into closer alignment, thus improving our ability to protect vulnerable humans and nonhumans alike. The next section explores that possibility.

III. Protecting the Vulnerable

To be fair, the Humane Society is usually at the forefront of efforts to advance human and animal welfare simultaneously. Indeed, the organization grew out of the intersection of animal and child abuse. Its history begins, famously, with the story of Mary Ellen Wilson. Mary Ellen was ten years old in 1874, when she was rescued from the home of Mary Connolly by the American Society for the Prevention of Cruelty to Animals (ASPCA). The Connolly family had been keeping the girl prisoner in a dark, cramped tenement and subjecting her to severe beatings. Eventually, rumors of the girl's situation came to the attention of mission worker Etta Wheeler, who tried to get help from her church, from local charities, and from the police. But the charities explained that they had no authority to enter a private residence. The police needed evidence of abuse, not hearsay. In desperation, she turned to the ASPCA, which was happy to help. Mrs. Wheeler found several neighbors who could testify to the girl's abuse, and that was enough for ASPCA director Henry Bergh. On April 9, 1874, an ASPCA agent entered the Connolly's home and carried Mary Ellen to the chambers of a New York Supreme Court judge. The subsequent prosecution of Mary Connolly for assault and battery earned her a year in prison. But the other notable result of the case was the creation, by Henry Bergh and Elbridge Gerry, of the New York Society for the Prevention of Cruelty to Children. This organization prompted the creation of the first Humane Societies, devoted to the welfare of both animals and children.[59]

The advantage of linking child protection to animal protection was that animal protection societies were unique among the reform and charity groups of the day: They had investigative and prosecutorial powers. Although there was a state law against child abuse, the police were often reluctant to get involved with domestic relations. But animal welfare activists did so routinely. Their agents were trained to enter homes, investigate, and prosecute violations of the animal welfare laws. Their power to penetrate the curtain of domestic privacy made them well positioned to address other kinds of domestic abuse. Thus child protection groups adopted the organizational models and some of the statutory precedents of animal protection.[60] Historian Susan Pearson argues further that the ASPCA's talk of animal rights—rights that are held by dependent, nonrational beings—helped to lay the foundation for the concept of children's rights and to support the view that the state has a duty to protect the welfare of children.[61] In short, creating institutions and laws to protect animal welfare thus resulted in institutions and laws aimed at protecting vulnerable humans.

To be sure, the Humane Societies aimed to protect children, in part, by extending the reach of the criminal justice system—precisely the strategy I criticized above. But I think this story is only superficially about criminal justice. The work of the Humane Societies cannot be reduced to simply putting more people in jail. The reason the ASPCA was well positioned to help Mary Ellen Wilson was that it had developed investigative expertise and organizational capacity that other reform societies didn't have. Contemporary humane societies continue in that tradition, developing community-based programs that range from running animal shelters and mobile veterinary clinics, providing disaster relief for animals, running wildlife rehabilitation centers, working with corporations to adopt animal-friendly policies, organizing pet adoption programs, and engaging in an array of public education initiatives. Thus many of its programs are aimed not at punishing animal mistreatment but at making it easier for people to take care of animals, supporting and promoting mutually beneficial animal/humans relationships, and strengthening the human/animal community. Reform efforts aimed at this goal—improving our social capacity to protect the vulnerable and support the flourishing of all members of the community—harmonize animal and human interests rather than promoting one at the expense of the other.

A good example of this approach is taking shape among people concerned about domestic violence. An increasing number of animal welfare and domestic violence workers are recognizing that cruelty to animals is often part of a pattern of domestic abuse. Abusers of spouses and children often include the family pets among their victims, or threaten or torture a victim's pet as a way to control the human victim. In one study, 52 percent of the battered women reported that their partners had threatened their pets (compared to 16.7 percent of nonbattered women). And 54 percent of the battered women reported that their partners had actually hurt or killed the pet (compared to 3.5 percent of nonbattered women). The same study suggested that abusing pets inflicted emotional trauma on the woman and children in the home and that concern for the pet's safety often delayed the decision to leave the home. This suggests that domestic violence may be best addressed in conjunction with efforts to address animal abuse.[62]

Accordingly, the Humane Society launched its "First Strike" program in 1997 to facilitate coordinated approaches to domestic violence.[63] The HSUS recommends providing for pets at shelters, allowing animals to be included in protection orders, developing reporting systems that help animal welfare investigators notify police or social services of animal abuse or neglect, adopting interagency protocols for dealing with domestic and animal abuse, cross-training, and pursuing coordinated intervention strategies that involve animal control agencies. These institutional changes can increase the capacity of law enforcement and social service agencies to protect vulnerable humans and nonhumans in domestic situations.

Importantly, however, such reforms must go well beyond improving the coercive power of the state. Domestic violence is often shockingly cruel and offers some of the best candidates for imprisonment. But even in this domain, imprisoning offenders is a small part of addressing the problem. Domestic violence is often rooted in socioeconomic stressors, in problematic gender ideologies, in women's lack of opportunity and earning power outside the home, in mental health and substance abuse issues, in lack of community support for families—all problems that call for programs aimed at public education and community development rather than improved criminal enforcement. As scholar Claire Renzetti explains, much domestic violence is the result of weak or dysfunctional communities. Changing those community contexts may include investing resources in making neighborhoods afflicted with high abuse rates more livable and stable, improving relationships with the police, and improving coordination and provision of social services (especially during recessions).[64] And in pursuing these broader goals of community stabilization and development, we necessarily turn to the noncoercive power of the state, the power to provide resources and facilitate collective action. The same is true of efforts to improve animal welfare. Once we conceptualize our goal more broadly—not as prohibiting mistreatment but as increasing our social capacity to protect vulnerable members of the community and to help them flourish—it becomes clear that these creative, facilitative state powers are more central to our project than state coercion is.

Unfortunately, the creative powers of the state have not received much attention in liberal political theory. As I've suggested above, liberal theorists have traditionally taken as their central task justifying coercive state power, and particularly criminal sanctions like imprisonment. Such coercive state action does require strong justification in a liberal state, but the modern state's noncoercive powers arguably are more pervasive and can have a significant *positive* impact on individual liberty. These powers include, for example, providing social services or funding civic organizations that do so, gathering data and making it publicly available, identifying and certifying "best practices," creating guidelines for government purchases, making changes to regulatory laws in order to make it easier for civic organizations to carry out their work, bringing together different civic actors on public commissions and the like to facilitate coordination, and making official statements of public values. The original federal Humane Slaughter Act, passed in 1958, is an example of this power: The federal government, reluctant to intrude on traditional state powers, did not actually prohibit nonhuman methods of slaughter. Rather, it specified that the federal government would buy meat only from slaughterhouses that complied with the Act, and it declared that humane slaughter is the public policy of the United States. The government thus used its purchasing power and legitimacy to shape industry practice, which made the expansion of the Act to all federally inspected slaughterhouses in 1978 much less controversial.[65] Even the bare statement of public policy was significant, because such policy statements could be used by courts to justify interpreting other laws to support that value (to conclude, for example, that protecting animal welfare is a compelling government interest).

To be sure, some of these powers (like the provision of social services) rest on the power to tax, which is backed by the state's coercive power. But as I argued in chapter 2, spending tax dollars is considerably less of an assault on individual autonomy than being subject to imprisonment or even heavily fined. Indeed, what is significant for liberal theorists about these powers is that their use can greatly *facilitate* individual liberty. By supporting stronger communities, animal-friendly workplaces, and more functional families, such policies can help to create a public culture that supports animal companionship and offers many opportunities for individuals to develop their capacities to take care of animals.

IV. Conclusion

Even the most compassionate liberal state cannot by itself create a supportive animal welfare society. It must work in partnership with a vibrant, active, and diverse civil society that provides individuals with the collective goods necessary to conceive and pursue a better, richer vision of the good life. This point returns us to the value of cultural diversity. Cultural development depends, in part, on generating new ideas, practices, and institutions. Diversity among the civic associations involved in animal welfare issues can help to produce this creativity. As innovative as the Humane Society has been, its efforts surely would be complemented by an animal welfare association that reflected, for example, the spiritual views of Santeria or the historical perspective and experiences of African Americans.

A preference for cultural diversity gives us another reason to favor the creative powers of the state, which can do a great deal to promote a more diverse array of civic associations. In contrast, expanding the coercive power of the state can create a hostile environment in which minority cultures are marginalized and cultural differences are suppressed. For example, imagine the consequences of banning animal sacrifice. Such a ban would be extremely difficult to enforce and would undoubtedly create tensions between the Cuban immigrant community and the broader public. Practitioners of Santeria might take their practices underground, thus becoming more isolated from the rest of the community. The resulting climate of hostility and distrust would make it very difficult for animal welfare organizations to work with this community to regulate or modify the practice. Animal welfare is unlikely to be enhanced under these conditions. In contrast, helping a cultural institution like the Santeria church to prosper—through tax breaks, accommodating zoning ordinances, and the like—could strengthen the Cuban immigrant community. A strong Santeria church would give animal welfare advocates a partner to work with in addressing animal welfare issues in that community. And Santeria priests are likely to have better ideas about how to address these issues than outsiders would.

In sum, the liberal state's coercive powers can play only a limited role in moving us toward a better, more fully realized animal welfare society. The limits of the liberal state, the fact and value of cultural pluralism, and the persistent inequities in our criminal justice system all should lead us to disfavor reliance on criminal prohibitions to improve protection for animal welfare. Indeed, focusing on criminal law betrays far too narrow a conception of the progressive goals of the animal welfare/rights movement: to create a more humane society where humans and nonhumans can flourish together. The liberal state cannot force its citizens to conform to a particular ideal conception of that society. It can, however, promote the conditions for progress toward such an ideal, namely, a healthy and culturally diverse civil society. For all the emphasis on laws and government institutions in this book, the fact remains that civil society is the principal sphere in which different conceptions of mixed human/animal community are developed, proposed, and debated and new institutional and social practices are invented. It is not the liberal state but liberal citizens, acting together in the vast array of community, professional, educational, religious, and advocacy organizations, that will provide the creative energy needed to guide the evolution of human/animal relations.

Conclusion

The animal kingdom turns out to be at the heart of the contemporary debate on the relationship between man and nature.

—LUC FERRY, *The New Ecological Order*

ONE OF THE paradoxes I have discovered while writing this book is that everyone is interested in animals but no one thinks they're important. More precisely, despite the size and complexity of our animal governance apparatus, political scientists and political philosophers have devoted very little attention to how and why we govern animals. It should be clear by now that I think that's a mistake; animals are interesting and important enough in their own right to warrant scholarly attention, quite apart from their contribution to human well-being. Many of the animals we live with are sentient, intelligent beings that make moral demands on us every day. Why shouldn't our studies of politics attend to them as well?

But one can also defend such attention on the grounds that animals and humans are so interdependent that one can't govern a political community humanely and justly without attending to its animal members. Indeed, shifting our scholarly focus from humans to animals should give us a new perspective on government and on our political values. As Luc Ferry has argued, animals are central to our relationship with the natural world; they occupy the critical space between human and nonhuman nature. Thinking about how we govern animals is a good way to approach the complex relationship between the human community and the biotic community. In short, a study like this one should offer insights into how we can better care for the welfare of animals just for their own sakes, but it should also help us better govern humans and our natural environment. Toward those dual ends, this chapter offers some conclusions about the future of the animal rights movement and the future of liberalism.

I. Whither Animal Rights?

In August 2009, the *Isthmus*, a newspaper in Madison, Wisconsin, ran a story about experiments being performed on sheep by researchers at the University of Wisconsin. The experiments involved putting live sheep into a hyperbaric chamber and then changing the atmospheric pressure to simulate what happens during a deep-sea dive. The sheep were then removed from the chamber and monitored for signs of decompression sickness (the bends). The *Isthmus* story noted, correctly, that some sheep died as a result of this treatment. Others suffered from the bends but then recovered. Some, too sick to recover, were euthanized by the researchers.

The furor over their work must have come as a surprise to the researchers. People have been studying decompression this way for decades; results of the first experiments, on goats, were published in 1908.[1] Similar experiments had been conducted at the University of Wisconsin at least since 1988 and had yielded several "important discoveries" (according to a university spokesperson), which were duly published in scholarly journals. Indeed, the researchers had every reason to believe their study was perfectly legal. The university, like any institution that accepts federal money, is subject to the Animal Welfare Act (AWA), and in accordance with that statute it has established Institutional Animal Care and Use Committees (IACUCs) for each of its schools. The committee is responsible for making sure all research on animals (well, the warm-blooded animals covered by the AWA and NIH regulations) is conducted in an ethical manner.

The university's IACUC had approved these experiments. But the research, according to a decision by the Dane County District Attorney's office, violated a different law. This state statute, passed in 1985, reads quite simply, "No person may kill an animal by means of decompression."[2] In light of this opinion, the university decided to suspend the experiments.

The university didn't give in without a fight, though. The university's position was that the state law doesn't apply. The researchers, after all, weren't *trying* to kill the sheep. The deaths were just "unanticipated" consequences of their experiments. The district attorney seemed to think this was quibbling; it was certainly predictable that *some* deaths would occur. The better argument, perhaps, was that the people who wrote the statute didn't intend for it to apply to this sort of research. It was aimed at ending the use of decompression as a means of euthanasia by dog pounds, pet shops, and animal shelters. The legislative history isn't very clear, but the university's position is probably correct. Other states were passing similar laws during the 1980s, and they generally concerned the destruction of abandoned animals. Nevertheless, the attorney general concluded that he couldn't ignore the provision's broad language. The legislature could have included an exemption for research, but it didn't, and he had to apply the law as written.

But he didn't. Exercising his prosecutorial discretion, he decided not to pursue the matter. He clearly thought the law was stupid. It imposed a penalty (five hundred dollars) on anyone who caused the death of an animal by decompression, regardless of their intent or lack thereof, and regardless of whether the death was ethically justified. Instead of enforcing it, he suggested that the university ask the legislature to amend the law to include a research exemption (as, indeed, some other states do).[3] The university's decision to suspend the experiments was thus a matter of prudence (or public relations) rather than a direct response to government regulation.[4]

From the perspective of a typical animal rights activist, this case may look like an excellent example of how our haphazard and totally inadequate regulatory system only accidentally works to protect animal welfare. Given an apparent conflict between human and animal welfare, the regulatory regime clearly favors humans. Under the AWA, human interests trump animal interests; the statute aims at ensuring that animals don't suffer more than necessary, but the IACUCs aren't authorized to stop experiments just because the harm to the animals outweighs the benefits to humans. Moreover, the IACUC's approval of the research seemed to influence the district attorney's decision not to prosecute, even if it didn't protect the university from public pressure. The university found itself in trouble mostly because a poorly drafted state law superseded the more carefully crafted federal regulatory system, flatly prohibiting a practice that the federal system would have allowed. The sheep just got lucky.

But maybe that conclusion is too simple. After all, the university did suspend the experiments, not because they were illegal but because they were unpopular. The legal flap created an opportunity for papers like the *Isthmus* to bring the experiments to public attention. The *Isthmus*, in turn, was alerted to the story by an animal welfare group, the Alliance for Animals, which had been informed by a part-time lab assistant who witnessed the experiments.[5] It was public pressure from civic groups and the press, rather than the threat of legal sanctions, that ended the experiments. But the regulatory regime gave the newspaper something to write about; it created a set of expectations that university research would be attentive to animal welfare. More generally, the regulatory regime helped to create the social context in which this drama unfolded. And that, I would argue, is exactly what the regulations protecting animal welfare should do.

Animal rights activists generally call for a flat prohibition on animal experimentation. But, as I've argued, there are limits to what a liberal state can legitimately and effectively prohibit. In the absence of a broad consensus about the legitimacy of animal experimentation, the best we can do is to create a regulatory structure that aims to *build* a reasonable, well-considered consensus—a structure that shapes the institutional and broader social context in which medical research is carried out. To be sure, our regulatory system is hardly perfect in this respect; it is the product of too many compromises. But it isn't bad. Instead of relying on flat prohibitions, the system requires the scientific community to develop ethical guidelines, to educate and police itself, and to open its practices to public scrutiny.

This approach, combined with heightened activism by animal rights advocates, has resulted in a significant change in the scientific community's approach to animal experimentation over the last fifty years. Traditionally, American scientists have put up strong resistance to any governmental interference into experimentation on animals.[6] Great Britain, under pressure from its active antivivisectionist movement, created government licensing and oversight of laboratories as early as 1876. But in the United States, such measures were consistently defeated by the medical research community. That resistance began to weaken in the 1960s, however. One factor, as I have discussed, was the *Life* magazine article exposing conditions on dog farms and particularly the risk that unclaimed dogs could be seized and experimented on by laboratories. But the 1960s also witnessed changing attitudes among scientists. Several British studies published during that decade questioned the scientific value of medical research on animals, and in 1961 a group of veterinarians working for Chicago-area research institutions formed the Animal Care Panel. Two years later that group published a Guide for the Care and Use of Laboratory Animals—perhaps an attempt to head off government regulation, but also indicating some real interest among scientists in establishing standards of good practice.

Congressional opinion was also moving in the direction of federal regulation. The passage of the Laboratory Animal Welfare Act (the precursor to the Animal Welfare Act) in 1966 led the National Institute of Health (NIH) to address the issue of animal experimentation more systematically. In 1971 it issued a policy on the care and treatment of laboratory animals, and these initial federal efforts received further public support in 1976, when animal rights activist Henry Spira led a campaign exposing research conducted at the American Museum of Natural History in New York City. The controversial research concerned brain function in cats, and Spira persuaded a weekly New

York paper to publish graphic descriptions of the experiments, arguing that they were cruel and had little scientific merit. The campaign attracted national attention; Congressman Ed Koch denounced the experiments (comparing them to the Nazis' experiments on human subjects), and even *Science* magazine published an article by Nicholas Wade questioning whether the current standards of scientific practice gave sufficient weight to the interests of the animal.[7]

As a result of this activism, government action, and self-regulation by the scientific community, the climate of opinion had changed substantially by the time Congress amended the AWA in 1985 to mandate the creation of IACUCs in institutions receiving federal research funds. Under the current regulations, the IACUC is directed to evaluate and report on all of the institution's programs and facilities for activities involving animals at least twice each year and is required to review the care and use of animals in federally supported activities. Its chief function is to review proposed experiments in order to determine whether they are consistent with federal ethical guidelines. But the committee is also required to provide training or instruction for scientists, laboratory technicians, and other personnel involved in animal care, treatment, or use. This training or instruction must include information on the humane practice of animal care and use as well as training in research or testing methods that minimize the number of animals required to obtain valid results and minimize animal distress.

To be sure, many animal rights activists insist that these regulations don't go far enough, and scientific practice undoubtedly is still in need of further reform. But this regulatory approach makes continuing reforms more likely by requiring the scientific community to talk to each other and to the public about the ethics of animal experimentation, and to address ethics when training scientists. Such ethical discourse (combined with continued political activism by animal welfare/animal rights activists) has resulted in several professional organizations devoted to developing ethical standards and finding alternatives to animal research, such as the National Toxicology Program's Interagency Center for the Evaluation of Alternative Toxicological Methods, the Interagency Coordinating Committee on the Validation of Alternative Methods, and the Physicians Committee for Responsible Medicine. Even the Food and Drug Administration, which has traditionally supported animal testing, is now moving toward testing practices that would reduce the use of animals. This system of self-policing, public discussion, and education has created a common ground where the less radical animal welfare advocates can have productive conversations with the more enlightened scientists about alternatives to using animals, the scientific validity and usefulness of animal experimentation, and ways to better manage lab animals to protect their welfare.[8] Indeed, this regulatory regime aims at shaping the attitudes and expectations of the scientific community itself. And the animal rights movement complements that work: By informing and mobilizing the public, it subjects the scientific community to constant critical scrutiny and helps to create alternative practices. Overall, this transformation of the scientific community, incomplete though it is, serves as a pretty good model of how a vigorous animal rights movement, together with moderate institutional and legal reforms, can increase protections for animal welfare without violating the basic principles of liberal government.

An important point to take away from this history is that much of the regulatory and political activity described above was aimed at creating the context in which scientists could *publicly justify* their treatment of animals. As I argued in the introduction, the concept of the "political" is deeply attached to the act of justifying the use of force; only when the justification of power includes reference to the animals' welfare, interests, or rights does our rule deserve to be called "political" in the best sense, as something to be achieved by the best regimes. The most valuable political work of the animal welfare/rights movement aims at creating practices and institutions that call forth such justifications—justifications that are addressed to the public in their role as citizens and that take into account the perspectives of the animals themselves.

The animal welfare/animal rights movement has thus played a critical role in bringing laboratory animals into the political community—in giving them political representation—by helping to create public spaces and opportunities to discuss, collectively, the ethical status of animals and our duties as citizens toward them. This is not to diminish the importance of reforming how we actually treat animals, of course. The more radical animal rights activists may be frustrated that despite the improving political status of animals, we still perform experiments on them, we still raise them for food, and we still treat them too often as mere property. They're right; these practices raise ethical concerns that our laws should address. But my analysis has important implications for how we should pursue that goal.

Traditionally, animal rights advocates have pursued not just animal welfare but animal liberation—a goal that seems to require ending animal husbandry, pet ownership, and other forms of human companionship with animals. Under my analysis, this is the wrong aim, and the wrong way to understand the purpose and meaning of animal rights. As Joseph Raz argues, we shouldn't view legal rights as devices to protect animals' individual interests against the demands of the community. Rather, rights are aimed at protecting the *collective* goods necessary to liberty—the common culture we need to realize our ideals. So we protect freedom of speech not because the individual's right to speak is more important than the welfare of the community, but because protecting that right creates for the community a culture of free, critical, and creative public debate, a culture supportive of the search for truth and creative self-expression. In the same way, protecting animal rights is justified to the extent it helps us to create a culture in which human/animal relations can flourish, in which we can realize the goods that are unique to that sort of relationship. To be sure, animal rights rest on the animals' interests in their own welfare—interests that humans are morally bound to consider—but protecting those interests in turn depends on maintaining a public culture supportive of good, enriching human/animal relations. Understanding this point allows us to avoid pitting animal rights *against* human welfare. Our aim is a public culture in which human and animal interests align, which would benefit all of us.

Under this view, the animal rights/animal welfare movement should aim not to end human domination of animals but to protect and maintain good institutions and sound practices of animal husbandry and companionship. Indeed, our very concept of animal rights makes sense only against a background of animal husbandry and companionship. Recognizing animal rights assumes, for example, extensive government regulation of our treatment of animals—regulation that in turn assumes the government has a duty to protect animals, that animals are members of the community the government is bound to protect. The concept of animal rights also assumes that we know what rights animals need, a knowledge that grows out of long-standing husbandry practices. Most obviously, the right to protection against cruelty or neglect refers to an ideal of animal care that makes sense in light of our practice of domesticating animals. A society that relates to animals primarily through hunting, I submit, would never grant, nor even conceptualize, such rights. Members of hunting and gathering societies recognize duties to animals, but those duties involve other ways of showing respect for the prey animal. They certainly don't focus on preventing violence to or requiring affirmative care of the animal.

This is not to suggest that our existing practices of animal care cannot be criticized. Many of our practices—most notably, the relatively new practice of large-scale, confined livestock production—are not consistent with our best traditions of animal husbandry; they do not promote the flourishing of human/animal relations and need to be reformed. But, under my view, legal rights are a very late step in the reform process. The first steps involve developing better practices and institutions, ones that better realize our ideals. Only then should we create legal rights to protect them.[9] For example, developing and supporting more humane methods of raising livestock is more important than simply prohibiting particular bad practices in a piecemeal fashion. Encouraging self-examination and self-policing in the scientific community is more effective than trying to ban animal experimentation. In general, the primary focus of reform must be supporting the various good traditions of animal care and husbandry that we find in civil society and building new institutions and practices that bring animal and human interests into harmony. The result should promote good animal/human relationships and our mutual flourishing.

II. Whither Liberalism?

I began this study by asking whether liberal political theory can be revised to recognize the proper moral status and social meaning of animals. I conclude that it can, and indeed liberalism needs no radical alteration to accommodate our fellow creatures. However, my argument does suggest that certain versions of liberalism are going to be more useful to us as we come to terms with our obligations toward nonhumans and with our own animal nature—our nonrational capacities, vulnerabilities, and dependencies. Specifically, my analysis favors varieties of liberalism that are explicit about their social foundations and not very insistent on their metaphysical foundations. That is, I have found it useful to draw on liberal theorists like Raz, Elizabeth Anderson, Don Herzog, and Eric Freyfogle, all of whom acknowledge that our liberal principles are derived not solely from reason but also from experience. These are principles that have worked *for us*, not principles that must be universally valid for all societies throughout time. Our liberalism must be suited to a twenty-first-century America in which humans and (some) animals live together in long-standing relations of mutual dependence. Given this social foundation, we must reject versions of liberalism that insist on dividing the world into persons and things, with no place for fellow-creatures. We need a liberalism that respects the moral status of nonhumans, recognizes important differences among animals, and is sensitive to the varying kinds of relationships that humans have with animals. Such a public philosophy can, I believe, be conducive to human flourishing as well.

Most significantly, some varieties of modern social contract theory are not going to prove very useful. Theories that conceptualize the end of the social contract narrowly, as individual rational autonomy, are not particularly good guides to governing a mixed human/animal community. Instead, we must conceptualize the social contract in ways consistent with classic liberals such as John Locke, but also informed by noncontractarian theorists such as Joseph Raz and Martha Nussbaum: The aim of the social contract is to protect the community and to create a culture in which community members can realize important values. Those values certainly include rational autonomy, which is essential for most human adults. But they also include other varieties of individual flourishing. For our animal members, the end of the social contract is a healthy interdependence with other community members—an interdependence that allows each being to flourish in its characteristic way. Indeed, that is an appropriate end for many humans as well (for all humans, in fact, at certain stages of their lives). So focusing on the status of animals provides us with guidance in properly conceptualizing the end of the social contract for everyone.

Similarly, liberal theories of property need not serve as an obstacle to animal welfare. But we should reject theories that oversimplify the world we live in, recognizing only persons (who cannot be owned) and things (which can). This requires us to reject the view that property is a natural right conferring a kind of unlimited sovereignty over a piece of the world. Indeed, it is difficult to find a serious theorist who endorses this caricature of liberal property rights. Such boundless property rights are hardly workable, and this understanding of property has never been reflected in our legal system. As Freyfogle has argued, liberal regimes have traditionally recognized only limited and qualified property rights, defined according to what kind of good is in question and its role in social relations. So there is nothing in liberal theory or practice that prevents us from recognizing limited property rights in animals, defined in a way that protects the animal's "equitable self-ownership." Owners of animals are essentially trustees or guardians for the animal, a relation well established in liberal legal regimes.

This understanding of property does not mean we can revert to treating humans as property as well. That experiment failed dismally, for good reason. Indeed, America's failed experiment with human slavery is an important part of the history on which our current liberal regime is built. But the flexible concept of property I'm advocating does open up other possibilities. For example, it allows us to redefine rights in land and other environmental goods in terms of this trustee relation, as Freyfogle suggests. Here I suggest we take Anderson's value theory as our guide and recognize that the specific content of property rights must be determined by the social meaning of the good in question. Rights in land, animals, natural wonders, creative works, and other kinds of property should be fashioned not according to some metaphysical principle but with the aim of protecting the kinds of relationships and practices we value. This approach would go a long way toward ensuring that liberalism remains relevant and useful for a twenty-first-century postindustrial society.

Similarly, there is no outstanding difficulty in providing political or legal representation for animals. Again, we must conceptualize representation somewhat differently, not as a second-best form of political agency but as a way to *create* a kind of political agency for all members of the community. Political agency is not a natural fact, for animals or for humans. Our political practices and institutions help to constitute political agents and should be designed with this aim in mind: to give voice to the voiceless and ensure that their interests are considered in policy deliberations. Indeed, as Michael Saward has perceptively argued, representatives play a key role in creating the political community, in determining who exactly is included in "We, the people." Recognizing that creative function, I think, can help us to ensure a more inclusive democracy for everyone.

Finally, I have emphasized in the last chapter that pursuing a more fully realized animal welfare society *can but need not* conflict with human welfare. Pursuing animal welfare through aggressive campaigns to extend criminal prohibitions, toughen criminal penalties, and increase enforcement tends to put animal welfare at odds with human welfare. These campaigns are particularly problematic when they target minority communities, many of which have already been devastated by America's addiction to mass incarceration. Indeed, there is little evidence that increasing criminal enforcement actually has much impact on crime rates anyway. Instead of turning to criminal prohibitions, we should ensure that minority cultural traditions have the space and support to develop in a humane fashion, and so enrich our repertoire of social practices. Then we can put our resources toward legal and social reforms aimed at increasing our social capacity to protect the vulnerable and allowing different kinds of beings to flourish. That program promises to create a more humane society that can benefit all of its members, not just the nonhuman ones. We are all animals, after all; we are all, at some stages in our lives, vulnerable, interdependent, not very rational, and lacking voice and agency. A liberal theory along the lines I've outlined here is appropriate for such creatures. And a liberal regime designed to allow such creatures to thrive can serve the cause of human freedom better, I think, than a regime designed solely for its fully rational, autonomous members.

Liberalism is not, however, infinitely flexible; it is not oriented toward achieving rapid and dramatic social change. For example, the variety of liberalism I am promoting can be a good guide to dealing with one of the most serious long-term challenges facing the United States: the need for better environmental management. However, the liberalism I am describing may not be compatible with more comprehensive environmental reform agendas advocated by theorists such as Robyn Eckersley and David Schlosberg.[10] They endorse a conception of environmental citizenship that carries duties to all animals, to ecosystems, to the earth in general. Under my view, even duties to noncitizens in other parts of the world should be considered, at best, supererogatory. My concern is that the expansive list of duties proposed by these theorists seems likely to fuel an extraordinary expansion of state power—an expansion wholly at odds with the liberal tradition.

Nevertheless, my understanding of liberalism does not rule out the possibility of recognizing a broader range of duties to other kinds of nonhuman beings, including trees, mountains, or even whole ecosystems. The version of liberalism proposed in this study is explicitly grounded on social practice. Therefore, as social practices change, membership in the social contract can change as well. If we develop social practices that accord moral status to mountains, so that we can meaningfully talk to one another about treating such nonhuman beings as members of the community, it would make sense to include them in the social contract. We must not underestimate the creative power of representative practices, like Joanna Macy's Council of All Beings. If we start to see ourselves as plain citizens and members of the land community, that understanding should and will be reflected in our political practices. Such radical changes in our moral sympathies are not only possible, they are to be expected—especially in a liberal polity that aims at the flourishing of humans in community with all our fellow-creatures.

I will leave it to other theorists to work out what this more fully green liberalism might look like. But I think our explorations suggest a few points that can be a useful starting place for that project. First, we should begin from the premise that the subject of liberal political theory is not the isolated and autonomous human individual but ecological and socially interdependent beings: humans in relation to the nonhuman world. Our thinking about the state should begin from this ecologically grounded conception of the human political actor. A second principle is that maintaining the nonhuman world in good condition requires keeping that human/nonhuman relationship in good condition. Because they have extraordinary power to affect nonhuman beings and systems, humans play a critical stewardship role in relation to nonhuman nature. Supporting that stewardship role requires not simply prohibiting a list of bad behaviors but cultivating and maintaining a culture of stewardship, in which good practices and institutions can develop and thrive. Finally, then, liberal theory should focus less on the coercive power of the state and more on its role in facilitating the emergence of creative, diverse civil society—a society that supports the welfare of *all* its members.

Notes

PREFACE

1. Lévi-Strauss was explaining that animals are chosen as totems not because they are good to eat ("bonnes à manger") but because they are good to think ("bonnes à penser"). *Totemism*, trans. Rodney Needham (Boston: Beacon Press, 1963), p. 89.

INTRODUCTION

1. Cong. Rec., 107th Cong., 2nd sess. (2002), vol. 148, pt. 12: 616–617.

2. The statute in question, the Federal Property and Administrative Service Act (40 USC sec. 101 et seq), was amended in 1997 to allow other federal dog handlers, like Drug Enforcement Administration officers, to adopt their dogs.

3. Cong. Rec., 106th Cong., 2nd sess. (2000), vol. 146, no. 125: 9600.

4. "City of Saint Paul Considers Innovative Solution to Feral Felines." February 24, 2007, http://network.bestfriends.org/news; Denise LeBeau, "St. Paul Votes for Pro Feral Cat Ordinance!" September 27, 2007, http://network.bestfriends.org/4507/news.aspx.

5. *Animal Lovers Volunteer Association (ALVA) vs. Weinberger*, 765 F.2d. 937 (9th Cir., 1985). See the ALBC website for more information about the San Clemente goat conservation program: www.albc-usa.org/cpl/sanclementegoat.html.

6. A few prominent examples include Peter Singer, *Animal Liberation* [1975] (New York: HarperCollins, 2002); Tom Regan, *The Case for Animal Rights* (Berkeley: University of California Press, 1983); Mary Midgley, *Animals and Why They Matter* (Athens: University of Georgia Press, 1983); Rosemary Rodd, *Biology, Ethics and Animal* (Oxford: Clarendon Press, 1990).

7. *Animal Rights*, ed. Cass Sunstein and Martha Nussbaum (Oxford: Oxford University Press, 2004); Martha Nussbaum, *Frontiers of Justice* (Cambridge, MA: Belknap Press, 2006); Alisdair MacIntyre, *Dependent Rational Animals* (Chicago: Open Court, 1999); Marcel Wissenburg, *Green Liberalism* (London: Routledge, 1998); Robert

Garner, *The Political Theory of Animal Rights* (Manchester: Manchester University Press, 2005).

8. Several scholars of the liberal tradition have made this point. See, e.g. Elizabeth Anderson, *Value in Ethics and Economics* (Cambridge, MA: Harvard University Press, 1993), p. 9.

9. The term "animal" has a strict biological meaning, but that meaning isn't particularly relevant to this analysis. As will become clear throughout the book, my argument applies to beings that are considered animals, or fellow creatures, by the given society. In some communities, this could include bacteria, or even spiritual entities.

10. John Rawls, *Political Liberalism*, exp. ed. (New York: Columbia University Press, 2005), pp. 9, 10.

11. See, e.g., *In Defense of Animals: The Second Wave*, ed. Peter Singer (Malden, MA: Blackwell, 1006).

12. Regan, *The Case for Animal Rights*, p. 153.

13. I will provide empirical support for this point in more depth in chapter 1, and address the issue of cultural difference in some depth in chapter 5.

14. Regan makes this point in the context of mammals, but it holds for many other sorts of animals as well. Regan, *The Case for Animal Rights*, p. 82.

15. Ibid., p. 199.

16. Frey, "Rights, Interests, Desires and Beliefs," *American Philosophical Quarterly* 16, no. 3 (1979): 233–239.

17. David Hume, *An Enquiry Concerning the Principles of Morals*, ed. Tom Beauchamp (Oxford: Clarendon Press, 1998), p. 18.

18. Rawls, *Political Liberalism*, p. 21.

19. Raz, *The Morality of Freedom* (Oxford: Clarendon Press, 1988), p. 3.

20. Hector St. John de Crèvecoeur, *Letters from an American Farmer* [1782] (New York: Penguin Classics, 1986), p. 57.

21. Midgley, *Animals and Why They Matter*, p. 67; Rodd, *Biology, Ethics and Animals*, pp. 35, 206.

22. John Locke, "Second Treatise," in *Two Treatises of Government* [1690] (New York: Hafner, 1947), para. 3.

23. "Politics as a Vocation" [1919], in *Political Writings*, ed. Peter Lassman and Ronald Spiers (Cambridge: Cambridge University Press, 1994), pp. 310–311.

24. E.g., Susan Okin, *Justice, Gender, and the Family* (New York: Basic Books, 1989).

25. Joseph Raz, *The Morality of Freedom* (Oxford: Clarendon Press, 1986), p. 24.

26. The generalization may be overbroad; some primates may recognize obligation, and even some canine behavior might be so described. See Rodd, *Biology, Ethics and Animals*, pp. 35, 206. It follows that to the extent an animal does recognize an obligation to obey, we may hold authority over it. Whether that authority is political depends on other factors, such as whether it is backed by the legitimate use of force and, perhaps, whether state action is involved.

27. Raz, *The Morality of Freedom*, p. 25.

28. The legal arguments turned on other points entirely, of course: whether the navy had properly conducted its environmental impact assessment. But those arguments were clearly not ALVA's true concern.

29. This is a central argument in Marcel Wissenburg, *Green Liberalism*.

30. See chapter 2 for more discussion of this point.

31. Midgley, *Animals and Why They Matter*, p. 70.

32. This argument was forwarded by Louis Hartz in *The Liberal Tradition in America* (New York: Harcourt, Brace, 1955). It has been widely debated ever since, but the basic point that liberalism has had a very strong influence on American political traditions hasn't been seriously challenged.

33. The animal welfare movement is older and less radical than the animal rights movement, but they are certainly closely related. I will often conflate the two, distinguishing between them only when their differences are relevant to my argument.

CHAPTER 1

1. Roderick Nash, *The Rights of Nature* (Madison: University of Wisconsin Press, 1989), p. 7.

2. Endangered Species Act, 16 USC sec. 1531(a). See chapter 2 for discussion of the significance of this anthropocentric language.

3. David Moore, "Public Lukewarm on Animal Rights," Gallup News Service, May 21, 2003, www.gallup.com/poll/8461/public-lukewarm-animal-rights.aspx (accessed November 20, 2010).

4. Nash, *Rights of Nature*, p. 4.

5. Ibid.

6. E. P. Evans, *The Criminal Prosecution and Capital Punishment of Animals* (New York: E. P. Dutton & Co., 1906), p. 38.

7. Ibid., pp. 38–49.

8. Records from this period are incomplete, but Evans lists, for example, thirty-three proceedings in the fifteenth century and fifty in the sixteenth (mostly from France). Ibid., pp. 265–286.

9. Esther Cohen, "Law, Folklore and Animal Lore," *Past and Present* 110 (1986): 17; J. J. Finkelstein, "The Ox That Gored," *Transactions of the American Philosophical Society* 71, no. 2 (1981): 67.

10. Evans, *Criminal Prosecution*, pp. 40–41.

11. Walter Woodburn Hyde, "The Prosecution and Punishment of Animals and Lifeless Things in the Middle Ages and Modern Times," *University of Pennsylvania Law Review and American Law Register* 64 (May 1916): 698, 701, 708.

12. Finkelstein, "The Ox That Gored," pp. 64–65, 69.

13. Cf. Piers Biernes, "The Law Is an Ass," *Society and Animals* 2, no. 1 (1994): 43–44.

14. Finkelstein, "The Ox That Gored," p. 70. His interpretation, of course, raises the uncomfortable thought that our modern practice of "putting down" dangerous or unwanted dogs also has a ritualistic dimension.

15. Cohen, "Law, Folklore and Animal Trials," p. 36. See also Biernes, "The Law Is an Ass"; Paul S. Berman, "Rate, Pigs, and Statues on Trial: The Creation of Cultural Narratives in the Prosecution of Animals and Inanimate Objects," *New York University Law Review* 69 (May 1994): 288–326 (interpreting these trials as ritualistic attempts to restore moral order).

16. *CEASE v. New England Aquarium*, 836 F.Supp. 45 (D.Mass 1993).

17. 906 F.Supp. 549 (D. Haw. 1991).

18. 16 USC sec. 1361 et seq.

19. 5 USC sec. 702.

20. 836 F.Supp., p. 49.

21. 836 F.Supp., p. 52.

22. Fox Butterfield, "Claiming Harassment, Aquarium Sues 3 Animal Rights Groups," *New York Times,* October 1, 1991.

23. See, e.g., Suzanne Fields, "Gorillas in the Nursery," Townhall.com, July 6, 2007.

24. The Constitution does impose a limit on the Court's discretion to decide who has standing to bring suit. Article III of the Constitution authorizes federal courts to decide "cases and controversies," which the Supreme Court interprets to mean that it can act only when parties with real injuries bring suit. But it has broad discretion to decide who, or what, counts as a "party" and an "injury."

25. For further discussion of this issue, see Christopher Stone, *Should Trees Have Standing?* (Los Altos, CA: William Kaufman, 1974); Cass Sunstein, "A Tribute to Kenneth L. Karst: Standing for Animals (With Notes on Animal Rights)," *UCLA Law Review* 47 (June 2000): 1333–1368.

26. Gary Francione, *Animals, Property, and the Law* (Philadelphia: Temple University Press, 1995), pp. 65–90. See also Katherine Burke, "Can We Stand for It? Amending the Endangered Species Act with an Animal-Suit Provision," *Colorado Law Review* 75 (Spring 2004): 633–666.

27. "The Doctrine of Standing as an Essential Element of the Separation of Powers," *Suffolk University Law Review* 17 (1983): 892–893.

28. 765 F.2d. 937 (9th Cir., 1985), p. 937.

29. Nash, *The Rights of Nature*, p. 17.

30. Peter Singer, *The Expanding Circle* (New York: Farrar, Straus and Giroux, 1981), frontispiece, pp. 111–124 (quoting Lecky, *History of European Morals from Augustus to Charlemagne*, 1869).

31. Nash, *Rights of Nature*, p. 44 (quoting Charles Darwin, *The Descent of Man* [1886]).

32. Aldo Leopold, *A Sand County Almanac with Essay on Conservation from Round River* (New York: Ballantine, 1966), p. 238.

33. J. Baird Callicott, "The Conceptual Foundations of the Land Ethic," in *Companion to "A Sand County Almanac,"* ed. J. Baird Callicott (Madison: University of Wisconsin

Press, 1987), pp. 186–217. See also Bernard Rollin, "The Ascent of the Apes—Broadening the Moral Community," in *The Great Ape Project*, ed. Paolo Cavalieri and Peter Singer (New York: St. Martin's Griffin, 1993), pp. 206–219.

34. Nash, *Rights of Nature*, pp. 16–17.

35. Stephen Quilley, "The Land Ethic as an Ecological Civilizing Process: Aldo Leopold, Norbert Elias, and Environmental Philosophy," *Environmental Ethics* 31 (Summer 2009): 124, 131 (drawing on Norbert Elias, *The Civilising Process* [1939] (New York: Urizen Books, 1978).

36. Quilley, "The Land Ethic," pp. 128–131. Quilley speaks simply of increasing interdependence, but I have added "conscious," since the process he describes seems to require that people be aware of these interdependencies, at some level. This of course complicates the application of this theory to the nonhuman world—presumably human interdependence with nature has always been extremely salient. But we should not read this as a highly deterministic theory; other responses to that interdependence are presumably possible (as suggested below). In other words, conscious interdependence may be a necessary but not sufficient condition for the emergence of ethical relations.

37. Quilley, "The Land Ethic," p. 125.

38. Seminal works on American political development include Oscar and Mary Handlin, *Commonwealth*, rev. ed. (Cambridge, MA: Belknap Press of Harvard University Press, 1969); Stephen Skowronek, *Building a New American State* (Cambridge: Cambridge University Press, 1983); and Theda Skocpol, *Protecting Soldiers and Mothers* (Cambridge, MA: Belknap Press of Harvard University Press, 1992).

39. Walter Dunn, *Frontier Profit and Loss* (Westport, CT: Greenwood Press, 1998), pp. 10–12.

40. Richard Andrews, *Managing the Environment, Managing Ourselves* (New Haven, CT: Yale University Press, 1999), pp. 46–49; William Cronon, *Changes in the Land* (New York: Hill & Wang, 1983), pp. 92–98, 101. The French and British governments regulated the fur trade principally by limiting trade beyond garrisoned posts and controlling how much alcohol could be distributed to natives, but such policies were not consistently adhered to, nor effectively enforced. Dunn, *Frontier Profit and Loss*, pp. 29–33, 50–52.

41. Massachusetts Body of Liberties, secs. 92, 93 (1641).

42. Virginia Anderson, *Creatures of Empire* (Oxford: Oxford University Press, 2004), pp. 91–93.

43. Ibid., pp. 46–51, 94–95.

44. Cronon, *Changes in the Land*, pp. 134–137; Anderson, *Creatures of Empire*, pp. 142, 158–163.

45. Percy Bidwell and John Falconer, *History of Agriculture in the Northern United States, 1620–1860* (Washington: Carnegie Institution, 1925), pp. 23–24.

46. Anderson, *Creatures of Empire*, pp. 114, 124.

47. Terry Jordan, *North American Cattle-Ranching Frontiers* (Albuquerque: University of New Mexico Press, 1993), pp. 113, 118.

48. On folklore in nineteenth-century American culture, see Charles Joyner, *Shared Traditions* (Urbana: University of Illinois Press, 1999); David Hackett Fischer, *Albion's Seed* (New York: Oxford University Press, 1989); John Blassingame, *The Slave Community*, 2nd ed. (Oxford: Oxford University Press, 1979).

49. Blackstone, *Commentaries on the Laws of England* (1765–1769) (Chicago: University of Chicago Press, 1979), introduction, sec. 2.

50. Ibid., Book 3, sec. 3.

51. Ibid., Book 3, sec. 5.

52. Russell Weigley, *History of the United States Army* (Bloomington: Indiana University Press, 1967), pp. 8–9, 70–71.

53. Ibid., pp. 139, 159.

54. Ibid., pp. 171, 184, 267; James Arnold, *Jeff Davis' Own: Cavalry, Comanches and the Battle for the Texas Frontier* (New York: John Wiley & Sons, 2000), pp. 12–14.

55. Weigley, *History of the United States Army*, pp. 220–221.

56. John Otto, *Southern Agriculture during the Civil War Era, 1860–1880* (Westport, CT: Greenwood Press, 1994), p. 37.

57. Otto, *Southern Agriculture*, p. 74.

58. Andrew Isenberg, *The Destruction of the Bison* (Cambridge: Cambridge University Press, 2000), pp. 104–105.

59. Stuart Marks, *Southern Hunting in Black and White* (Princeton, NJ: Princeton University Press, 1991), pp. 28–37.

60. Ibid., pp. 26–28.

61. Jordan, *North American Cattle-Ranching Frontiers*, pp. 123–169 and passim.

62. Biddell and Falconer, *History of Agriculture*, pp. 187–193, 223; Peter McClelland, *Sowing Modernity* (Ithaca, NY: Cornell University Press, 1997), pp. 210–215, 233.

63. Biddell and Falconer, *History of Agriculture*, pp. 185–186, 190–193.

64. McClelland, *Sowing Modernity*, pp. 232–233.

65. William Novak, *The People's Welfare* (Chapel Hill: University of North Carolina Press, 1996), pp. 221–227; Andrews, *Managing the Environment*, p. 110.

66. Susan Pearson, "'The Rights of the Defenseless': Animals, Children, and Sentimental Liberalism in Nineteenth-Century America" (PhD diss., University of North Carolina, 2004), pp. 58–59; Katherine Grier, *Pets in America* (Chapel Hill: University of North Carolina Press, 2006), p. 57.

67. Grier, *Pets in America*, p. 56.

68. Harriet Ritvo, *The Animal Estate* (Cambridge, MA: Harvard University Press, 1987), p. 86.

69. Grier, *Pets in America*, pp. 26–57, 231–242, 262–264.

70. Ibid., pp. 46–57.

71. *Sentell v. New Orleans and Carrollton Railroad Co*, 166 US 698 (1897), p. 700. The Court is not using "intrinsic value" here as modern philosophers would; it simply

means that the market value of a dog depends on its breed and peculiar characteristics, so dogs have no general value for the law to protect.

72. For a discussion of the law in this area, see S. Waisman, P. Frasch, and B. Wagman, *Animal Law: Cases and Material*, 3rd ed. (Durham, NC: Carolina Academic Press, 2006), pp. 22–37.

73. James Jasper and Dorothy Nelkin, *The Animal Rights Crusade* (New York: Free Press, 1992), p. 57.

74. Grier, *Pets in America*, pp. 214, 217.

75. Pearson, "Rights of the Defenseless," pp. 187–196.

76. Nash, *Rights of Nature*, pp. 6–7.

77. Andrews, *Managing the Environment*, p. 112; Grier, *Pets in America*, p. 151.

78. *Broadway etc Stage Co. v. ASPCA*, 15 Abbot 51 (New York 1873). Susan Pearson argues that the common law only prevented public acts of cruelty, which constituted a breach of the peace; Bergh's law went further and prohibited private acts of cruelty and neglect. Her interpretation of the common law has some support in other legal commentary of the era. See Pearson, "Rights of the Defenseless," pp. 137–138. I believe that the common law's focus on public acts of cruelty reflects concerns about the proper reach of state power, not a more limited ethic of kindness to animals. See chapter 2 for more discussion of that point.

79. Handlin and Handlin, *Commonwealth*, pp. 229–244; Skocpol, *Protecting Soldiers and Mothers*, pp. 102–159.

80. Julie Novkov, *Constituting Workers, Protecting Women* (Ann Arbor: University of Michigan Press, 2001), p. 226 (discussing *Adkins v. Children's Hospital*, 261 US 525 [1923]).

81. Skocpol, *Protecting Soldiers and Mothers*, pp. 102–159.

82. On the logic of such alliances, see Lani Guinier and Gerald Torres, *The Miner's Canary* (Cambridge, MA: Harvard University Press, 2002).

83. Grier, *Pets in America*, pp. 89–90, 151, 214–217.

84. Willard Cochrane, *The Development of American Agriculture* (Minneapolis: University of Minnesota Press, 1979), pp. 244–245. Cochrane points out that by 1965, private funding of agricultural research had increased to 55 percent of total research expenditures for agriculture. However, the State still funds a substantial portion of the total, which is well over $1 billion per year.

85. Curt Meine, *Aldo Leopold: His Life and Work* (Madison: University of Wisconsin Press, 1988), p. 148. Of uncertain constitutionality, the Weeks-McLean Act was replaced in 1918 by the Migratory Bird Treaty Act.

86. Ibid., pp. 147–150.

87. See, e.g., California Constitution, article 1, section 25, 1910; Vermont Constitution, chapter 2, part 67, 1777; Minnesota Constitution, article 13, sec. 12 (1998); North Dakota Constitution, article 11, sec. 27 (2000); Wisconsin Constitution, article 1, sec. 26 (2003).

88. Meine, *Aldo Leopold*, pp. 154–155, 241. See the Animal Damage Control Act, 7 USCA secs. 426–426c.

89. US Department of Agriculture, Census of Agriculture. www.ers.usda.gov/news/
    BSECoverage.htm; www.agcensus.usda.gov/Publications/Historical_
    Publications/1920/Livestock_Products.pdf (both accessed January 14, 2012).

90. Andrews, *Managing the Environment*, p. 132.

91. 7 USC sec. 1901; Jasper and Nelkin, *Animal Rights Crusade*, p. 140. The law did not
    criminalize inhumane slaughter; rather, it provided that federal agencies could buy
    meat only from companies that complied with the law. This created considerable
    financial pressure on the large meat-processing companies to comply.

92. Unlike state governments, Congress has no general "police" power (power to pro-
    tect the public safety and welfare). Its authority over animals derives in large part
    from its authority to regulate interstate commerce. The leading case is *Rupert
    v. United States*, 181 F. 87 (8th Cir., 1910) (affirming Congress's authority to pass the
    first national legislation for the protection of game animals, the Lacey Act, 16 USC
    secs. 3371–3378).

93. Grier, *Pets in America*, p. 269.

94. *Code of Federal Regulations*, vol. 9, sec. 1.1 (defining "animal" as "any live or dead
    dog, cat, nonhuman primate, guinea pig, hamster, rabbit, or any other warm-
    blooded animal, which is being used, or is intended for use for research, teaching,
    testing, experimentation, or exhibition purposes, or as a pet. This term excludes
    birds, rats of the genus Rattus, and mice of the genus Mus, bred for use in research;
    horses not used for research purposes; and other farm animals").

95. *Rabideau v. City of Racine*, 243 Wis. 2d 486 (2001); Tennessee Code Ann., sec.
    44-17-403.

96. Waisman et al., *Animal Law*, pp. 570–572, 616–618.

97. "Germany Votes for Animal Rights," CNN, May 17, 2002, articles.cnn.com/2002-
    05-17/world/germany.animals_1_animal-rights-human-rights-lawmakers?_
    s=PM:WORLD; "EU Bans Battery Hen Cages," BBC News Online, January 28,
    1999, news.bbc.co.uk/2/hi/uk_news/264607.stm; Sally Pook, "Animal Law
    Will Give Pets Their Own 'Bill of Rights,'" *Telegraph*, January 31, 2006, www.
    telegraph.co.uk/news/uknews/1509284/Animal-law-will-give-pets-their-own-
    bill-of-rights.html.

98. Jennifer Koons, "Ecuador's New Constitution Gives Inalienable Rights to Nature,"
    Greenwire, September 30, 2008, www.greenchange.org/article.php?id=3389; Erin
    Evans, "Constitutional Inclusion of Animal Rights in Germany and Switzerland,"
    paper presented at the annual meeting of the Western Political Science Association,
    Manchester Hyatt, San Diego, CA, March 20, 2008.

CHAPTER 2

1. Douglas Brinkley, *The Great Deluge* (New York: HarperCollins, 2006), p. 517.

2. Letter from Judy Chase, president of the Animal Shelter Aid Program, to Lincoln
   Chaffee, September 29, 2005, www.congress.org/congressorg/bio/userletter
   (stating that the most common reason cited for refusing to evacuate was the need

to care for pets); Rebecca Simmons, "No Pet Left Behind," April 20, 2006, www.hsus.org/pets/pets_related_news_and_events.

3. PETS Act, PL 109–308 (2006).

4. Remarks of Rep. Tom Lantos, Cong. Rec., September 20, 2006, H6806; Simmons, "No Pet Left Behind."

5. Cong. Rec., September 20, 2006, H6806–H6808.

6. Bob Kemper, "Pet-Loving Georgians Call Bill a Disaster," *Atlanta Journal-Constitution*, May 23, 2006.

7. New York Rev. Stat., Ch. 374, sec. 1–10 (1867).

8. *Broadway etc. Stage Co. v. ASPCA*, 15 Abbott 51 (New York, 1873).

9. McShane, "Gelded Age Boston," *New England Quarterly* 74 (June 2001): 274–302, quote on p. 294.

10. Bergh, "The Cost of Cruelty," *North American Review* 133 (July 1882): 75–81. Bergh doesn't address why government regulation is needed to protect the owners of the livestock from these losses, but it's likely that he and his audience saw the railroads as far too powerful to be restrained through private actions in tort or contract.

11. Humane Methods of Livestock Slaughter Act, 7 USC sec. 1901 (1958); Animal Welfare Act, 7 USC sec. 2131(b) (1966); Endangered Species Act, 16 USCA 1531(a) (3) (1973).

12. The evidence of a link between animal abuse and violence toward humans is actually much weaker than these advocates usually recognize, but the link between domestic abuse and mistreatment of pets has better support. For an overview of the literature, see Mark Dadds, "Conduct Problems and Cruelty to Animals in Children: Where Is the Link?," in *The International Handbook of Animal Abuse and Cruelty*, ed. Frank Ascione (West Lafayette, IN: Purdue University Press, 2008). On domestic and animal abuse, see Catherine Faver and Elizabeth Strand, "Unleashing Compassion: Social Work and Animal Abuse," and Barbara Boat, Lynn Loar, and Allie Phillips, "Collaborating to Assess, Intervene, and Prosecute Animal Abuse," both in Ascione, *International Handbook of Animal Abuse and Cruelty*.

13. Remarks of Mr. Monroney, Cong. Rec. vol. 104, pt. 5, 85th Cong., 2nd sess. (1958): 6490–6491; Remarks of Mr. Poage, Cong. Rec. vol. 104, pt. 2, 85th Cong., 2nd sess. (1958): 1653–1656; Remarks of Mr. Reid, Cong. Rec. vol. 112, pt. 4, 89th Cong., 2nd sess. (1966): 5042.

14. The difficulty of justifying animal welfare laws under liberal principles is discussed by Robert Garner in *The Political Theory of Animal Rights* (Manchester, UK: Manchester University Press, 2005). His analysis focuses more on liberals' general support for moral pluralism than on the specific concerns about political obligation and state power raised here, but we are largely in agreement on the basic point.

15. Rawls, *A Theory of Justice*, rev. ed. (Cambridge, MA: Harvard University Press, 1999), pp. 18–19, 42.

16. Raz, *The Morality of Freedom* (Oxford: Clarendon Press, 1986), pp. 42–57, 58–59. Raz considers reasons for extending political authority beyond such cases, but this is his basic test of legitimacy in the normal case.

17. Ibid., pp. 288–320 (discussing the relationship between autonomy and well-being).

18. Ibid., pp. 412–420.

19. Ibid., pp. 417–418.

20. Raz says at one point that political authority is ultimately based on the moral duty individuals owe their fellow *humans*, but he later accepts that we may have moral duties toward nonhuman animals as well. Ibid., pp. 72, 176–178.

21. Minnesota Statutes 2001, Chapter 343, subd. 9.

22. Raz, *Morality of Freedom*, p. 418.

23. Immanuel Kant, *Lectures on Ethics*, trans. P. Heath and J. B. Schneewind (Cambridge: Cambridge University Press, 1997), p. 240.

24. Alisdair MacIntyre, *Dependent Rational Animals* (Chicago: Open Court, 1999), pp. 134–138.

25. As noted above, the evidence for this assertion is weak, nor is it entirely clear how criminalizing this behavior would help in treating the disorder.

26. Raz, *Morality of Freedom*, pp. 86–87.

27. I will take John Locke, *Two Treatises of Government* [1690] (New York: Hafner, 1947), as my principal classic liberal social contract theorist. I will use T. M. Scanlon, *What We Owe to Each Other* (Cambridge, MA: Belknap Press, 1998), and John Rawls, *A Theory of Justice*, rev. ed. (Cambridge, MA: Belknap Press, 1999), as examples of contemporary contract theories. On the influence of social contract theory in the United States, see Mark Hulliung, *The Social Contract in America* (Lawrence: University Press of Kansas, 2008).

28. German Basic Law, Article 20a. Switzerland, too, amended its constitution in 1992 to protect the dignity of animals (*Wurde der Kreatur*). On both constitutional movements, see Erin Evans, "Constitutional Inclusion of Animal Rights in Germany and Switzerland," paper presented at the annual meeting of the Western Political Science Association, Manchester Hyatt, San Diego, CA, March 20, 2008.

29. As one would expect, the meaning of the provision is disputed. Consumer Affairs Minister Renate Kunast insists that animal welfare will not trump human interests: "People remain the most important," she said. "Germany Votes for Animal Rights," CNN.com, May 17, 2002, http://archives.cnn.com/2002/WORLD/europe/05/17/germany.animals/index.html.

30. Regan, *The Case for Animal Rights* (Berkeley: University of California Press, 1983).

31. Rosemary Rodd, *Biology, Ethics, and Animals* (Oxford: Clarendon Press, 1990), p. 240.

32. Robert K. Merton, *Social Theory and Social Structure* (Glencoe, IL: Free Press, 1957). Merton coined the term "middle-range theory" to refer to descriptive theories that are more general than bare empirical data gathering but less comprehensive and abstract than grand theory. My use of the term for normative theory is somewhat idiosyncratic, but I think it captures the way we ordinarily deal with moral issues in social life.

33. John Rawls, *Political Liberalism*, exp. ed. (New York: Columbia University Press, 2005), pp. xviii–xix. A reasonable comprehensive doctrine has three main features:

it covers the major religious, philosophical, and moral aspects of human life in a more or less consistent and coherent manner; it specifies which values count as especially significant and how to balance them when they conflict; and it belongs to or draws upon a tradition of thought and doctrine. Rawls, *Political Liberalism*, p. 59.

34. According to the American Pet Products Association, 39 percent of US households include at least one dog, and 35 percent include at least one cat. American Pet Products Association, Industry Statistics and Trends (2008), http://americanpetproducts. org/press_industrytrends.asp (accessed December 15, 2008). A widely cited opinion survey conducted in 1985 found that 87 percent of respondents considered pets family members, a finding confirmed by a more recent Harris poll, in which 88 percent of pet owners called their pets "members of the family." K. Bulcroft, "Pets in the American Family," *People, Animals, Environment* 8, no. 4 (1990): 13–14; Harris Interactive, "Pets Are 'Members of the Family' and Two-Thirds of Pet Owners Buy Their Pets Holiday Presents," December 25, 2007, www.humanespot.org/content/pets-are-members-family-and-two-thirds-pet-owners-buy-their-pets-holiday-presents.

35. See chapter 1 for empirical support for this claim.

36. Martha Nussbaum, *The Frontiers of Justice* (Cambridge, MA: Belknap Press, 2006). Nussbaum, it should be noted, does not believe the ends of the social contract can be reformulated as I suggest here and therefore rejects social contract theory altogether. We could also follow Rodney Peffer, who argues that the government's responsibility for welfare arises out of the value of human worth or dignity. "A Defense of Rights to Well-Being," *Philosophy and Public Affairs* 8, no. 1 (1978): 65–87. Worth and dignity are concepts that can apply to nonhuman animals as well. However, the concept of flourishing is better suited to our purposes, given the interdependence of human and animal welfare. Dignity is an attribute of an individual; flourishing happens in community with others.

37. *Women and Human Development* (Cambridge: Cambridge University Press, 2000), pp. 78–80.

38. John Locke, *Two Treatises of Government* [1690] (New York: Hafner, 1947), secs. 56, 134; *Letter Concerning Toleration* [1689] (Indianapolis: Hackett, 1983), pp. 38–39 (arguing that magistrates should tolerate churches, which allow men to "perform such . . . things in Religion as cannot be done by each private man apart").

39. Rawls actually limits this condition to the hypothetical contracting parties; the actual citizens of a well-ordered society, he acknowledges, must be educated into a robust sense of justice for the social contract to hold. Rawls, *Political Liberalism*, pp. 85–86.

40. Scanlon, *What We Owe to Each Other*, pp. 5, 180–181.

41. John Rawls, *Political Liberalism*, exp. ed. (New York: Columbia University Press, 2005), p. 18; T. M. Scanlon, *What We Owe to Each Other* (Cambridge, MA: Belknap Press, 1998), pp. 110, 129, 180–181.

42. Several moral philosophers have attempted to include animals in the social contract. The most successful include Mark Rowlands, *Animal Rights*, 2nd ed. (New York: Palgrave Macmillan, 2009), and Matthew Talbert, "Contractualism and Our

Duties to Nonhuman Animals," *Environmental Ethics* 28 (Summer 2006): 201–215. Their analyses are consistent with mine. Talbert, for example, suggests that we wish to live in relations of mutual justification with animals as well as humans. For animals, this would require respecting their welfare. Thus he agrees that the social contract can obligate us to attend to the welfare of those who aren't capable of rational autonomy, which is my position (and Rowlands's). In contrast, some theorists have tried to bring animals into Rawls's social contract simply by modifying the original position to prevent the parties from knowing whether they are humans or nonhumans. Donald Vandeveer, "Of Beasts, Person, and the Original Position," *Monist* 62, no. 3 (1979): 368–377; Michael Pritchard and Wade Robison, "Justice and the Treatment of Animals: A Critique of Rawls," *Environmental Ethics* 3 (Spring 1981): 55–61; Robert Elliot, "Rawlsian Justice and Non-Human Animals," *Journal of Applied Philosophy* 1, no. 1 (1984): 95–106; Brent Singer, "An Extension of Rawls's Theory of Justice to Environmental Ethics," *Environmental Ethics* 10 (Fall 1988): 217–231. But that modification necessarily requires us also to modify the end of the social contract, which for Rawls is developing humans' capacity to honor fair terms and their capacity to pursue the good (capacities that only humans have). Rawls, *Political Liberalism*, p. 301. There is no reason to include animals in the original position unless the social contract they would be helping to form has something to do with their welfare. Therefore, including animals in the social contract requires us to accept that the purpose of the social contract goes beyond protecting the welfare of rational, autonomous agents.

43. Tom Regan, "Duties to Animals," *Ethics and Animals* 2 (1981): 76–81, quote on p. 79.

44. To be fair, Locke did not deny the possibility of animal minds, only the higher-order cognitive capacities necessary to discover and knowingly follow God's law. John Locke, *An Essay concerning Human Understanding* [1690], ed. Roger Woolhouse (New York: Penguin, 1997), book 2, chap. 11, secs. 5–12.

45. Dale Jamieson, *Morality's Progress* (Oxford: Clarendon Press, 2002), pp. 47–86. Jamieson and Bekoff provide philosophical justification for cognitive ethology, whose emergence in the 1970s reflected a growing recognition among scientists that the best explanations of animal behavior include attention to animals' mental states.

46. Paul Shepard, *The Others: How Animals Made Us Human* (Washington, DC: Island Press, 1996), p. 17; Alisdair MacIntyre, *Dependent Rational Animals* (Chicago: Open Court, 1999), p. 51.

47. Mary Midgley, *Animals and Why They Matter* (Athens: University of Georgia Press, 1983), p. 70. Philip Pettit defines domination as the capacity to interfere arbitrarily with a choice an individual is about to make. Pettit, *Republicanism* (Oxford: Clarendon Press, 1997), p. 52. To apply this concept to animals, of course, we must acknowledge that animals can have the mental capacity to make choices.

48. I specify that human parties must recognize these moral qualities of animals because our public philosophy must have a firm basis in public sentiment or it simply won't be effective.

49. Jean-Jacques Rousseau, "Discourse on Inequality" [1755], in *The First and Second Discourses, Together with the Replies to Critics and Essay on the Origin of Languages*, ed. Victor Gourevitch (New York: Harper and Row, 1986), p. 146.

50. Nussbaum, *Frontiers of Justice*, p. 334.

51. Mary Midgley, *Animals and Why They Matter* (Athens: University of Georgia Press, 1983), pp. 87–88; Rosemary Rodd, *Biology, Ethics and Animals* (Oxford: Clarendon Press, 1990), p. 228.

52. J. Baird Callicott, "Animal Liberation and Environmental Ethics: Back Together Again," in *The Animal Rights/Environmental Ethics Debate*, ed. Eugene Hargrove (Albany: SUNY Press, 1992), p. 256. See also Rollin and Rollin, "Dogmaticisms and Catechisms," in Armstrong and Botzler, *The Animal Ethics Reader*, p. 72; Catherine Larrère and Raphaël Larrère, "Animal Rearing as a Contract?," *Journal of Agriculture and Environmental Ethics* 12, no. 1 (2000): 51–58.

53. Clare Palmer, "The Idea of the Domesticated Animal Contract," *Environmental Values* 6, no. 4 (1997): 411–425; Clare Palmer, *Animals in Context* (New York: Columbia University Press, 2010), pp. 59–62.

54. Rawls, *Political Liberalism*, p. 288.

55. The situation of livestock (animals raised for food) involves additional complexities, which I will address below.

56. Carole Pateman, *The Sexual Contract* (Stanford: Stanford University Press, 1988); Charles Mills, *The Racial Contract* (Ithaca, NY: Cornell University Press, 1997).

57. The following account is based largely on Eric Stoykovich, "Of a Predatory Nature? Dogs and the Protection of Sheep in the Eastern United States," paper presented at the ASEH conference, Baton Rouge, LA, 2007.

58. Similar laws were passed in England and France in the late eighteenth century. Harriet Ritvo, *The Animal Estate* (Cambridge, MA: Harvard University Press, 1987), pp. 188–190; Kathleen Kete, *The Beast in the Boudoir* (Berkeley: University of California Press, 1994), pp. 40–54.

59. Stoykovich, "Of a Predatory Nature?," p. 8 (quoting the Fifth Annual Report of the Secretary of the Maine Board of Agriculture, 1860 [Augusta: Stevens and Sayward, 1860], pp. 41–43).

60. Ibid. (quoting "Dogs and Dog Laws," Report of the Commissioner of Agriculture for the Year 1863 [Washington, DC: GPO, 1863], pp. 454–455).

61. Kete, *The Beast in the Boudoir*, p. 54. A similar debate over dog taxes in England began with an effort to discourage people, and especially the poor, from owning dogs. But it resulted in a tax that fell less heavily on the poor, acknowledging their right to own dogs for work or companionship. Ingrid Tague, "Eighteenth-Century English Debate on a Dog Tax," *Historical Journal* 51, no. 4 (2008): pp. 901–920.

62. William Root, "'Man's Best Friend': Property or Family Member?" *Villanova Law Review* 47, no. 2 (2002): 423–450; Gerry Beyer, "Pet Animals: What Happens When Their Humans Die?," *Santa Clara Law Review* 40: 617–676 (2000). Most courts also refuse to enforce wills providing for the destruction of an animal. The

leading case is *Smith v. Avanzino*, no. 225698, Cal. Super. Ct., San Francisco Cty., June 17, 1980.

63. See, e.g., Robyn Eckersley, *The Green State* (Cambridge, MA: MIT Press, 2004), p. 111.

64. Some ethicists attempt to limit our duties to animals by rooting them in relationships. For example, Clare Palmer argues that we have a moral duty to assist animals we affect but not animals outside our sphere of influence. Palmer, *Animals in Context*. Her moral theory is largely compatible with my political theory and with liberal theories of political obligation generally. But I remain skeptical that a purely theoretical approach to determining political membership is practical. Palmer's theory, for example, suggests that we have moral obligations that extend well beyond the political community of the nation state, and it is not clear to me that this would be a viable approach to political obligation.

65. Don Herzog, *Without Foundations* (Ithaca, NY: Cornell University Press, 1985), pp. 24–25.

66. Ibid., pp. 21–22.

67. Elizabeth Anderson, "Animal Rights and the Values of Nonhuman Life," in *Animal Rights: Current Debates and New Directions*, ed. Cass Sunstein and Martha Nussbaum (Oxford: Oxford University Press, 2004), p. 288.

68. See, e.g., Ruth Youngblood, "New England Town Adopts Swan Flock," *Los Angeles Times*, May 18, 1984 (Durham, NH, names and protects a flock of swans, appointing official "Keepers of the Swans," and sets up a swan fund).

69. For a recent study of farm animal production in the United States, see "Putting Meat on the Table: Industrial Farm Animal Production in America," *Report of the Pew Commission on Industrial Farm Animal Production* (2008).

70. Those feral populations would in turn cause environmental problems that might well lead to culling, as we did with the San Clemente goats. It is hard to see how we can escape responsibility for managing populations of animals (that is, killing individuals), when we introduced them into the ecosystem and deliberately bred them to replace the wild animals that we exterminated.

71. The next chapter will discuss in depth the ethical problems involved in commodification of animals.

72. Wendell Berry, *The Gift of Good Land* (San Francisco: North Point Press, 1981), pp. 226–227, 215.

73. Michael Pollan, *The Omnivore's Dilemma* (New York: Penguin, 2006), p. 225.

74. Reese, "Jonathan Safran Foer's Annoying Argument against Eating Meat," Double XX, November 11, 2009, www.doublex.com.

75. For the view that we should allow domesticated animals to die off, see Peter Wenz, *Environmental Justice* (Albany: SUNY Press, 1988), p. 328; Marti Kheel, *Nature Ethics* (New York: Rowman and Littlefield, 2008), p. 232.

76. "City of Saint Paul Considers Innovative Solution to Feral Felines," Best Friends Network, February 24, 2007, network.bestfriends.org/news.

77. Courtney Mabeus, "Local CATNiPP Could Help Reduce City's Feral Cat Population," *Examiner*, October 20, 2006, www.examiner.com.

78. Cong. Rec., 85th Cong., 2nd sess. (1958), vol. 104, pt. 2: 1657.

79. Cong. Rec., 89th Cong., 2nd sess. (1966), vol. 112, pt. 5: 19754.

CHAPTER 3

1. "The HSUS Applauds Vermont Officials for Tightening the Lid on Captive Hunting," www.hsus.org/wildlife_abuse (accessed December 18, 2008).

2. Dennis Jenson, "Clock Ticking for Elk Farmer," *Times Argus*, August 23, 2009.

3. 10 *Vermont Statutes Annotated*, App. Sec. 19.4.

4. "Vermont Man May Be Separated from the Moose He Loves," PeoplePets newsletter, August 6, 2009, www.peoplepets.com/news/strange/.

5. John Locke, "Second Treatise," in *Two Treatises of Government* [1690] (New York: Hafner, 1947), chap. 5.

6. Martin Balluch and Eberhart Theuer, "Trial on Personhood for Chimp, 'Hiasl,'" *Altex: Alternatives to Animal Experimentation* (April 2007). Austria has also banned experimentation on gibbons. Andrew Knight, "The Beginning of the End for Chimpanzee Experiments?," *Philosophy, Ethics, and Humanities in Medicine* 3 (2008): 16–21.

7. "It's Official: In Austria, a Chimp Is Not a Person," Associated Press, January 15, 2008.

8. Gary Francione, *Animals, Property and the Law* (Philadelphia: Temple University Press, 1995), pp. 14, 24; *Animal Rights: Current Debates and New Directions*, ed. Cass Sunstein and Martha Nussbaum (Oxford: Oxford University Press, 2004), p. 117.

9. Steve Wise, *Rattling the Cage* (New York: Basic Books, 2000), pp. 4–5.

10. Sunstein and Nussbaum, *Animal Rights*, pp. 148–149.

11. Jeremy Waldron, *The Right to Private Property* (Oxford: Clarendon Press, 1988), p. 103.

12. Ibid., pp. 38–39. As Waldron points out, this is not to suggest that all property is held this way in a private property system. This is merely the "organizing idea," the point of reference by which the system's operation should be understood. Ibid., p. 42.

13. Locke, "Second Treatise," para. 27.

14. Waldron, *The Right to Private Property*, pp. 188–189.

15. Jean-Jacques Rousseau, "Discourse on Inequality" [1755], in *The First and Second Discourses, Together with the Replies to Critics and Essay on the Origin of Languages*, ed. Victor Gourevitch (New York: Harper and Row 1986), p. 44. For additional critiques of Locke's argument, see Alan Carter, *The Philosophical Foundations of Property Rights* (New York: Harvester Wheatsheaf, 1989), pp. 15; Waldron, *The Right to Private Property*, pp. 185–191.

16. James Tully, *A Discourse on Property* (Cambridge: Cambridge University Press, 1980), pp. 61–62, 72.

17. Locke, "Second Treatise," para. 6, 26, 27; "First Treatise of Government," in *Two Treatises of Government* [1690] (New York: Hafner, 1947), para. 30.

18. Jeremy Waldron, *God, Locke and Equality* (Cambridge: Cambridge University Press, 2002), pp. 71–82.

19. Balluch and Theuer, "Trial on Personhood for Chimp, 'Hiasl.'"

20. Alan Carter discusses such theories in *The Philosophical Foundations of Property Rights*, pp. 27–37.
21. Carter, *Philosophical Foundations*, pp. 29–30. Waldron raises further problems with desert in *The Rights to Private Property*, pp. 201–207.
22. This summary of Hegel's property theory is based on Alan Ryan, *Property and Political Theory* (Oxford: Basil Blackwell, 1984), pp. 118–141, and Waldron, *The Right to Private Property*, pp. 343–389.
23. Hegel is not, however, offering a theory of natural property rights; he is explaining the point of a system of legal property rights.
24. Carter, *Philosophical Foundations*, pp. 89–90; Waldron, *The Right to Private Property*, pp. 352–357.
25. Waldron, *The Right to Private Property*, pp. 30, 33, 45.
26. Eric Freyfogle, *Agrarianism and the Good Society* (Lexington: University Press of Kentucky, 2007), p. 98.
27. Elizabeth Anderson, *Value in Ethics and Economics* (Cambridge, MA: Harvard University Press, 1993), p. 11.
28. Ibid., pp. xiii, 6, 10.
29. Ibid., pp. 17, xiii.
30. "Ideals" are conceptions of what kind of a person one wants to be, what kind of character and commitments one should aspire to. Ibid, p. 6.
31. Ibid., pp. 12, 144.
32. Ibid., p. 7.
33. Ibid, p. 92. On contextual justification, see chapter 2, above.
34. The literature on animal friendship is almost too vast to cite; it ranges from Anna Sewell's classic *Black Beauty* (Chicago: M. A. Donohue, 1877) to more sophisticated treatments like Vicki Hearne's *Animal Happiness* (New York: HarperCollins, 1994).
35. Anderson, *Value in Ethics and Economics*, p. 146.
36. Ibid., p. 209.
37. Ibid., pp. 9–10.
38. Ibid., pp. 147, 150.
39. David Schlosberg, *Defining Environmental Justice* (Oxford: Oxford University Press, 2007), pp. 14–20.
40. Ibid., pp. 138–142.
41. Francione, *Animals, Property and the Law*, p. 14.
42. Ariel Gross, *Double Character* (Princeton, NJ: Princeton University Press, 2000).
43. Francione, *Animals, Property and the Law*, pp. 4–5.
44. David Favre, "A New Property Status for Animals," in Sunstein and Nussbaum, *Animal Rights*, pp. 240–241.
45. Sonia Waisman, Pamela Frasch, and Bruce Wagman, *Animal Law: Cases and Material*, 3rd ed. (Durham, NC: Carolina Academic Press, 2006), pp. 566–577.
46. Favre, "A New Property Status for Animals," pp. 243–244.

47. The following is based on the series by Pat Stith and Joby Warrick, all in the *Raleigh News and Observer*: "Corporate Takeover," February 21, 1995; "Murphy's Law," February 22, 1995; "Hog-Tied on Ethics," February 23, 1995; "The Smell of Money," February 24, 1995; and "Pork Barrels," February 26, 1995; and Daniel Roth, "The Ray Kroc of Pigsties," *Forbes*, October 13, 1997. A similar, more detailed account of the Nebraska hog industry is told in Carolyn Johnsen, *Raising a Stink* (Lincoln: University of Nebraska Press, 2003).

48. "Smithfield Foods, Inc. Shareholders Approve Acquisition of Murphy Family Farms," Smithfield Foods press release, December 22, 1999. See also Johnsen, *Raising a Stink*, p. 5, on scientific production methods.

49. Stith and Warrick, "Murphy's Law."

50. Roth, "The Ray Kroc of Pigsties"; Johnsen, *Raising a Stink*, p. 15.

51. Marlene Halverson, "Farm Animal Health and Well-Being," Supp. Literature Summary and Technical Working Paper prepared for the Minnesota Planning Agency Environmental Quality Board, St. Paul, MN, June 30, 2001, pp. 150–174; Johnsen, *Raising a Stink*, p. 6.

52. Halverson, "Farm Animal Health and Well-Being," pp. 167–169.

53. Paul Thompson, "Getting Pragmatic about Farm Animal Welfare," in *Animal Pragmatism*, ed. E. McKenna and A. Light, pp. 140–155 (Bloomington: Indiana University Press, 2004); Johnsen, *Raising a Stink*, p. 6.

54. One might wish to call this failure a "misexpression" rather than a misvaluation: one values a thing appropriately but fails to express that value rationally. However, Anderson resists drawing hard lines between attitudes and behavior; valuation is not merely a feeling but a complex collection of feelings and actions. Anderson, *Value in Ethics and Economics*, pp. 11–12.

55. Harriet Ritvo, *The Animal Estate* (Cambridge, MA: Harvard University Press, 1987), pp. 93–94; Katherine Grier, *Pets in America* (Chapel Hill: University of North Carolina Press, 2006), pp. 231–242, 262–264.

56. Grier, *Pets in America*, p. 269.

57. B. Adams and J. Larson, "Animal Welfare Act Legislative History," www.nal.usda.gov/awic/pubs/AWA2007/intro.shtml (accessed July 27, 2010).

58. American Pet Products Association, "2008 Industry Statistics and Trends," americanpetproducts.org/press_industrytrends.asp (accessed December 15, 2008).

59. The API investigated sixty-four randomly selected stores in four California cities. Animal Protection Institute, "Little Shop of Sorrows" (2005), pp. 5–6, www.bornfreeusa.org/downloads/pdf/PetShops_Report.pdf (accessed January 14, 2012).

60. See, e.g., Laura Italiano, "$4.4M Puppy Mill Scandal," *New York Post*, September 22, 1996.

61. Reliable data on euthanasia rates is hard to come by, but a well-designed 2003 study of Michigan animal shelters estimates that the euthanasia rate for adoptable dogs was about 2.6 percent of the total dog population of the state, and the euthanasia rate for adoptable cats was 3.1 percent of the total cat population. In raw numbers,

56,972 dogs and 76,321 cats were euthanized by animal shelters in Michigan in 2003. P. Bartlett, A. Bartlett, S. Walshaw, S. Halstead, et al., "Rates of Euthanasia and Adoption for Dogs and Cats in Michigan Animal Shelters," *Journal of Applied Animal Welfare Science* 8, no. 2 (2005): 97–104.

62. See, e.g., Born Free USA and Animal Protection Institute, "Take Action: How You Can Help" www.api4animals.org/a5a4_action.php (accessed December 29, 2008); Humane Society of the United States, "Puppy-Buying Tips," www.stoppuppymills. org/puppy_buying_tips.html (accessed December 15, 2008); Companion Animal Protection Society, "Companion Animal Protection Society Plans Nationwide Protest," www.caps-web.org/get_article.php?id=61 (accessed December 16, 2008).

63. Born Free USA and Animal Protection Institute, "The Current State of Pet Shop Laws," www.api4animals.org/b4a1_petshoplaws_currentstate.php (accessed July 27, 2010).

64. Francione, *Animals, Property and the Law,* pp. 119, 208–249; Cass Sunstein, "A Tribute to Kenneth L. Karst: Standing for Animals (with Notes on Animal Rights)," *UCLA Law Review* 47 (2000): 1333–1368.

65. J. Reaser and M. Meyers, *Doing It Right* (Washington, DC: Pet Industry Joint Advisory Council, 2006), pp. 10–11.

66. Broad prohibitions on commerce in pet animals have occasionally been proposed. See, e.g., Maria La Ganga, "Fur and Feathers Fly as San Francisco Weighs Ban on Pet Sales," *Los Angeles Times,* July 26, 2010.

67. Petco, "Pet Adoptions," www.petco.com/petco_Page_PC_petadoptionshome_Nav_ 313.aspx (accessed July 27, 2010).

68. In 2002 Florida banned gestation crates. Arizona, Colorado, Oregon, California, and Maine have subsequently passed livestock welfare regulations, over a great deal of industry opposition. HSUS, "Maine Becomes Sixth State to Ban Extreme Confinement," May 13, 2009, www.humanesociety.org/news/news/2009/05/maine_ veal_gestation_crates_051309.html.

69. Alexei Barrionuevo, "Pork Producer Says It Plans to Give Pigs More Room," *New York Times,* January 26, 2007.

70. "The Petersons Talk about Pasturelands Pigs," www.awionline.org/www.awionline. org/farm/peterson.htm (accessed July 27, 2010).

71. Anderson, *Values in Ethics and Economics,* p. 172.

72. On the other hand, the same respect for pluralism should lead to the state to recognize the special status of pets as family members in tort and family law.

73. Anderson, *Value in Ethics and Economics,* p. 141.

74. Grier, *Pets in America,* p. 317.

75. Reaser and Meyers, "Doing It Right," pp. 6, 10, 11, 14; Petco, "Company Info," www. petco.com/Content/Content.aspx?PC=companyinfo&;Nav=142 (accessed December 29, 2008).

76. Johnsen, *Raising a Stink,* p. 7.

77. Deborah Rudacille, *The Scalpel and the Butterfly* (New York: Farrar, Straus and Giroux, 2000), pp. 306–313.

CHAPTER 4

1. Joanna Macy, "Welcome to All Beings," www.joannamacy.net/aboutjoannamacy. html (accessed July 27, 2010).

2. Joanna Macy and Molly Young Brown, *Coming Back to Life* (Gabriola Island, BC: New Society, 1998), pp. 163–164; Joanna Macy, "The Council of All Beings," in *The Encyclopedia of Religion and Nature*, ed. Bron Taylor (Bristol: Thoemmes Continuum, 2005), pp. 427–428.

3. Elizabeth Bragg, *Manual for the Council of All Beings*, www.rainforestinfo.org.au/ deep-eco/cabcab.htm (accessed September 2, 2010).

4. Macy, "The Council of All Beings," pp. 425, 427.

5. David Schlosberg, *Defining Environmental Justice* (Oxford: Oxford University Press, 2007), p. 195; personal communication, July 2, 2010.

6. Alice Walker, *The Temple of My Familiar* (New York: Harcourt Brace Jovanovich, 1989), p. 199.

7. 2004 PETA Proggy Awards, www.peta.org/feat/proggy/2004/winners.html#visionary (accessed June 30, 2010).

8. Temple Grandin and Catherine Johnson, *Animals in Translation* (New York: Scribner, 2005), pp. 51–52; Temple Grandin, *Thinking in Pictures* (New York: Doubleday, 1995), pp. 159–160; quote on 172.

9. Grandin, *Thinking in Pictures*, pp. 143–144.

10. Hannah Pitkin, *The Concept of Representation* (Berkeley: University of California Press, 1967), pp. 8–9.

11. Robyn Eckersley, *The Green State* (Cambridge, MA: MIT Press, 2004), pp. 111–120. See also Michael Saward, "Representation," in *Political Theory and the Ecological Challenge*, ed. Andrew Dobson and Robyn Eckersley (Cambridge: Cambridge University Press, 2006); Schlosberg, *Defining Environmental Justice*, pp. 193–195; Andrew Dobson, "Representative Democracy and the Environment," in *Democracy and the Environment*, ed. William Lafferty and James Meadowcroft (Cheltenham, UK: Edward Elgar, 1996), pp. 124–137; John Dryzek, *Deliberative Democracy and Beyond* (Oxford: Oxford University Press, 2000), pp. 152–154; Mike Mills, "Green Democracy," in *Democracy and Green Political Thought*, ed. Brian Doherty and Marius de Geus (London: Routledge, 1996), pp. 102–110.

12. Marlene Halverson, "Farm Animal Health and Well-Being," Supp. Literature Summary and Technical Working Paper prepared for the Minnesota Planning Agency Environmental Quality Board, St. Paul, MN, June 30, 2001, p. 14 (summarizing the literature).

13. Eckersley, *The Green State*, pp. 125, 131–132; Mills, "Green Democracy," p. 110; Rosemary Rodd, *Biology, Ethics and Animals* (Oxford: Clarendon Press, 1990), pp. 102–103; Martha Nussbaum, *Frontiers of Justice* (Cambridge, MA: Belknap Press, 2006), pp. 354–355.

14. Pitkin, *The Concept of Representation*, pp. 209, 211.

15. Ibid., pp. 231–232.

16. Ibid., pp. 112–143, 168–189.

17. Madison, "Federalist #10," in *The Federalist Papers*, ed. Isaac Kramnick [1788] (New York: Penguin Classics, 1987), pp. 126–127.

18. Michael Saward, "The Representative Claim," *Contemporary Political Theory* 5, no. 3 (2006): 301, 313. The following argument is also substantially informed by Nancy Schwartz, *The Blue Guitar* (Chicago: University of Chicago Press, 1988).

19. Jennifer Rubenstein, "The Ethics of NGO Advocacy," paper presented at the APSA Annual Meeting, Boston, MA, August 2008, p. 15. See also Clarissa Riel Hayward, "Making Interest: On Representation and Democratic Legitimacy," in *Political Representation*, ed. Ian Shapiro, Susan Stokes, Elisabeth Jean Woods, and Alexander Kirshner (Cambridge: Cambridge University Press, 2009), pp. 111–135.

20. Saward, "The Representative Claim," p. 303.

21. See the discussion of Alice Walker's essay on a Balinese chicken, below.

22. Personal communication, July 1, 2010.

23. Bylaws, www.charlottelaws.org/DAW percent20Bylaws.htm (accessed September 2, 2010).

24. Party for the Animals website, www.partyfortheanimals.info/content/view/300 (accessed July 23, 2010).

25. Party for the Animals Manifesto, www.partyfortheanimals.info/content/view/303 (accessed July 23, 2010).

26. Party for Animals website, www.partyfortheanimals.nl/content/view/321 (accessed July 23, 2010).

27. Animals Count website, www.animalscount.org/about/ (accessed September 2, 2010).

28. Vote4animals website, www.vote4animals.org.uk/intro.htm (accessed September 2, 2010).

29. Humane Party website, www.humaneparty.org/five-things-that-make-us-unique.htm (accessed July 8, 2010); Alix Kroger, "Dutch Raise Animal Rights to New Level," BBC News, December 4, 2006, news.bbc.co.uk/2/hi/europe/6198676.stm.

30. Mike Mills, "Green Democracy," pp. 109–110.

31. Jane Mansbridge, "Rethinking Representation," *American Political Science Review* 9 (November 2003): 522.

32. Dobson, "Representative Democracy and the Environment," pp. 132–133.

33. Jennifer Rubenstein, "Accountability in an Unequal World," *Journal of Politics* 69 (August 2007): 616–632.

34. Mansbridge, "Rethinking Representation," p. 520.

35. Personal communication, July 1, 2010.

36. Yates, "Animal Rights Activists Get Official Roles in City and County Dog Law Enforcement," *Whole Dog News*, September 25, 2008, http://thewholedog.org/wholedognews/?p=151.

37. Andrew Rehfeld, "Toward a General Theory of Political Representation," *Journal of Politics* 68 (February 2006): 5.

38. Ibid., pp. 6–7.

39. Rubenstein, "The Ethics of NGO Advocacy," pp. 16–23.

40. Personal communication, July 1, 2010.

41. Ibid.

42. Saward, "The Representative Claim," p. 302.

43. Leo Hickman, "The Lawyer Who Defends Animals," *Guardian*, March 5, 2010; Deborah Ball, "Scales of Justice," *Wall Street Journal*, March 6, 2010; "Swiss TV: Voters Reject Legal Representation for Animals." *USA Today*, March 7, 2010.

44. Ball, "Scales of Justice."

45. Antonin Scalia, "The Doctrine of Standing as an Essential Element of the Separation of Powers," *Suffolk University Law Review* 17 (1983): 892–893.

46. *Sierra Club v. Morton*, 405 US 727 (1972) (Douglas, dissenting); Cass Sunstein, "A Tribute to Kenneth L. Karst: Standing for Animals," *UCLA Law Review* 47 (June 2000): 1360–1361.

47. Katherine Burke, "Can We Stand for It?: Amending the Endangered Species Act with an Animal-Suit Provision," *University of Colorado Law Review* 75 (Spring 2004): 633–666.

48. Alice Walker, "Am I Blue?" in *Living by the Word* (New York: Harcourt Brace Jovanovich, 1988), pp. 3–8.

49. Ibid., p. 7.

50. Ibid.

51. Aristotle, *The Politics*, trans. Carnes Lord (Chicago: University of Chicago Press, 1984), book 5, chap. 11.

52. "Why Did the Balinese Chicken Cross the Road?" in *Living by the Word*, p. 170.

CHAPTER 5

1. "10 Questions for Ray Kurzweil," *Time*, December 6, 2010, p. 8.

2. *Merced v. Kasson*, 577 F.3d 578 (5th Cir., 2009), p. 582.

3. Ibid., pp. 582–583.

4. Euless Ord. sec. 10-3, sec. 10-68.

5. David O'Brien, *Animal Sacrifice and Religious Freedom: Church of the Lukumi Babalu Aye v. City of Hialeah* (Lawrence: University Press of Kansas, 2004), p. 35.

6. Ibid., p. 41.

7. Ibid., pp. 46–47; *Church of the Lukumi Babalu Aye v. City of Hialeah*, 508 US 520 (1993). Specifically, the city enacted Ordinance 87-52, which defined "sacrifice" as "to unnecessarily kill, torment, torture, or mutilate an animal in a public or private ritual or ceremony not for the primary purpose of food consumption" and prohibited possession of an animal for this purpose. But it restricted application of this prohibition to "ritual" killings and exempted licensed slaughterhouses. The city also adopted Ordinance 87-71, which provided that "it shall be unlawful for any person, persons, corporations or associations to sacrifice any animal within the corporate limits of the City of Hialeah, Florida."

8. O'Brien, *Animal Sacrifice and Religious Freedom*, pp. 83–84.

9. Ibid., pp. 92–93.

10. *Church of the Lukumi Babalu Aye v. City of Hialeah*, 723 F.Supp 1467, pp. 1472–1473, 1486 (SD Fla 1989).

11. O'Brien, *Animal Sacrifice and Religious Freedom*, pp. 101–102.

12. *Church of the Lukumi Babalu Aye*, 508 US 520, pp. 546–547 (1993).

13. Merced also challenged the law under the federal Religious Land Use and Institutionalized Persons Act, RLUIPA 42 USC 2000cc(a)(1). That challenge was dismissed because the ordinance in question was not a land use regulation. *Merced v. Euless*, 2008 US Dist. LEXIS 3685 (ND Tex, 2008).

14. These cases involve religious freedom, which some scholars believe has a special constitutional significance; they might treat religious diversity differently from cultural diversities not rooted in religious belief. However, I think the distinction between religious belief and other kinds of values and cultural perspectives is too problematic to rely on, so the following analysis doesn't give religious belief special status.

15. Claire Jean Kim, "Slaying the Beast: Notes on the Intersections of Race, Culture, and Species," paper delivered at the APSA Annual Meeting, Washington, DC, September 2–5, 2010, p. 2.

16. O'Brien, *Animal Sacrifice and Religious Freedom*, pp. 21–22.

17. Ibid., pp. 19–20.

18. Kim, *Slaying the Beast*.

19. Will Kymlicka, *Multicultural Citizenship* (Oxford: Clarendon Press, 1995), pp. 81, 89.

20. Ibid., pp. 102–103.

21. Brian Barry, *Culture and Equality* (Cambridge, MA: Harvard University Press, 2001).

22. Macedo, "The Perils of Diversity," *American Prospect* (December 30, 2002), p. 36.

23. Barry, *Culture and Equality*, pp. 41–42, 47.

24. William Galston, *The Practice of Liberal Pluralism* (Cambridge: Cambridge University Press, 2005), p. 3.

25. Kymlicka, *Multicultural Citizenship*, pp. 152, 167–168.

26. Galston, *The Practice of Liberal Pluralism*, p. 189.

27. 7 USCA. § 1902.

28. Barry, *Culture and Equality*, pp. 41–44; Peter Singer, *Animal Liberation* (New York: HarperCollins, 2002), pp. 150–154.

29. Galston, *The Practice of Liberal Pluralism*, p. 4.

30. Mercedes Sandoval, *Worldview, the Orichas, and Santeria* (Gainesville: University Press of Florida, 2006), p. 113.

31. Joseph Murphy, *Santeria: An African Religion in America* (Boston: Beacon Press, 1988), p. 44; Professor Thabiti Willis, Carleton College, personal communication, January 19, 2011.

32. O'Brien, *Animal Sacrifice*, p. 150.

33. Dogfighting is illegal in forty-eight states, and it is a federal crime to transport dogs across state lines for this purpose. Vick also faced state felony dogfighting charges, to which he eventually pled guilty.

34. George Dohrmann, "The House on Moonlight Road," *Sports Illustrated*, June 4, 2007. Wayne Pacelle discusses the Humane Society's role in the case in *The Bond* (New York: HarperCollins, 2011), pp. 135–176.

35. www.peta.org/b/thepetafiles/archive/2007/10/03/Vick-at-the-Office-Part-2.aspx (accessed January 21, 2012).

36. Kim, "Slaying the Beast," p. 13.

37. Steve Gorman, "Whoopi Goldberg Defends Vick's Dog-Fighting Role," Reuters, September 5, 2007.

38. "PETA Says Vick Took, Passed Course on Preventing Animal Cruelty," www.alop.org/2008/04/peta-says-vick-took-passed-course-on-preventing-animal-cruelty/ (accessed January 20, 2011).

39. Kim, "Slaying the Beast," p. 15, quoting Dyson's remarks on NPR's *Tell Me More*.

40. "Vick Case Divides African-American Leaders," August 23, 2007, www.msnbc.msn.com (accessed January 20, 2011).

41. Loïc Wacquant, *Punishing the Poor* (Durham, NC: Duke University Press, 2009), pp. 60, 113, 119; Michael Tonry and David Farrington, "Punishment and Crime across Space and Time," *Crime and Justice* 33 (2005): 1.

42. Wacquant, *Punishing the Poor*, p. 61; Marc Mauer and Ryan S. King, *Uneven Justice: State Rates of Incarceration by Race and Ethnicity* (Washington, DC: The Sentencing Project, July 2007), p. 4.

43. Mary Patillo, David Weiman, and Bruce Western, introduction to *Imprisoning America: The Social Effects of Mass Incarceration*, ed. Mary Pattillo, David Weiman, and Bruce Western (New York: Russell Sage Foundation, 2004), pp. 1, 5–7; Wacquant, *Punishing the Poor*, pp. 51, 61, 197.

44. Michelle Alexander, *The New Jim Crow* (New York: New Press, 2010), p. 99.

45. Ibid., p. 4.

46. Ibid., p. 92; Wacquant, *Punishing the Poor*, p. 125. Hispanics are also disproportionately incarcerated. Marc Mauer and Ryan S. King report that "in 2005, Hispanics comprised 20 percent of the state and federal prison population, a rise of 43 percent since 1990. As a result of these trends, one of every six Hispanic males and one of every 45 Hispanic females born today can expect to go to prison in his or her lifetime." *Uneven Justice*, p. 3.

47. Anthony Doob and Cheryl Marie Webster, "Sentencing Severity and Crime: Accepting the Null Hypothesis," *Crime and Justice* 30 (2003): 143; Michael Jacobson, *Downsizing Prisons* (New York: New York University Press, 2005), pp. 109–111.

48. Alexander, *The New Jim Crow*, pp. 83–86.

49. Ibid., p. 92; Jacobson, *Downsizing Prisons*, pp. 131–172.

50. Patillo, Weiman, and Western, *Imprisoning America*, pp. 4–5; James Lynch and William Sabol, "Effects of Incarceration on Informal Social Control in Communities," in ibid, pp. 135–164. Lynch and Sabol make it clear that the effects of mass incarceration on a neighborhood are complex. Their study suggests that increases in incarceration can reduce crime at least temporarily by removing offenders from the vicinity, but they do not necessarily enhance community organization or promote informal social control.

51. They may also believe it is an effective fund-raising tool, offering a specific, well-defined goal that's easy to explain to potential donors. That would not, however, justify adopting an ill-conceived and racially divisive legislative agenda.

52. Orlando Patterson, *Rituals of Blood* (Washington, DC: Counterpoint, 1998), p. 191.

53. Alice Walker, *In Search of Our Mothers' Gardens* (New York: Harcourt, 1983), p. 26.

54. PETA has stated publicly that it does not believe Vick can be rehabilitated. The Humane Society, however, is more optimistic and is cooperating with Vick on an anti-dogfighting campaign targeting urban areas. Lindsay Barnett, "Is Michael Vick in Talks to be PETA's Spokesman?" LA Times blog *LA Unleashed*, May 1, 2009, http://latimesblogs.latimes.com/unleashed/2009/05/peta-denies-michael-vick-in-talks-to-be-spokesman.html; Lindsay Barnett, "Michael Vick to Work with the Humane Society on Its Campaign against Dogfighting," LA Times blog *LA Unleashed*, May 20, 2009, http://latimesblogs.latimes.com/unleashed/2009/05/michael-vick-to-work-with-humane-society.html; Pacelle, *The Bond*, pp. 135–176.

55. Keith Guzik, "Abusers' Narratives Following Arrest and Prosecution for Domestic Violence," in *Violence against Women in Families and Relationships*, vol. 1, ed. Evan Stark and Eve Buzawa (Santa Barbara: Praeger, 2009).

56. Michael Rempel, "Batterer Programs and Beyond," in Stark and Buzawa, *Violence against Women in Families and Relationships*, vol. 1.

57. See David Anderson, *Sensible Justice: Alternatives to Prison* (New York: New Press, 1988), for a discussion of other prison alternatives.

58. See Sue Ellen Brown, "The Under-representation of African American Employees in Animal Welfare Organizations in the United States," *Society and Animals* 13, no. 2 (2005): 153–162.

59. Susan Pearson, "'The Rights of the Defenseless': Animals, Children, and Sentimental Liberalism in Nineteenth-Century America" (PhD diss., University of North Carolina, 2004), pp. 1–5.

60. Bernard Unti, "Cruelty Indivisible," in *The International Handbook of Animal Abuse and Cruelty*, ed. Frank Ascione (West Lafayette, IN: Purdue University Press, 2008), pp. 10–11.

61. Pearson, *Rights of the Defenseless*, p. 144.

62. Frank Ascione, Claudia Weber, and David Wood, "Animal Welfare and Domestic Violence," report submitted to the Geraldine R. Dodge Foundation, April 25, 1997.

63. Humane Society of the United States Animal Sheltering website, www.animalsheltering.org/programs_and_services/first_strike/ (accessed December 15, 2010).

64. Claire Renzetti, "Intimate Partner Violence and Economic Disadvantage," in *Violence against Women in Families and Relationships*, vol. 3, ed. Evan Stark and Eve Buzawa (Santa Barbara: Praeger 2009), pp. 85–87.

65. Geoffrey Becker, "USDA Meat Inspection and the Humane Methods of Slaughter Act," Congressional Research Service, February 26, 2008.

CONCLUSION

1. Robert Ball, Charles Lehner, and Erich Parker, "Predicting Risk of Decompression Sickness in Humans from Outcomes in Sheep," *Journal of Applied Physiology* 86 (1999): 1920–1929.

2. Wisconsin Statute sec. 951.025.

3. Letter from Dane County District Attorney Brian Blanchard to Attorney Ben Griffiths, University of Wisconsin, October 2, 2009, www.allanimals.org/files/ UW_sheep_reply.pdf; Bill Lueders, "The Decompression of Sheep," *Isthmus,* August 27, 2009; Deborah Ziff, "No Fines for Sheep Deaths at UW-Madison," October 8, 2009, host.madison.com; Bill Lueders, "US Responds to Dane County DA on Sheep Decompression Experiments," *Isthmus*, September 24, 2009.

4. The animal rights groups haven't given up, however. PETA and the Alliance for Animals petitioned a Wisconsin court to see that the law was enforced, which resulted in appointment of a special prosecutor investigating whether criminal charges should be brought. Valerie Strauss, "Sheep Deaths in University Research Lead to Probe," *Washington Post*, June 3, 2010.

5. Bill Lueders, "The Decompression of Sheep," *Isthmus*, August 27, 2009.

6. *Institutional Animal Care and Use Guidebook,* 2nd ed., ed. Marky Pitts et al. (Bethesda, MD: Applied Research Ethics National Association, 2002), pp. 5–8.

7. Deborah Rudacille, *The Scalpel and the Butterfly* (New York: Farrar, Straus and Giroux, 2000), pp. 129–133.

8. Ibid., pp. 294–296, 301–313.

9. Joseph Raz, *The Morality of Freedom* (Oxford: Clarendon, 1988), pp. 246, 256.

10. Robyn Eckersley, *The Green State* (Cambridge, MA: MIT Press, 2004); David Schlosberg, *Defining Environmental Justice* (Oxford: Oxford University Press, 2007).

Selected Bibliography

CASES

Animal Lovers Volunteer Association (ALVA) v. Weinberger, 765 F.2d. 937 (9th Cir. 1985).
Broadway etc. Stage Co. v. ASPCA, 15 Abbot 51 (New York 1873).
CEASE v. New England Aquarium, 836 F.Supp. 45 (D. Mass. 1993).
Church of the Lukumi Babalu Aye v. City of Hialeah, 508 U.S. 520 (1993).
Hawaiian Crow v. Lujan. 906 F.Supp. 549 (D. Haw. 1991).
Merced v. Euless, 2008 U.S. Dist. LEXIS 3685 (ND Tex., 2008).
Merced v. Kasson, 577 F.3d 578 (5th Cir., 2009).
Rabideau v. City of Racine, 243 Wis. 2d 486 (2001).
Rupert v. United States, 181 F. 87 (8th Cir., 1910).
Sentell v. New Orleans and Carrollton Railroad Co, 166 US 698 (1897).
Sierra Club v. Morton, 405 US 727 (1972).
Smith v. Avanzino, No. 225698 (Cal. Super. Ct., San Francisco Cty., June 17, 1980).

STATUTES

Animal Welfare Act, 7 USC sec. 2131(b) (1966)
Endangered Species Act, 16 USCA 1531(a)(3) (1973)
Humane Methods of Livestock Slaughter Act, 7 USC sec. 1901 (1958)

BOOKS AND ARTICLES

Alexander, Michelle. *The New Jim Crow*. New York: New Press, 2010.
Anderson, David. *Sensible Justice: Alternatives to Prison*. New York: New Press, 1988.
Anderson, Elizabeth. *Value in Ethics and Economics*. Cambridge, MA: Harvard University Press, 1993.
Anderson, Virginia. *Creatures of Empire*. Oxford: Oxford University Press, 2004.

Andrews, Richard. *Managing the Environment, Managing Ourselves.* New Haven, CT: Yale University Press, 1999.

Aristotle. *The Politics.* Trans. Carnes Lord. Chicago: University of Chicago Press, 1984.

Armstrong, Susan, and Richard Botzler, eds. *The Animal Ethics Reader.* London: Routledge, 2003.

Arnold, James. *Jeff Davis' Own: Cavalry, Comanches and the Battle for the Texas Frontier.* New York: John Wiley & Sons, 2000.

Ascione, Frank, ed. *International Handbook of Animal Abuse and Cruelty.* West Lafayette, IN: Purdue University Press, 2008.

Barry, Brian. *Culture and Equality.* Cambridge, MA: Harvard University Press, 2001.

Bartlett, P., A. Bartlett, S. Walshaw, S. Halstead, et al. "Rates of Euthanasia and Adoption for Dogs and Cats in Michigan Animal Shelters." *Journal of Applied Animal Welfare Science* 8, no. 2 (2005): 97–104.

Berman, Paul S. "Rate, Pigs, and Statues on Trial: The Creation of Cultural Narratives in the Prosecution of Animals and Inanimate Objects." *New York University Law Review* 69 (May 1994): 288–326.

Berry, Wendell. *The Gift of Good Land.* San Francisco: North Point Press, 1981.

Beyer, Gerry. "Pet Animals: What Happens When Their Humans Die?" *Santa Clara Law Review* 40 (2000): 617–676.

Bidwell, Percy, and John Falconer. *History of Agriculture in the Northern United States, 1620–1860.* Washington: Carnegie Institution, 1925.

Biernes, Piers. "The Law Is an Ass." *Society and Animals* 2, no. 1 (1994): 27–46.

Blackstone. *Commentaries on the Laws of England* [1765–1769]. Chicago: University of Chicago Press, 1979.

Blassingame, John. *The Slave Community.* 2nd ed. Oxford: Oxford University Press, 1979.

Brinkley, Douglas. *The Great Deluge.* New York: HarperCollins, 2006.

Brown, Sue Ellen. "The Under-representation of African American Employees in Animal Welfare Organizations in the United States." *Society and Animals* 13, no. 2 (2005): 153–162.

Bulcroft, K. "Pets in the American Family." *People, Animals, Environment* 8, no. 4 (1990): 13–14.

Burke, Katherine. "Can We Stand for It?: Amending the Endangered Species Act with an Animal-Suit Provision." *University of Colorado Law Review* 75 (Spring 2004): 633–666.

Callicott, J. Baird, ed. *Companion to "A Sand County Almanac."* Madison: University of Wisconsin Press, 1987.

Carter, Alan. *The Philosophical Foundations of Property Rights.* New York: Harvester Wheatsheaf, 1989.

Cavalieri, Paolo, and Peter Singer, eds. *The Great Ape Project.* New York: St. Martin's Griffin, 1993.

Cochrane, Willard. *The Development of American Agriculture.* Minneapolis: University of Minnesota Press, 1979.

Cohen, Esther. "Law, Folklore and Animal Lore." *Past and Present* 110 (1986): 6–37.

Cronon, William. *Changes in the Land*. New York: Hill & Wang, 1983.

De Crèvecoeur, Hector St. John. *Letters from an American Farmer* [1782]. New York: Penguin Classics, 1986.

Dobson, Andrew, and Robyn Eckersley. *Political Theory and the Ecological Challenge*. Cambridge: Cambridge University Press, 2006.

Doherty, Brian, and Marius de Geus, eds. *Democracy and Green Political Thought*. London: Routledge, 1996.

Doob, Anthony, and Cheryl Marie Webster. "Sentencing Severity and Crime: Accepting the Null Hypothesis." *Crime and Justice* 30 (2003): 143–195.

Dryzek, John. *Deliberative Democracy and Beyond*. Oxford: Oxford University Press, 2000.

Dunn, Walter. *Frontier Profit and Loss*. Westport, CT: Greenwood, 1998.

Eckersley, Robyn. *The Green State*. Cambridge, MA: MIT Press, 2004.

Elliot, Robert. "Rawlsian Justice and Non-Human Animals." *Journal of Applied Philosophy* 1, no. 1 (1984): 95–106.

Evans, E. P. *The Criminal Prosecution and Capital Punishment of Animals*. New York: Dutton, 1906.

Ferry, Luc. *The New Ecological Order*. Trans. Carol Volk. Chicago: University of Chicago Press, 1992.

Finkelstein, J. J. "The Ox That Gored." *Transactions of the American Philosophical Society* 71, no. 2 (1981): 1–89.

Fischer, David Hackett. *Albion's Seed*. New York: Oxford University Press, 1989.

Francione, Gary. *Animals, Property, and the Law*. Philadelphia: Temple University Press, 1995.

Frey, R. G. "Rights, Interests, Desires and Beliefs." *American Philosophical Quarterly* 16, no. 3 (1979): 233–239.

Freyfogle, Eric. *Agrarianism and the Good Society*. Lexington: University Press of Kentucky, 2007.

Galston, William. *The Practice of Liberal Pluralism*. Cambridge: Cambridge University Press, 2005.

Garner, Robert. *The Political Theory of Animal Rights*. Manchester, UK: Manchester University Press, 2005.

Grandin, Temple. *Thinking in Pictures*. New York: Doubleday, 1995.

Grandin, Temple, and Catherine Johnson. *Animals in Translation*. New York: Scribner, 2005.

Grier, Katherine. *Pets in America*. Chapel Hill: University of North Carolina Press, 2006.

Gross, Ariel. *Double Character*. Princeton, NJ: Princeton University Press, 2000.

Guinier, Lani, and Gerald Torres. *The Miner's Canary*. Cambridge, MA: Harvard University Press, 2002.

Halverson, Marlene. "Farm Animal Health and Well-Being." Supp. Literature Summary and Technical Working Paper prepared for the Minnesota Planning Agency Environmental Quality Board, St. Paul, MN, June 30, 2001.

Handlin, Oscar, and Mary Handlin. *Commonwealth*. Rev. ed. Cambridge, MA: Belknap Press of Harvard University Press, 1969.

Hargrove, Eugene, ed. *The Animal Rights/Environmental Ethics Debate*. Albany: SUNY Press, 1992.

Hartz, Louis. *The Liberal Tradition in America*. New York: Harcourt, Brace, 1955.

Hearne, Vicki. *Animal Happiness*. New York: HarperCollins, 1994.

Herzog, Don. *Without Foundations*. Ithaca, NY: Cornell University Press, 1985.

Hulliung, Mark. *The Social Contract in America*. Lawrence: University Press of Kansas, 2008.

Hume, David. *An Enquiry Concerning the Principles of Morals*. Ed. Tom Beauchamp. Oxford: Clarendon Press, 1998.

Hyde, Walter Woodburn. "The Prosecution and Punishment of Animals and Lifeless Things in the Middle Ages and Modern Times." *University of Pennsylvania Law Review and American Law Register* 64 (May 1916): 696–730.

Isenberg, Andrew. *The Destruction of the Bison*. Cambridge: Cambridge University Press, 2000.

Jacobson, Michael. *Downsizing Prisons*. New York: New York University Press, 2005.

Jamieson, Dale. *Morality's Progress*. Oxford: Clarendon Press, 2002.

Jasper, James, and Dorothy Nelkin. *The Animal Rights Crusade*. New York: Free Press, 1992.

Johnsen, Carolyn. *Raising a Stink*. Lincoln: University of Nebraska Press, 2003.

Jordan, Terry. *North American Cattle-Ranching Frontiers*. Albuquerque: University of New Mexico Press, 1993.

Joyner, Charles. *Shared Traditions*. Urbana: University of Illinois Press, 1999.

Kant, Immanuel. *Lectures on Ethics*. Trans. P. Heath and J. B. Schneewind. Cambridge: Cambridge University Press, 1997.

Kete, Kathleen. *The Beast in the Boudoir*. Berkeley: University of California Press, 1994.

Kheel, Marti. *Nature Ethics*. New York: Rowman and Littlefield, 2008.

Kim, Claire Jean. "Slaying the Beast: Notes on the Intersections of Race, Culture, and Species." Paper delivered at the APSA Annual Meeting, Washington, DC, September 2–5, 2010.

Kymlicka, Will. *Multicultural Citizenship*. Oxford: Clarendon Press, 1995.

Lafferty, William, and James Meadowcroft, eds. *Democracy and the Environment*. Cheltenham, UK: Edward Elgar, 1996.

Larrère, Catherine, and Raphaël Larrère. "Animal Rearing as a Contract?" *Journal of Agricultural and Environmental Ethics* 12, no. 1 (2000): 51–58.

Leopold, Aldo. *A Sand County Almanac with Essays on Conservation from Round River*. New York: Ballantine, 1966.

Lévi-Strauss, Claude. *Totemism*. Trans. Rodney Needham. Boston: Beacon Press, 1963.

Locke, John. *An Essay Concerning Human Understanding* [1690]. Ed. Roger Woolhouse. New York: Penguin, 1997.

———. *Letter Concerning Toleration* [1689]. Indianapolis: Hackett, 1983.

———. *Two Treatises of Government* [1690]. New York: Hafner, 1947.

Macedo, Stephen. "The Perils of Diversity." *American Prospect*, December 30, 2002, 36.

MacIntyre, Alisdair. *Dependent Rational Animals.* Chicago: Open Court, 1999.

Mansbridge, Jane. "Rethinking Representation." *American Political Science Review* 9 (November 2003): 515–528.

Marks, Stuart. *Southern Hunting in Black and White.* Princeton, NJ: Princeton University Press, 1991.

Mauer, Marc, and Ryan S. King. *Uneven Justice: State Rates of Incarceration by Race and Ethnicity.* Washington, DC: The Sentencing Project, July 2007.

McClelland, Peter. *Sowing Modernity.* Ithaca, NY: Cornell University Press, 1997.

McKenna, E., and Andrew Light, eds. *Animal Pragmatism.* Bloomington: Indiana University Press, 2004.

McShane, Clay. "Gelded Age Boston." *New England Quarterly* 74 (June 2001): 274–302.

Meine, Curt. *Aldo Leopold: His Life and Work.* Madison: University of Wisconsin Press, 1988.

Merton, Robert K. *Social Theory and Social Structure.* Glencoe: Free Press, 1957.

Midgley, Mary. *Animals and Why They Matter.* Athens: University of Georgia Press, 1983.

Mills, Charles. *The Racial Contract.* Ithaca, NY: Cornell University Press, 1997.

Murphy, Joseph. *Santeria: An African Religion in America.* Boston: Beacon Press, 1988.

Nash, Roderick. *The Rights of Nature.* Madison: University of Wisconsin Press, 1989.

Novak, William. *The People's Welfare.* Chapel Hill: University of North Carolina Press, 1996.

Novkov, Julie. *Constituting Workers, Protecting Women.* Ann Arbor: University of Michigan Press, 2001.

Nussbaum, Martha. *Frontiers of Justice.* Cambridge, MA: Belknap Press, 2006.

———. *Women and Human Development.* Cambridge: Cambridge University Press, 2000.

O'Brien, David. *Animal Sacrifice and Religious Freedom: Church of the Lukumi Babalu Aye v. City of Hialeah.* Lawrence: University Press of Kansas, 2004.

Okin, Susan. *Justice, Gender, and the Family.* New York: Basic Books, 1989.

Otto, John. *Southern Agriculture during the Civil War Era, 1860–1880.* Westport, CT: Greenwood Press, 1994.

Pacelle, Wayne. *The Bond.* New York: HarperCollins, 2011.

Palmer, Clare. "The Idea of the Domesticated Animal Contract." *Environmental Values* 6, no. 4 (1997): 411–425.

———. *Animals in Context.* New York: Columbia University Press, 2010.

Pateman, Carole. *The Sexual Contract.* Stanford: Stanford University Press, 1988.

Patillo, Mary, David Weiman, and Bruce Western. *Imprisoning America: The Social Effects of Mass Incarceration.* New York: Russell Sage Foundation, 2004.

Patterson, Orlando. *Rituals of Blood.* Washington, DC: Counterpoint, 1998.

Pearson, Susan. "'The Rights of the Defenseless': Animals, Children, and Sentimental Liberalism in Nineteenth-Century America." PhD diss., University of North Carolina, 2004.

Pettit, Philip. *Republicanism*. Oxford: Clarendon Press, 1997.

Pew Commission on Industrial Farm Animal Production. *Putting Meat on the Table: Industrial Farm Animal Production in America*. N.p.: Pew Commission, 2008.

Pfeffer, Rodney. "A Defense of Rights to Well-Being." *Philosophy and Public Affairs* 8, no. 1 (1978): 65–87.

Pitkin, Hannah. *The Concept of Representation*. Berkeley: University of California Press, 1967.

Pollan, Michael. *The Omnivore's Dilemma*. New York: Penguin, 2006.

Pritchard, Michael, and Wade Robison. "Justice and the Treatment of Animals: A Critique of Rawls." *Environmental Ethics* 3 (Spring 1981): 55–61.

Quilley, Stephen. "The Land Ethic as an Ecological Civilizing Process: Aldo Leopold, Norbert Elias, and Environmental Philosophy." *Environmental Ethics* 31 (Summer 2009): 115–134.

Rawls, John. *Political Liberalism*. Exp. ed. New York: Columbia University Press, 2005.

———. *A Theory of Justice*. Rev. ed. Cambridge, MA: Harvard University Press, 1999.

Raz, Joseph. *The Morality of Freedom*. Oxford: Clarendon Press, 1986.

Regan, Tom. *The Case for Animal Rights*. Berkeley: University of California Press, 1983.

Rehfeld, Andrew. "Toward a General Theory of Political Representation." *Journal of Politics* 68 (February 2006): 1–21.

Ritvo, Harriet. *The Animal Estate*. Cambridge, MA: Harvard University Press, 1987.

Rodd, Rosemary. *Biology, Ethics and Animal*. Oxford: Clarendon Press, 1990.

Root, William. "'Man's Best Friend': Property or Family Member?" *Villanova Law Review* 47, no. 2 (2002): 423–450.

Rousseau, Jean-Jacques. *The First and Second Discourses, Together with the Replies to Critics and Essay on the Origin of Languages*. Ed. Victor Gourevitch. New York: Harper and Row, 1986.

Rubenstein, Jennifer. "The Ethics of NGO Advocacy." Paper presented at the APSA Annual Meeting, Boston, MA, August 2008.

———. "Accountability in an Unequal World." *Journal of Politics* 69 (August 2007): 616–632.

Rudacille, Deborah. *The Scalpel and the Butterfly*. New York: Farrar, Straus and Giroux, 2000.

Ryan, Alan. *Property and Political Theory*. Oxford: Basil Blackwell, 1984.

Sandoval, Mercedes. *Worldview, the Orichas, and Santeria*. Gainesville: University Press of Florida, 2006.

Saward, Michael. "The Representative Claim." *Contemporary Political Theory* 5, no. 3 (2006): 297–318.

Scalia, Antonin. "The Doctrine of Standing as an Essential Element of the Separation of Powers." *Suffolk University Law Review* 17 (1983): 892–893.

Scanlon, T. M. *What We Owe to Each Other*. Cambridge, MA: Belknap Press of Harvard University Press, 1998.

Schlosberg, David. *Defining Environmental Justice*. Oxford: Oxford University Press, 2007.

Schwartz, Nancy. *The Blue Guitar.* Chicago: University of Chicago Press, 1988.

Shapiro, Ian, Susan Stokes, Elisabeth Jean Woods, and Alexander Kirshner, eds. *Political Representation.* Cambridge: Cambridge University Press, 2009.

Shepard, Paul. *The Others: How Animals Made Us Human.* Washington, DC: Island, 1996.

Singer, Brent. "An Extension of Rawls' Theory of Justice to Environmental Ethics." *Environmental Ethics* 10 (Fall 1988): 217–231.

Singer, Peter, ed. *In Defense of Animals: The Second Wave.* Malden: Blackwell, 2006.

———. *The Expanding Circle.* New York: Farrar, Straus and Giroux, 1981.

———. *Animal Liberation* [1975]. New York: HarperCollins, 2002.

Skocpol, Theda. *Protecting Soldiers and Mothers.* Cambridge, MA: Belknap Press of Harvard University Press, 1992.

Skowronek, Stephen. *Building a New American State.* Cambridge: Cambridge University Press, 1983.

Stark, Evan, and Eve Buzawa, eds. *Violence against Women in Families and Relationships.* 4 vols. Santa Barbara: Praeger, 2009.

Stone, Christopher. *Should Trees Have Standing?* Los Altos, CA: William Kaufman, 1974.

Stoykovich, Eric. "Of a Predatory Nature? Dogs and the Protection of Sheep in the Eastern United States." Paper presented at the ASEH conference, Baton Rouge, LA, 2007.

Sunstein, Cass. "A Tribute to Kenneth L. Karst: Standing for Animals (with Notes on Animal Rights)." *UCLA Law Review* 47 (2000): 1333–1368.

Sunstein, Cass, and Martha Nussbaum. *Animal Rights: Current Debates and New Directions.* Oxford: Oxford University Press, 2004.

Tague, Ingrid. "Eighteenth-Century English Debate on a Dog Tax." *Historical Journal* 51 (2008): 901–920.

Talbert, Matthew. "Contractualism and Our Duties to Nonhuman Animals." *Environmental Ethics* 28 (Summer 2006): 201–215.

Tonry, Michael, and David Farrington. "Punishment and Crime across Space and Time." *Crime and Justice* 33 (2005): 1–39.

Tully, James. *A Discourse on Property.* Cambridge: Cambridge University Press, 1980.

Vandeveer, Donald. "Of Beasts, Person, and the Original Position." *Monist* 62, no. 3 (1979): 368–377.

Wacquant, Loïc. *Punishing the Poor.* Durham, NC: Duke University Press, 2009.

Waisman, Sonia, Pamela Frasch, and Bruce Wagman. *Animal Law: Cases and Material.* 3rd ed. Durham, NC: Carolina Academic Press, 2006.

Waldron, Jeremy. *God, Locke and Equality.* Cambridge: Cambridge University Press, 2002.

———. *The Right to Private Property.* Oxford: Clarendon Press, 1988.

Walker, Alice. *Living by the Word.* New York: Harcourt Brace Jovanovich, 1988.

———. *In Search of Our Mothers' Gardens.* New York: Harcourt, 1983.

Weber, Max. *Political Writings*. Ed. Peter Lassman and Ronald Spiers. Cambridge: Cambridge University Press, 1994.

Weigley, Russell. *History of the United States Army*. Bloomington: Indiana University Press, 1967.

Wenz, Peter. *Environmental Justice*. Albany: SUNY Press, 1988.

Wise, Steven. *Rattling the Cage*. New York: Basic, 2000.

Wissenburg, Marcel. *Green Liberalism*. London: Routledge, 1998.

Index